THE POVERTY CURTAIN:
CHOICES FOR THE THIRD WORLD

THE POVERTY CURTAIN

•

CHOICES
FOR
THE
THIRD
WORLD

•

MAHBUB UL HAQ

COLUMBIA
UNIVERSITY
PRESS
NEW YORK

Library of Congress
Cataloging in Publication Data
Haq, Mahbub ul.
  The poverty curtain.
  Bibliography: p.
  Includes index.
  1. Underdeveloped areas.   2. Poverty.
3. Economic development.   I. Title.
HC59.7.H35   330.9′172′4   76-7470
ISBN 0-231-04062-8
ISBN 0-231-04063-6 pbk.

Columbia University Press
New York   Guildford, Surrey
Copyright © 1976 Columbia University Press
Printed in the United States of America
10 9 8 7 6 5 4 3

To

B A N I

What I give to you
Is yours by right everlasting.
What I give to you is your own gift—
Fuller your acceptance, the deeper my debt.

CONTENTS

FOREWORD

BY BARBARA WARD

AS THE 1970S ADVANCE, THERE IS AN INDEFINABLE BUT deepening sense of a profound change in human affairs. Those who have profited from earlier arrangements are fearful and their fear can go on to violence and aggression. Those who suffered before are hopeful but their hope, if too long deferred, can also turn to violence. So this is a time of growing unsteadiness in the world's understanding of itself. Some people talk of the "blood-dimmed tide of anarchy," others of "the dawn" in which it is "bliss to be alive." But whether it is fear or hope that stirs the depths, profound movements are at work in planetary politics, movements as vast, and perhaps as irreversible as, say, a geological adjustment of continental plates.

The analogy is not wholly inappropriate for in terms of politics it is a sort of continental shift that seems to be taking place. The continents of the wealthy white earthlings of European descent—from Vancouver to Vladivostock—are seeing the end of the submergence of the "continents of poverty." In Latin America, in Africa, in Asia, the formal closing down of the old colonial system is being followed by a deepening realization of the economic and social consequences of what has been, so far, a primarily political act. The call for a "new economic order" is precisely what it says it is, a demand that the legacy of three hundred years of European dominance should give way——to what? This is where all the tensions of fear and hope gather. This is where the question, anarchy? or new dawn? has to find an answer.

There are no safe scientific guides or predictions in politics. But there is a vast amount of history to examine and even if Santayana's comment "that those who will not learn from history are destined to repeat it," has become a truism, truisms remain true. And in today's predicaments, the world has the advantage of not being too far removed from a very relevant stretch of history—an earlier version of today's traumatic

events. When all the exceptions are admitted, all the differences
of culture, climate and historical experience, when full allow-
ance is made for the unrepeatability of exact human events (you
cannot step into the same river twice) it is still broadly true to
say that as this century ends, the whole planet is being drawn
into the industrializing, urbanizing, technological order just as
the peoples of Western Europe, then America, then Russia were
drawn into it during the nineteenth century.

Admittedly, the firstcomers had enormous advantages—slow
growth of population (though the cause, high death rates, is not
enviable), vast resources of empty land opening up for settlement and for food supplies, and a fair match between work force
and technology (there were no petrochemical complexes in early
Lancashire costing $24 million and providing only 40 jobs).
Yet the economic and social consequences of the new system,
say in the 1840s, after three to four decades of intensive development, do bear a family resemblance to world conditions in
the 1970s, some thirty years after the end of World War II and
the beginnings of political decolonisation.

The fundamental affinity lies in the realization that the vast
increases in wealth are enriching a small proportion of the population and that there is a good chance that a much larger mass
of people are actually worse off. The historical reason for this
fact can be said to go back to the earliest years of technological
transformation, in fact to the great debates in Britain under
Cromwell about the nature of property and the rights attached
to it. There were two strands to the argument. One was a passionate opposition to royal despotism, ruling by divine right
and rigging the economy for royal courtiers and monopolists.
Only private property rights would secure the citizen against
these encroachments. The other thread was the argument that a
man has a right to property because his work alone has worked
it up from its virgin, unusable, and valueless state.

But, said the more radical wing of Cromwell's men, the
Levellers, what about the workers?—the ploughmen, the shep-
herds, the harvesters who actually do the work? Should they not
have a share as well?

The fateful and unhappy conclusion of the debate was that servants are not more separate from a master than his arms and his legs and thus enjoy no separate rights. This definition dominated the eighteenth century start to the industrial revolution. Manchester's mill workers were simply "hands"—a significant, unconscious extension of the mistaken biological analogy. Even though pioneers like Robert Owen or, later, the Rochdale founders of the cooperative movement, proved that bringing the workers into partnership in the enterprise actually increased productivity and hence profits, the leaders of the new system, in part from genuine conviction over the risks of outside interference, in part from unbridled self-interest (since they were making vast fortunes), stuck to the narrow, traditional interpretation of property rights. Property alone, now extended from land to capital, determined the rewards of industrialism and, in the new competitive free market, unskilled labor was simply a commodity finding its own price—the minimum needed to keep a pauper child alive, so not a very large sum. Skilled men still lacked organization to enforce their claims. Although statistics are uncertain, it seems clear that throughout the first half of the nineteenth century, the working class as a whole gained no increase in standards from the new system and the poorest, perhaps 20 to 30 percent of the population (displaced cottagers, starving weavers) were actually worse off. The truly inhuman conditions in the new industrial cities received official confirmation in Britain's first Blue Book on *The Sanitary Condition of the Labouring Population in Great Britain,* published in 1842. Yet Britain's cities were held to be less lethal than many in Europe or America.

This was the background of the Hungry '40s and 1848, the Year of Revolutions. Thereafter, political roads began to divide. Where traditions of free politics had taken root, the next century was one of piecemeal but decisive reform—extension of the franchise, recognition of unions, the beginning of public health and housing, the progressive income tax, the emergence of every kind of mix of social democracy. In other societies—in Russia, in parts of Germany, in Central Europe—the despotic tradition was retained and proved a prime factor in a terrible century of wars and revolutions.

This vast debate over shares and justice and cooperation within fully industrialized societies is still unfinished even now. But it is as nothing compared with the eruption on a planetary scale of the old questions of the 1840s. After centuries of colonialism which developed little save the raw materials needed in the Atlantic world, after thirty years of intensive efforts to develop a modern technological order, the discovery has been made (the equivalent of the 1842 Report) that the mass of people in the developing world have gained little from their economic and social involvement in what is still an Atlantic-dominated world economy and that the poorest are actually poorer still. And the reason for this imbalance in the world of the 1970s is precisely the same as the reasons in 1842. A market system, wholly uncorrected by institutions of justice, sharing, and solidarity, makes the strong stronger and the weak weaker. Markets as useful tools in a functioning social order have a positive and decentralizing role to play. Markets as masters of society enrich the rich and pauperize the poor.

So, today, the whole world is confronted with the old challenge of the Hungry '40s. Which route will the nations follow? Will they institutionalize their highest principles of justice, cooperation, and responsibility? Or will they leave interest and power alone to determine the outcome? This, in essence, is the fundamental choice to be made in discussing and deciding upon any "new international economic order." It can follow the creative route. It can "extend the franchise" by bringing the poor nations into the decision-making that determines their future. It can recognize their right to organize and see in, say, stable world commodity prices the beginnings of collective bargaining. It can institute automatic transfers of resources—through Special Drawing Rights, for instance, or taxes on raw material imports, or tolls on international transport systems—and they can be the first sketch of an indirect tax system. World aid, as an agreed proportion of GNP, would be the equivalent of introducing planetary income tax. Steady investment in water and

energy and education and health would repeat at the world level
the civic spending everywhere undertaken within the nation. In
short, such policies can extend to the whole of human society
the rights and responsibilities of a just and cooperative economic system.

None of this is strange or unlikely. Every part of it is now
the day-to-day routine of civilized countries. But the block, like
the class block of Disraeli's Britain in the 1840s with "its nation of the rich and nation of the poor," is the inability to accept the need for these institutions on a scale transcending national frontiers. We are therefore still set for the second
route—of indifference to planetary need, of belief in automatic
processes, of reliance upon mechanisms which do not and cannot, of themselves, secure the public good. And at the end of
that route lies deepening anarchy, a widening breakdown of
order and—who knows how soon?—the terrorist with the plu-
tonium bomb.

There is therefore no more urgent issue for the world than to
invent speedily, generously, and confidently the kind of new
economic order which spares humanity the all but certain risk of
auto-destruction. It is the great merit of Dr. Mahbub ul Haq's
study that it discusses this central need with a rationality, an
experience, and a controlled force that should appeal to all governments and peoples now profoundly engaged in the dialogue
about their own future. Reason, truth, a willingness to learn
from past mistakes, and a complete lack of rancor are the chief
tools of this debate. They are all of them most vigorously put to
work in this admirable book.

PREFACE

A POVERTY CURTAIN HAS DESCENDED RIGHT ACROSS THE face of our world, dividing it materially and philosophically into two different worlds, two separate planets, two unequal humanities—one embarrassingly rich and the other desperately poor. This invisible barrier exists within nations as well as between them, and it often provides a unity of thought and purpose to the Third World countries which otherwise have their own economic, political and cultural differences. The struggle to lift this curtain of poverty is certainly the most formidable challenge of our time.

This book is about this struggle. Most of the required changes lie right within the control of the Third World—whether in the restructuring of domestic political power, or in the fashioning of new development styles and strategies, or in the search for new areas of collective self-reliance. A part of the struggle is at the international level—to change the past patterns of hopeless dependency to new concepts of equality, partnership and interdependence.

The struggle is primarily a political one, as all such struggles always are whenever a major readjustment in internal and external power structures is at stake. But it also requires a breakthrough in our perceptions, a change in the intellectual climate in which new thinking must take shape. The aim of this book is a modest one: to cover just a small part of such a revolution in mankind's perceptions.

In a way, this is not a book in the standard sense of the term. It is more an evolution of ideas over time. I have tried to relate them as honestly as I could, including my own agonizing mistakes and rediscoveries. I personally believe that ideas have a life of their own and there is nothing more fascinating than to watch their growth.

Two clarifications are in order. First, the definition of Third World, as used in this book, covers all developing countries of

Asia, Africa, Middle East and Latin America. The confusing multiplicity of terms used recently, dividing these countries economically into several different worlds, is ignored here as it has little relevance to the main message of this book. Second, I have expressed my views here neither as a Pakistani nor as a World Bank official but only as a private citizen of the Third World. One of the most attractive features of the World Bank is the freedom it allows its officials to express their personal opinions even when some of these opinions may be at odds with the official policy.

The book is divided into three parts, though any such division is necessarily arbitrary in case of ideas which have an essential unity. However, to provide some background to my readers—and to indulge my own considerable vanity at times—I have added a brief introduction to each part ("In Retrospect") which traces the evolution of my own thinking and, I hope, that of the world on these issues of development strategies and international order.

The ideas expressed in this book evolved in numerous discussions with many friends and colleagues who, of course, bear no responsibility for the final product but whom I must thank for their intellectual stimulation: Richard Gardner, James Grant, Robert Triffin, Gamani Corea, Hollis B. Chenery, Ernest Stern, William Clark, Maurice Strong, Barbara Ward, Enrique Iglesias, Lal Jayawardena, Jan Tinbergen, Manuel Perez Guerrero, to mention only a few. Barbara Ward added to the many debts that I already owe her by writing a perceptive foreword to this book, placing the demand for equality of relationships between the rich and the poor in its long-term, historical perspective.

I am particularly grateful to Shahid Javed Burki for his constant help and support at all stages of the work. Professor Howard Wriggins, Director of the Southern Asian Institute at Columbia University, was also most helpful with his constructive comments and advice on earlier drafts.

It would not have been possible to complete this manuscript in the short time available but for the untiring, selfless and invaluable help of my secretary, Viviana Batzella, and the efficient assistance of Barbara Morrisey, Feli Favis, and Aurora Gamboa. To all of these lovely and uncomplaining souls, my grateful thanks. I also appreciate the assistance of Ines Garcia and Josefina Valeriano in compiling the statistical appendix and the index.

I simply cannot conclude without acknowledging my profound debt to two persons who have had the greatest influence on my life and my thoughts: my mother, who always regarded the telling of truth as the greatest test of one's courage; and my father, who gave me, through his own personal life, the best example of uncompromising integrity.

WASHINGTON, D.C.   MAHBUB UL HAQ
MARCH 1976

NEW DEVELOPMENT STRATEGIES

PART

·1·

"There exists a functional justification for inequality of income if it raises production for all and not consumption for a few. . . . The road to eventual equalities may inevitably lie through initial inequalities."
—Mahbub ul Haq, 1963.

"It is time to stand economic theory on its head, since a rising growth rate is no guarantee against worsening poverty. . . . Divorce between production and distribution policies is false and dangerous: the distribution policies must be built into the very pattern and organization of production."
—Mahbub ul Haq, 1971

IN RETROSPECT

ABOUT EIGHTEEN YEARS AGO, AS I EMERGED FROM THE campuses of Cambridge and Yale, I had few doubts about the right path to economic development. I returned to Pakistan in 1957 and got immediately engaged in the formulation and implementation of Pakistan's five-year development plans. Those were the happy days. My sights were set, my horizon was clear, and there was no hesitancy in my views about economic development. I expressed them in my first book with a youthful exuberance and conviction which is one of the few privileges of the inexperienced:

NEED FOR A GROWTH PHILOSOPHY

It is well to recognize that economic growth is a brutal, sordid process. There are no short cuts to it. The essence of it lies in making the labourer produce more than he is allowed to consume for his immediate needs, and to invest and reinvest the surplus thus obtained. It is immaterial what one chooses to call this surplus—whether "surplus value," as Marx usually did; or "savings" or "capital formation," in the terminology of modern economic analysis; or "comrades' voluntary contribution to national growth," as it may perhaps be described by some apologists for the communist technique of exacting this surplus. It is equally immaterial who owns this surplus—whether "the capitalists," as in a free enterprise economy, or "the State," as in a communist economy. What is important and intellectually honest is to admit frankly that the heart of the growth problem lies in maximizing the creation of this surplus. Either the capitalist sector should be allowed to perform the role, or, if this is found inefficient because of the nature of the capitalist sector in a particular country or is distasteful politically, the State should undertake it. It would be wrong to dub the consequent emergence of surplus value as "exploitation": its justification is economic growth. Ironically enough, economic growth has come about almost in a similar fashion in America and Russia,

3

despite the charges of "capitalistic exploitation" and the coun-
tercharges of "state tyranny." More ironically still, there is no es-
cape from the emergence of "surplus value" even in a socialist or
communist state, though Marx condemned it bitterly as a capitalist phenomenon.

Our intention is not to be polemical. Nor should we raise any
ideological controversies. This is a luxury that only developed
countries can enjoy, having left behind in the debris of history the
crimes and excesses of their initial periods of growth. The underdeveloped countries have no choice but to admit that these excesses
are inevitable. Of course, such a frank admission is politically distasteful in a world where the clamour for better distribution is preceding increases in production and where vague "welfare state"
ideas undermine a firm commitment to growth philosophy. But it
is well to relearn the lesson of history. It would be tragic if policies
appropriate to a Keynesian era were to be tried in countries still
living in a Smithian or Ricardian world.

It is interesting to note the transition in Keynes's own thinking
on growth philosophy as one growth stage melted into another.
Thus, describing the flourishing capitalism of the nineteenth century, he wrote:

"In fact, it was precisely the inequality of the distribution of
wealth which made possible those vast accumulations of fixed
wealth and of capital improvements which distinguished that age
from all others. . . . If the rich had spent their new wealth on
their own enjoyments, the world would long ago have found such a
regime intolerable. But like bees they saved and accumulated, not
less to the advantage of the whole community because they themselves held narrower ends in prospect." (J. M. Keynes, *The Economic Consequences of the Peace,* New York, 1920, p. 19.)

Yet, in 1936, his vision quickly adjusting to the harsh realities
of the 1930s, he could argue with equal force:

"Thus our argument leads towards the conclusion that in con-
temporary conditions the growth of wealth, so far from being
dependent on the abstinence of the rich, as is commonly supposed,
is more likely to be impeded by it." (J. M. Keynes, *The General
Theory of Employment, Interest and Money,* New York, 1936, p. 373.)

The breathlessness with which Keynes makes his "discovery"
holds out a warning for planners in the underdeveloped countries.
The policy emphasis in the developed countries is moving toward

"distribution" and "welfare state" considerations. Such a tendency is understandable when the average income levels have risen high enough to yield a saving margin for growth and social attitudes and economic institutions have changed in such a way as to permit an effective mobilization of these saving margins. In fact, such a change in emphasis may even become necessary if growth is being hampered not by lack of capital but by lack of effective demand. It would be unfortunate, however, if this change in policy emphasis in the developed countries were to spill over, consciously or unconsciously, into the growth philosophy of economies still in a stage of "take-off." In this latter stage, the best (and, perhaps, the only) form of social security is a rapid extension of productive employment opportunities to all through the creation of sufficient capital by some. There exists, therefore, a functional justification for inequality of income if this raises production for all and not consumption for a few. The road to eventual equalities may inevitably lie through initial inequalities. The time for a Keynesian-type somersault is not just yet.[1]

Over the thirteen years of my association with Pakistan's economic planning, I was forced to reconsider many of these views as my convictions clashed with facts. The following chapters show the gradual evolution of my thinking, especially from 1970 onward as Pakistan's decade of rapid economic development during the 1960s was beginning to crumble, not because the pace of growth in the Gross National Product had been insufficient, but *in spite of* an enviable record of growth.

Chapter 1 reviews some of my experience with development planning in a light-hearted vein though the intent is deadly serious: some of these thoughts were first expressed in a lecture at McGill University early in 1968. This was only the beginning of a critical appraisal of the planning experience I had just lived through.

A few months later, in April 1968, I spoke again, this time in Karachi, alerting the country to the growing concentration of industrial income and wealth in the hands of only twenty-two

[1] Mahbub ul Haq, *The Strategy of Economic Planning* (New York: Oxford University Press, 1963), pp. 1–3.

family groups. I pointed out that these family groups controlled at that time about two thirds of the industrial assets, 80 percent of banking, and 70 percent of insurance in Pakistan. I also underscored the considerable political and social risks inherent in a pattern of development which, over the preceding decade, had led to a doubling of the disparity in the per capita income between East and West Pakistan and which had reduced the real wages of the industrial workers, concentrated in a few key urban areas, by about one third. It was evident that most of the population had remained virtually untouched by the forces of economic change since economic development had become warped in favor of a privileged minority. One of the most shocking indices of this distortion manifested itself in the distribution of certain public and private services. During the decade 1958–1968, Pakistan imported or domestically assembled private cars worth $300 million while it could spare only $20 million for public buses. During the same period, about 80–90 percent of private construction could only be described as "luxury housing" under any definition of the word.

It was not surprising that this speech created major shock waves within Pakistan.[2] It was not an easy decision for me to speak out publicly against the policies of the very government that I was serving. After all, I was Chief Economist of the National Planning Commission at that time and much of what I had to say was a summary indictment of the policies of the government during a period in which I was closely associated with planned development. But I have always believed that those who make a virtue out of institutional conformity and loyalty serve their institutions far more poorly than those who are willing to express their dissent and pay the necessary price for it.

In this instance, I did not have to pay the price that I was prepared to. After the first shock wore off, President Ayub

---

[2] While there was considerable excited debate in Pakistan, more serious work on this issue was initially undertaken by political scientists (like Wilcox, Dobell, Ziring) and sociologists (like Korson, Nicholas) than by economists who are only recently beginning to analyze the dimensions of this problem.

showed his foresight by asking me to draft an emergency program to redress some of the economic and social imbalances in the system. Unfortunately, he fell from power a few months afterward, before he could implement any of the needed changes. One of the bitter lessons he must have learned was that the alliances of privileged groups that he had forged to promote accelerated growth were totally unwilling to let him trim their privileges and that he had few political alliances at his disposal to engineer a meaningful change.

In the meanwhile, the debate on twenty-two family groups in Pakistan got completely out of control and these family groups were held responsible, individually and collectively, for all the economic and social ills of the country. Instead of carrying out fundamental institutional reforms in every sector of the economy, the new slogan was to liquidate the industrial family groups. I tried in a subsequent article to put the problem in its proper perspective:

If we are to evaluate the role of the 22 families in Pakistan today, we must see it in the perspective of the capitalistic system that the country has evolved over time. In blunt terms, Pakistan's capitalistic system is still one of the most primitive in the world. It is a system in which economic feudalism prevails. A handful of people, whether landlords or industrialists or bureaucrats, make all the basic decisions and the system often works simply because there is an alliance between various vested interests. Unfortunately, most of the criticism of the 22 families in the last five years has been directed to individual family groups rather than to the reform of the basic framework. . . .

What Pakistan badly needs today is to broaden the base of its economic and political power; to evolve a development strategy that reaches out to the bulk of the population; to innovate a new life style which is more consistent with its own poverty and its present stage of development. This is not going to be easy because, in the past, modernisation was foisted on a basically feudalistic structure in which political participation was often denied, growth of responsible institutions stifled and free speech curbed, and where all economic and political power gravitated towards a small minority. There is not much that can be done to save development from

being warped in favor of a privileged few in a system like this
unless the basic premises of the system are changed.[3]

While these controversies were still raging in Pakistan, I left
some of my own sins of development planning behind and came
to the World Bank (Washington, D.C.) in 1970 where I got
the opportunity to reflect on my past experience with somewhat
greater detachment and objectivity. It also became possible to
see Pakistan's experience in the comparative framework of other
developing countries. My reflections on development strategies
led me to increasing doubts and unease about some of the basic
premises and concepts of development which I had so readily accepted before. In the next few years, I began challenging many
of these premises, particularly the ones which totally conflicted
with the experience I had just lived through. Most of this
challenge was expressed in two speeches that I gave in 1971 and
1972 and which are reproduced in chapter 2.[4] In retrospect,
these speeches show a certain tone of belligerence which may
appear to be unduly shrill now but which was perhaps necessary
at that stage to challenge established thought.

I was not quite prepared for the furor that followed these
speeches. The academic community in the Western world
reacted in shocked disbelief: one of its own products had suddenly gone berserk. The reaction in the Third World, however,
was extremely encouraging, especially among the top policy
makers who were daily facing the same dilemmas as articulated
in these speeches, without being able to communicate them to
their own economists and without making a visible dent on the
elegant and arrogant frameworks that development planners had
so carefully built up. Some of the prominent leaders from the
Third World wrote me with a certain sense of relief, as if a
hardened sinner had finally confessed. This reaction spanned the
three continents. For instance, President Nyerere of Tanzania
sent a letter of appreciation, along with an autographed copy of

[3] The *London Times,* March 22, 1973.
[4] Keynote address to the 12th World Conference, Society for International
Development, Ottawa, May 1971; and address to the International Development Conference, Washington, D.C., April 1972.

his collected speeches, and wrote: "The points which you made in that speech—very succinctly and clearly—are very much in line with [my own] thinking." President Torrijos of Panama invited me over to address his top cabinet colleagues "to convert them to the new thinking." And the Prime Minister of India, Mrs. Indira Gandhi, paid a particularly flattering tribute by including many portions of these speeches, almost verbatim, in a major policy speech of her own on India's development strategy.[5]

I was also encouraged by the fact that the response in the Western world was progressively more understanding, after the first shock wore off. The secret visit of Henry Kissinger to China in March, 1971, which was revealed shortly after my first speech, made it somewhat easier to talk about China's development experience in American forums.[6] Moreover, many aid-giving agencies were coming to the same conclusions about the patterns of development in the developing world. Mr. McNamara spoke for many of them, and for the international development community as a whole, when he addressed the Board of Governors in September, 1972:

> The task, then, for the governments of the developing countries is to reorient their development policies in order to attack directly the personal poverty of the most deprived 40 percent of their populations. This the governments can do without abandoning their goals of vigorous overall economic growth. But they must be prepared to give greater priority to establishing growth targets in terms of essential human needs: in terms of nutrition, housing, health, literacy, and employment—even if it be at the cost of some reduction in the pace of advance in certain narrow and highly privileged sectors whose benefits accrue to the few. Such a reorientation of social and economic policy is primarily a political task,

[5] This led to some unfortunate embarrassment for her in the press which criticized her, unfairly, for quoting a Pakistani economist without acknowledgment. See the *London Times,* April 12 and 26, 1972.

[6] It is fascinating to watch the evolution of the Western world's understanding of China's development experience—from uncritical ridicule to greater sympathy and appreciation. There is now a growing volume of literature on China, but it is useful to see the works of Fairbank, Kuan-I Chen, Perkins and Chow to appreciate this rapid process of evolution.

and the developing countries must decide for themselves if they wish to undertake it. It will manifestly require immense resolve and courage. . . . We know, in effect, that there is no rational alternative to moving toward policies of greater social equity. When the highly privileged are few and the desperately poor are many—and when the gap between them is worsening rather than improving—it is only a question of time before a decisive choice must be made between the political costs of reform and the political risks of rebellion. That is why policies specifically designed to reduce the deprivation among the poorest 40 percent in developing countries are prescriptions not only of principle but of prudence. Social justice is not merely a moral imperative. It is a political imperative as well.[7]

The pendulum had begun to swing. In a way, I feel that it may have swung too far already since the concern for the bottom 40 percent is in danger of becoming an intellectual and political fashion rather than a serious policy issue. Conferences and seminars are being organized every day, with such breathless rapidity that almost the same participants stagger on from one place to the next bemoaning the fate of "the by-passed people," "the marginal men," "the bottom 40 percent," "the forgotten majority," etc., in relatively comfortable and exotic surroundings in which these conferences are increasingly held. There is little serious work on the dimensions of poverty and concrete policies to tackle, particularly in the developing world whose problem it basically is. On the political front, no political leader can afford not to pay at least some lip service to a program for a direct attack on mass poverty, yet the restructuring of political and economic power which is necessary for such a program has hardly begun in many developing countries. The most ardent supporters of poverty alleviation programs at present are generally the aid-giving agencies, but, with the best will in the world, their role in fashioning and implementing new development strategies can only be marginal and not very decisive. I return to this general theme in chapter 5.

[7] Robert S. McNamara, "Annual Speech to the Board of Governors," September 1972.

Having lived with the evolution of development strategies over the last two decades, my personal experience is that the emergence of any new idea goes through at least three distinct stages.

The first stage is characterized by organized resistance. As new ideas begin to challenge the supremacy of the old, all the organized wrath and scorn is heaped upon the heads of those who have had the audacity to think differently. Their thinking is described as mere rhetoric, demagoguery, devoid of analytical content, unsupported by empirical analysis, etc., and their personal credentials and motivations are often questioned. I say this with a certain twinge of personal hurt, but I have learnt over time that one must go through this phase with perfect stoicism since none of the insults are really meant personally and since it is an inevitable period for the trial of any new idea.

The second stage can generally be described as widespread and uncritical acceptance of new ideas. At some point, there is a sudden realization that the time for the new idea has arrived and all those who had opposed it thus far hurry over to adopt it as their own. Their advocacy becomes even more passionate than those of the pioneers, and they take great pains to prove that they discovered the idea in the first place. I have watched this phenomenon time and again, with great fascination and grudging admiration—whether it was the attack of twenty-two families in Pakistan, or the "dethroning" of the GNP and the "discovery" of poverty, or the understanding of the Chinese development experience in the Western world. The pendulum swings quite abruptly, from unlimited abuse of new ideas to their uncritical acceptance.

It is the third stage which is generally the most rewarding—a critical evaluation of ideas and their practical implementation. This is a much slower and more unpredictable process. It is my own belief that thinking on poverty issues (Part 1) is gradually entering this last stage. This is, unhappily, not true of the thinking on the new international economic order (Part 3) where we still seem to be standing on the threshold of new perceptions.

·1· SEVEN SINS OF DEVELOPMENT PLANNERS

In the late 1940s, there arose a new priesthood of develop- ment planners—men who had tremendous confidence in themselves but little confidence in their own societies which they all wanted to transform in a hurry. They promised every man a Mercedes, or at least a Honda, and then found that they could fulfill this promise only for themselves and for a privi- leged few. They were generally men of good intentions, often products of Western liberal education, who played the game of development with deadly seriousness.

While they sometimes managed to advance the average per capita income of their countries by a few dollars, they often left the masses more acutely aware of the inadequacy of the rewards of growth and of the socially disruptive nature of the entire pro- cess of development. Hailed at first as heroes, these priests of development were generally on the retreat toward the end of the 1960s. What went wrong, after all, with the process of plan- ning and development? What sins have been committed in the name of accelerated growth?

It will be useful to illustrate some of the mistakes of develop- ment planning from the experience of Pakistan—an experience with which I am familiar and to some of which mistakes I seem to have contributed quite handsomely. But Pakistan's experi- ence is by no means unique; other developing countries [1] have made similar mistakes, particularly in the Asian subcontinent [2]

[1] See, for instance, Albert Waterston, *Development Planning: Lessons of Expe- rience,* (Baltimore: Johns Hopkins University Press, 1965).

[2] For a good assessment of the Indian situation, see Paul Streeten and Michael Lipton, *The Crisis of Indian Planning: Economic Planning in the*

with which Pakistan's experience can be more usefully compared.

NUMBERS GAMES

One of the perennial sins of development planners has been their fascination with numbers. It is quietly assumed that whatever is measurable is relevant; what is nonmeasurable can be conveniently ignored. Thus, endless amount of work goes into econometric models; not enough into economic policy formulation or decent project appraisal. The planners will not be caught dead with an inconsistent plan; they are cheerfully oblivious to whether it is an empty one. And so empty economic boxes have abounded, with little policy or project content.

We committed less of this sin in Pakistan than do most countries, though we had our share. For one thing, there was endless preoccupation with the refinement of our national accounts; not enough work on the real problems of mass poverty. The five-year development plans tended to ignore problems of unemployment, rural poverty, urban unrest, and poor social services since there was so little quantitative information available in these areas. There was also a tendency to devote a good deal of time to theoretical concepts, much less to practical policies. It worried the planners no end whether the marginal rate of saving in Pakistan's Third Five-Year Plan should be fixed at 20 or 22 percent. Several weeks were spent in the National Planning Commission discussing such esoteric details. Yet the heart of the matter was Pakistan's taxation system which withdrew only about 8 percent of the Gross National Product. Without a thoroughgoing reform of this taxation system and without making it sufficiently elastic and progressive, high marginal rates of saving could only have been achieved if income distribution was

---

1960s (London: Oxford University Press, 1968); for Ceylon, see Don Snodgrass, *Ceylon: an Export Economy in Transition* (New Haven: Yale University Press, 1966); and for Burma, see Lucian Pye, *Politics, Personality and Nation Building: Burma's Search for Identity* (New Haven: Yale University Press, 1962).

allowed to become extremely skewed and if the rich chose to save rather than consume. The social and economic implications of such a strategy of obtaining high saving rates were tremendous but they received very little attention. Analysis of tax policy was often more cursory in each Annual Development Plan than the discussion of marginal saving rates.

Again, planners in Pakistan devoted even less of their time and skills to project selection and appraisal. This was regarded as dirty work which operators in the field must do. The link between planning at the macro-level and project selection at the micro-level was, therefore, often weak and uncertain. On the one hand, this led to a dearth of good projects, as Pakistan's aid consortia repeatedly pointed out. On the other, aggregative targets of income growth or employment generation and sectoral targets of production increases often carried little assurance that they would, in fact, be built into detailed project selection.

After spending a good deal of time with economic plan making, it is my conviction that the basic ingredients of a good development plan are economic policies, social and economic institutions, and project selection—certainly not the overall elegance of the plan models. In fact, it is just not worthwhile to invest a lot of time in constructing a perfectly consistent plan, since the real world defies many assumptions normally made in a development plan. One must ensure, of course, that the key assumptions of a development plan are, on the whole, sensible and not mutually contradictory. But this can be done without diverting the scarce time of the planners to unduly sophisticated consistency models.[3] In the last analysis, a development plan is just as good as its policy, institutional and project content.

EXCESSIVE CONTROLS

Another sin of the development planners is their curious love for direct economic controls. It is too readily assumed that development planning means encouragement of public sector and im-

[3] See Wouter Tims, "A Growth Model and Its Application—Pakistan" in Gustav F. Papanek, ed., *Development Policy: Theory and Practice* (Cambridge: Harvard University Press, 1968).

position of a variety of bureaucratic controls to regulate economic activity, particularly in the private sector. It is a strange phenomenon that the very societies which are generally short of good administration experiment with the most baffling array of administrative controls.

Pakistan groaned under fairly excessive direct controls in the 1950s.[4] All economic activities—imports, exports, investment and production—were subject to some administrative regulations, often at odds with one another. Strict foreign exchange and import controls were enforced on what could be imported and by whom; key imports such as steel and cement were rationed by the government; price controls were imposed on food grains and other essential consumption items; and compulsory procurement of food grains from the farmers at uneconomic prices was regarded almost as a matter of public necessity and responsibility.[5] The result was that the private sector, which had shown some dynamism in the early 1950s, shrank its investments in the later half of the decade. The growth rate of the Gross National Product fell behind population growth and per capita income declined during the decade of the 1950s.

Pakistan tried a bold experiment with liberal economic policies in the 1960s.[6] Direct controls were replaced by economic incentives in many sectors. An Export Bonus Scheme was introduced to stimulate manufactured exports by introducing favorable, multiple exchange rates for various exports.[7] Import controls were relaxed and administrative regulations substituted

---

[4] See Mahbub ul Haq, "Rationale of Government Controls and Policies in Pakistan," *Pakistan Economic Journal* 13, No. 1 (March 1963); also, Gustav Papanek, *Pakistan's Development* (Cambridge: Harvard University, 1967), pp. 106–44.

[5] It has been argued, with considerable justification, that the plethora of controls introduced in the 1950s greatly strengthened the position of bureaucracy in the framework of economic management in Pakistan. See Shahid Javed Burki, "Twenty Years of the Civil Service of Pakistan: A Reevaluation," *Asian Survey*, 9, No. 4 (April 1969):239–54.

[6] Mahbub ul Haq, *Towards Economic Liberalism*, 1967 (mimeographed).

[7] For a good description of the scheme, see Henry J. Bruton and Swadesh R. Bose, *The Pakistan Export Bonus Scheme* (Karachi: Pakistan Institute of Development Economics, 1965).

in many cases with higher effective tariffs or appropriate prices. Food rationing was abolished and incentive farm support prices introduced for wheat and rice. Agricultural inputs, particularly fertilizer, were heavily subsidized. Most of the specific price controls on individual commodities were abandoned in favor of fiscal subsidies. Industrial licensing system was simplified by introducing an Industrial Investment Schedule, permitting investments in a broad range of priority industries without cumbersome sanctioning procedures, and by setting up industrial investment and credit banks. In fact, there was hardly any sector of the economy which remained untouched by the forces of economic liberalism.

The response of the system was immediate and beyond expectations. The annual growth rate in the Gross National Product accelerated from 2 percent in the 1950s to over 5 percent in the 1960s (in fact, over 7 percent in West Pakistan). Exports moved away from their stagnation of the earlier decade and started growing at a healthy rate of 8 percent per annum. Even the vast majority of farmers (who were patronizingly regarded as ignorant and untouched by market forces) recognized what the incentive system meant: overall agricultural growth rate nearly tripled, from 1.3 percent in the 1950s to 3.5 percent in the 1960s (and even more dramatically in West Pakistan, from 2.6 percent to 6.2 percent). One should be careful in attributing the entire success of Pakistan in the economic field during the 1960s to the policies of economic liberalization, but there is no doubt that the replacement of direct controls by appropriate price signals and incentives played a large part in this success.

There were two mistakes, however, which cast a somber shadow on this courageous experiment in economic liberalization. First, the liberal economic policies were hedged in by too many qualifications and controls, particularly toward the later half of the 1960s, which diluted their earlier impact. The export bonus scheme became administratively cumbersome as it was required to perform a number of objectives besides export promotion, such as import regulation, regional balance, taxation of consumption, etc. Strict import licensing came back as foreign aid dwindled after the 1965 India-Pakistan war, since many administrators always interpreted import liberalization as implying more imports rather than the regulation of imports through the pricing system. It appears that the conviction for liberal economic policies did not run very deep within the system and was supported to a large extent by the generous availability of foreign assistance. As Pakistan's economic options narrowed down in the post-1965 period, signs of hesitancy and multiplicity of controls again appeared in the implementation of a liberal framework of economic policies.

Second, and even more important, policies of economic liberalism can work only if the fiscal system plays an aggressive role in ensuring social justice. Since the existing income distribution was considerably distorted in Pakistan, the free play of market mechanism naturally favored the richer regions as well as the richer income groups within these regions. Import liberalization directed imports to where the existing industrial capacity was located, i.e., West Pakistan in preference to East Pakistan. The existing credit institutions and market mechanism favored a handful of industrial family groups in the allocation of industrial sanctions and led to the emergence of the proverbial twenty-two industrial family groups [8] which enjoyed considerable power and influence. It became increasingly obvious toward the late 1960s that the policies of economic liberalism would command a high price from the system unless the existing imbalances in income and wealth were corrected and the gains from development were distributed more equitably.[9]

INVESTMENT ILLUSION

Among the many sins of development planners, a more amusing one is their constant preoccupation with investment levels.

---

[8] Mahbub ul Haq, *London Times,* March 22, 1973.

[9] In restrospect, it appears that the absence of any significant debate on the personal income distribution issues during this period was in part due to the great preoccupation with the question of regional imbalance between East and West Pakistan. Most of the articles in the *Pakistan Development Review,* the premier economic journal of Pakistan, were devoted to this latter issue.

Having learned two decades ago that capital formation is the heart of the development process,[10] the planners keep fussing continuously about the investment rate going up or down. It matters less what investment level really consists of; how productive it is; how far investment in human resources rather than in physical facilities is worthwhile; what physical facilities are lying idle for want of current inputs; and what priority current expenditures should have vis-à-vis future investment. This may appear to be a ruthless caricature of the real world, but unfortunately, one finds too many illustrations of this investment illusion to dismiss this concern lightly.

We often hear that capital is scarce in the developing countries. And yet we find that so much of the productive capital is lying idle in many poor societies. In Pakistan, underutilized industrial capacity was variously estimated at 50 to 60 percent in the 1960s at a time when its economic management was generally regarded as efficient. Schools and hospitals were often built without adequate provision of teachers and doctors to staff them. There was also considerable underutilization of economic infrastructure. Yet each time the economic decision makers confronted a choice between installing new capacity or fully utilizing the existing one, between capital imports or current imports, between allocating resources to the capital budget or to the current budget, their instinctive preference was for more investment. Shiny new industrial units were often added to the ones already lying underutilized. More schools were built each year while the requests of existing ones for adequate current expenditure to run them properly were rejected.

There were at least two reasons for such decisions which otherwise appear to be so irrational in the cold light of logic. First, there were separate administrative jurisdictions for current and capital expenditure in Pakistan—the Ministry of Finance was responsible for the former, the Planning Commission for the latter. While the Finance Ministry, with its inbuilt conser-

---

[10] Ragnar Nurkse, *Problems of Capital Formation in Underdeveloped Countries* (New York: Oxford University Press, 1953).

vatism, was interested in keeping down current expenditures, the Planning Commission was always pressing hard to increase investment. Let it be said to the credit of the planners that they did keep lamenting in their development plans the evidence of considerable underutilization of productive capacity and neglect of investment in human resources, but, since their jurisdiction extended only to the budgeting of development expenditure, their lamentations proved ineffective. In retrospect, it appears that the artificial distinction between development and non-development expenditure also created a good deal of confusion. Since development was regarded as synonymous with physical investment and since planners were supposed to look after investment decisions only, they often ended up creating more physical facilities while the existing ones remained underutilized. This was encouraged further by the prevalence of fairly low interest rates—the bank rate was generally below 4 percent during the 1960s—which conferred windfall profits on the users of scarce capital and which did not adequately penalize its wasteful use.

Second, it appears that the whole world loves investment. When Pakistan badly needed commodity assistance to utilize its industrial and agricultural capacity more fully, most donors were willing to offer it only project assistance. There was somehow a feeling among the donors that commodity assistance was likely to add to consumption while project assistance directly added to investment.[11] This was nothing but misplaced concreteness. So long as resources are fungible, project assistance also frees the country's own resources for other uses. Furthermore, there is hardly much logic in pumping more project assistance through capital machinery into countries which need current inputs to utilize existing production capacity. In such a situation, their savings and exports often depend on their current growth rate so that commodity assistance can get translated into investment via higher growth and saving rates. Thus, the

[11] Mahbub ul Haq, "The Transfer of Resources" in *The World Bank Group, Multilateral Aid, and the 1970's,* John P. Lewis, ed. (Lexington, Mass.: Lexington Books, 1973), pp. 85–87.

timely supply of adequate raw materials may make a greater contribution to future saving and export effort of the system by getting the production system moving than the supply of pieces of capital machinery. To insist on project assistance in such a situation is to carry investment illusion to its irrational limits.

DEVELOPMENT FASHIONS

One of the more pleasurable sins of development planners is their addiction to development fashions. We have seen a number of fashionable prescriptions sweep the world in the last two decades. The planners are often willing victims of these changing fashions, partly because they must keep up-to-date in the chase of development and partly because they may end up with very little foreign assistance if they do not subscribe to the currently fashionable thinking in the donor countries. Let us summarize a few ideas which have held the field so far, particularly in Pakistan:

1948–55 Import substituting industries are the key to development.[12]

1960–65 Import substitution is no good; export expansion is the real answer.[13]

1966–67 Industrialization is an illusion; rapid agricultural growth is the only answer.[14]

1967–68 Give top priority to population control policies as all development is likely to be submerged by population explosion.[15]

1971–75 The poor masses have not gained much from development. Reject GNP growth; distribution must come ahead of growth.[16]

[12] As reflected in the Industrial Policy announced in 1948.
[13] Coincided with the introduction of the Export Bonus Scheme in 1960.
[14] Resulted from the curtailment of PL480 food grain shipments and a serious drought in Pakistan.
[15] One of President Ayub's favorite themes toward the later half of the 1960s.
[16] As reflected in Pakistan's Fourth Five-Year Plan (1970–75).

It is probably too much to expect that development planners can remain immune to the current fashions, with their eyes fixed determinedly on their own systems and their unique characteristics, but constant shifts in development strategy are often fairly disruptive of the longer-term development process. This is likely to remain as the major dilemma of development planners: they need a fairly long time horizon to plan structural changes, yet national governments and international development community, for legitimate political compulsions, generally focus on the immediate problems and short-run solutions.

DIVORCE BETWEEN PLANNING AND IMPLEMENTATION

Development planners are quite fond of making a distinction between planning and implementation. When hard pressed, they generally argue that while development planning is their responsibility, its implementation is the responsibility of the entire political and economic system. This is no more than a convenient alibi. A good development plan often comes with a realistic blueprint for its own implementation. It must contain specific recommendations on all the detailed policies, institutional reforms, administrative framework and well-conceived projects which are necessary for its successful implementation. It should also be based on realistic political assumptions. The planners should keep evaluating the plan constantly during the course of its implementation so that timely corrections can be made in its direction.

In Pakistan, the functions of planning and plan evaluation were combined and located within the Planning Commission. This gave less of an excuse to the planners to disassociate themselves from the pace of plan implementation and, in fact, contributed to generally satisfactory implementation of development plans. Pakistan's five-year (or medium-term) development plans were also extended in two directions to ensure their orderly implementation. On the one hand, a long-term perspective plan was prepared, charting out the direction in which the society was expected to move over the next two decades. On the other, annual development plans were introduced, as a supplement to the budget, to accommodate changes in the internal and external economic situation and to translate the five-year plan targets into concrete policies, projects, and budgetary allocations. The preparation of Perspective Plans and Annual Development Plans was one of the main devices in Pakistan to bring planning and implementation into greater harmony.

It is not a sign of weakness, but of strength, that a development plan is continuously revised. Indeed, one should be quite suspicious of a five-year development plan which is implemented precisely according to its original schedule. So many assumptions change over a five-year period—export prospects, aid climate, weather, investment expectations—that it would be dishonest to pretend that all these changes can be foreseen and provided for in the original plan. If, by some coincidence, actual implementation turns out to be exactly as forecast in the plan, something may have gone wrong. It could well be like a stopped clock which gives the right time twice a day.

NEGLECT OF HUMAN RESOURCES

One particular sin of development planning which has persisted, despite some efforts in a few development plans to attend to it, is the general neglect of human resources. Notwithstanding any protests to the contrary, very little investment seems to have gone into the development of human resources in most developing countries, particularly in South Asia. Partly the reason is the presumed long gestation period of any such investment and the lack of any quantitatively established relationship between such investment and output.[17] And yet some

---

[17] This is being increasingly remedied by some recent work. See, for instance, G. Becker, "A Theory of Allocation of Time," *Economic Journal* vol. 75, No. 5, (September 1965), pp. 493–517, and Marcelo Selowsky and Lance Taylor, "The Economics of Malnourished Children: An Example of Disinvestment in Human Capital," *Economic Development and Cultural Change* 22, No. 1 (1973):17–30.

dramatic illustrations are available of what can be achieved by human resource development, probably the most dramatic one being that of China. Within a short period of time, the Chinese appear to have imparted technical and vocational skills to most of their labor force and elementary education to most of their population. The long gestation period was reduced by concentrating on functional, short-term training (for example, the well-known "barefoot doctors") rather than on liberal education or all-around training. Capital has been replaced by organization in many cases so that full employment exists despite meager supplies of capital. An abundant population and labor force have been transformed from a liability into an asset through judicious investments in human resources.[18]

Nothing ever discouraged me so much during my thirteen years as an economic planner in Pakistan as the callous neglect of the education sector in the actual implementation of the development plans. Whenever the financial resource situation was tight—which was often the case—the allocations for education were the first ones to be slashed. No wonder that Pakistan slid back from a literacy level of 18 percent in 1950, which was miserable enough, to a level of 15 percent by 1970, at the same time when China progressed from a similar literacy level to almost universal literacy. To compound the sin, not only the level but the content of education was generally wrong, focused as it was on producing a new generation of gentlemen.[19] It was often a tragic sight to watch a village child reciting some nursery rhymes with great pride while he did not know how to interpret the labels on a bag of fertilizer or to help his aging father decide which fertilizer would be more useful for what crop and at what time. Little was lost, therefore, when the parents withdrew their children from school after two to three years of schooling, making Pakistan's dropout ratio of 85 percent one of the high-

[18] For an excellent discussion, see Dwight Perkins, ed. *Agricultural Development in China, 1368–1968* (Edinburgh: Edinburgh University Press, 1969).

[19] Mahbub ul Haq, "Wasted Investment in Education," *Development Digest*, 1967.

est in the world. A dramatic illustration of how nonfunctional the education and training system had become was provided by one particular incident in the 1960s. Pakistan used to have a program of training intermediate-level medical doctors over a two-year period, mainly to man village dispensaries. The Medical Association of Pakistan agitated successfully that this intermediate level of training should be abolished since the rural areas also deserved the best-trained doctors. The result was that only the five-year specialized medical training courses survived, which certainly gave our doctors among the best training possible but 500 out of every 800 doctors trained every year sought employment abroad: almost none went to the rural areas! The system had successfully killed the intermediate training, which could have been expanded for the benefit of the bulk of the population, in favor of specialized training for the benefit of a privileged few.

It is my conviction that the most essential ingredient in a successful and harmonious development effort is a massive investment in functional literacy and training. Such an investment must be made as an act of faith, without any meticulous calculation of costs and benefits. The most important challenge for development planners is to devise a system of education which extends universal literacy, imparts relevant training, and is accessible to all irrespective of income levels. Without such a sound base, the pattern of development can easily get warped in favor of a privileged minority.

GROWTH WITHOUT JUSTICE

The most unforgivable sin of development planners is to become mesmerized by high growth rates in the Gross National Product and to forget the real objective of development. In country after country, economic growth is being accompanied by rising disparities, in personal as well as in regional incomes. In country after country, the masses are complaining that development has not touched their ordinary lives. Very often, economic growth has meant very little social justice. It has been accompanied by rising unemployment, worsening social services and increasing absolute and relative poverty.

Pakistan seemed to have made a fairly deliberate choice, when President Ayub took over in 1958, when it decided that all the energies of the system be devoted toward a faster pace of economic growth and that the issues of more equitable income distribution and a more democratic system of economic organization be deferred to a distant future. The first priority was growth; the other issues had to take a secondary place.

The commitment to a growth philosophy [20] was so wholehearted that all other policies were subordinated to it. President Ayub was fond of saying that his political manifesto was economic development—and he meant it. In this, he was no different from many of his contemporaries.[21] He had taken all precautions to ensure that the impulses for economic growth were not weakened by timid economic policies or political interference. The government had gone out of its way to encourage a handful of industrialists, big farmers, and capitalists to save and invest. Generous fiscal concessions were available and taxes were light and widely evaded. The National Planning Commission had been skillfully isolated from the political process—its only mandate being to devise policies for a high rate of growth. Policies of economic liberalism were followed, without adequate fiscal safeguards, so that incentives were often given to those who already had the basic economic strength to utilize them. International compulsions for "good performance," so as to be eligible for more aid, reinforced domestic pressures for such a pattern of growth. And since the economic scene changed rather dramatically, from less than 2 percent growth in the 1950s to

[20] About which I developed increasing doubts in the latter half of the 1960s: see my observations, for example, in *The Strategy of Economic Planning*, 1966, preface, and in "Pakistan's Choices for the 1970's," a paper presented to the Conference on Economic Growth and Distributive Justice in Pakistan, Rochester, New York, July 1970.

[21] For a good discussion of the choices made by national leaders in a number of different situations, see Howard Wriggins, *The Rulers Imperative* (New York: Columbia University Press, 1969).

over 5 percent growth in the 1960s, few questions were raised about the wisdom of such a total commitment to a growth philosophy.

Some doubts began to rise, however, after the 1965 India-Pakistan war. There was a sharp drop in resources available for development—both because higher defense spending preempted some badly needed resources and because there was a major decline in foreign assistance. This confronted the policy makers with some cruel choices between expansion of economic programs and improvement of social services, between protection of the existing saving rate and a further squeeze on real wages, between greater balance in regional development and more efficient use of reduced resources. In many such confrontations, generally the dictates of economic growth won. It was not surprising, therefore, that during the 1960s, regional and personal income disparities worsened, unemployment increased, real wages of industrial workers declined by about one-third, and there were major, and increasingly shrill, questions raised by East Pakistan about a pattern of development which was leaving it far behind West Pakistan. The 1960s decade ended with the overthrow of President Ayub, despite a fairly good record of efficient and effective economic management and despite an annual increase of nearly 6 percent in the GNP growth. This experience vividly raised the question, which was also being raised in many other developing countries, whether a rapid growth in the GNP was a sufficient condition for successful development—a question to which we turn in the next two chapters.

·2· NEW PERSPECTIVES ON DEVELOPMENT

THE SINS OF DEVELOPMENT PLANNERS came under consider-able attack in the early 1970s. This attack shaped up for a number of reasons—disillusionment with the results of the U.N.'s first development decade, evaluation of various national planning experiences (as described in the last chapter), and can-did self-analysis by many academics after spending some years in the developing world. There was a general demand for new development strategies as a consensus began to emerge that the old ones had largely failed to deliver any real improvement in the living conditions of the vast masses.

The new perspectives on development were rather slow to emerge. The dissatisfaction with the old was often no guarantee of the birth of anything particularly new. It was at this juncture of the debate, in 1971 and 1972, that I tried to advance a few propositions which sounded like heresies at that time but which have become quite respectable, and even fashionable, with the passage of time. For instance:

—growth in the GNP often does not filter down: what is needed is a direct attack on mass poverty;

—the market mechanism is often distorted by the existing distribution of income and wealth: it is generally an unre-liable guide to setting national objectives;

—institutional reforms are generally more decisive than ap-propriate price signals for fashioning relevant development strategies;

—new development strategies must be based on the satisfac-tion of basic human needs rather than on market demand;

—development styles should be such as to build development around people rather than people around development;

—distribution and employment policies must be an integral part of any production plan: it is generally impossible to produce first and distribute later;

—a vital element in the distribution policies is to increase the productivity of the poor by a radical change in the direction of investment toward the poorest sections of society;

—a drastic restructuring of political and economic power relationships is often required if development is to spread to the vast majority of the population.

I first expressed these thoughts in two speeches during the early 1970s. There is considerable overlap in these speeches since they were given within a year of each other and their idea was to drive home the basic message. I have resisted the temptation to change either their style or their substance: they have been reproduced faithfully below in order to trace the evolution of my own ideas on new development strategies.

The first speech was given in May, 1971, and was devoted mainly to the themes of employment and income distribution, though it went beyond this to define some elements of a strategy to tackle poverty. It is reproduced below.[1]

Ever since you asked me to make a presentation to this distinguished forum—on the very dubious assumption that since I was associated with Pakistan's economic planning for thirteen years, I ought to know something about employment strategy—I became conscious of a very deep responsibility. And despite all the gaps in my knowledge, I was determined not to let you down. So I went on a feverish search of the literature on employment strategy, all the theories and policy prescriptions

[1] Keynote address to the 12th World Conference of Society for International Development, Ottawa, May 1971. It was subsequently printed under the title "Employment in the 1970's: A New Perspective," in the *International Development Review*, No. 4, 1971.

that the economists and the practitioners in the field had to offer. And I came up with some distressing discoveries.

SOME DISTRESSING DISCOVERIES

First, it appears that we are assembled here to discuss a problem whose nature and dimensions we simply do not know. I looked at various estimates of unemployment and underemployment which had been prepared for the developing countries and was distressed to find that estimates of 5 to 10 percent unemployment and 20 to 25 percent underemployment were tossed around with a casualness which was simply frightening. There was no agreed methodology for measuring unemployment or underemployment, no definite ideas or projections on what had happened in this field in the 1960s or what might happen in the 1970s, and very poor knowledge about this "vital" concern even in some of the largest and most affected countries like India, Pakistan, and Brazil.

Second, while we economists knew so little about the nature and dimensions of the unemployment problem, we suffered from no modesty when it came to definitive policy prescriptions. The favorite prescription of the economists—besides the doubling or tripling of growth rates—is to correct the price system, particularly exchange rates, interest rates, terms of trade between agriculture and industry and prices of all factors of production. But has this faith in the price system been tested empirically? When various developing countries corrected their exchange rates or interest rates at various times, was this followed by a great surge in their employment situation or merely by better utilization of capital, larger output and higher labor productivity? In any event, how large a segment of the economy does the price adjustment affect when there is a large subsistence sector in these countries and the modern industrial sector generally contributes less than 10 percent to total output? No one will dare suggest that price corrections will not move these economies in the right direction. But are they decisive? Or do they make only a marginal impression on the unemployment problem? We need far more empirical evidence before we can pass any overall judgments.

Third, there is a fashion these days to talk about intermediate technology, something which is supposed to be more labor-intensive and more suited to the needs of the developing countries than the technology presently used in the developed world. But where does it exist? I found very little evidence of it in the developed countries, which have no real incentive for fashioning special technology for the developing countries and which export a good deal of their technology under tied assistance. There are no great improvisations going on in the developing countries themselves and no major research institutes devoting their energies to the development of intermediate technology. The only place where I found something resembling intermediate technology was in China, but there has not been much transfer of it to the developing countries, as China's trade and aid are fairly limited at present.

Fourth, I found in the literature on employment abundant suggestions that the developed world should open up its markets to the labor-intensive products of the developing countries. Here, at least, the evidence is fairly clear: no one has detected any impatience on the part of any developed country to follow this prescription.

Finally, looking at the national plans of the developing countries, it was obvious that employment was often a secondary, not a primary, objective of planning. It was generally added as an afterthought to the growth target in GNP but very poorly integrated in the framework of planning. I know from my own experience with the formulation of Pakistan's five-year plans that the chapter on employment strategy was always added at the end, to round off the plans and make them look complete and respectable, and was hardly an integral part of the growth strategy or policy framework. In fact, most of the developments which affected the employment situation favorably, such as the rural works program and the green revolution, were planned primarily for higher output, and their employment-generating potential was accidental and not planned. There were endless numbers of research teams, our own and foreign, fixing up our national accounts and ensuring that they adequately registered our rate of growth; there was not a fraction of this effort devoted to employment statistics.

The employment objective, in short, has been the stepchild of planning, and it has been assumed, far too readily, that high rates of growth will ensure full employment as well. But what if they don't? A sustained 6 percent rate of growth in Pakistan in the 1960s was accompanied by rising unemployment, particularly in East Pakistan. And what happens if the developing countries cannot achieve the high growth rates of 10 percent or more that it may take to eliminate unemployment and are confined to 5 or 6 percent over the present decade? Should they quietly accept rising unemployment, and the social and political unrest that accompanies it, as the inevitable price for not growing any faster?

There were uncomfortable questions of this kind which led me to a re-examination of the overall theory and practice of development. And I found it to be even in a sorrier state than the literature on employment.

HAS POVERTY DECREASED?

Here we stand after two decades of development, trying to pick up the pieces, and we simply do not know whether problems associated with dire poverty have increased or decreased or what real impact the growth of GNP has made on them. We do know that the rate of growth, as measured by the increase in GNP, has been fairly respectable in the 1960s, especially by historical standards. We also know that some developing countries have achieved a fairly high rate of growth over a sustained period. But has it made a dent on the problems of mass poverty? Has it resulted in a reduction in the worst forms of poverty—malnutrition, disease, illiteracy, shelterless population, squalid housing? Has it meant more employment and greater equality of opportunities? Has the character of development conformed to what the masses really wanted? We know so little in this field. There are only a few selected indices and they are rather disquieting.

A recent study in India shows that 40 to 50 percent of the total population has a per capita income below the official poverty line where malnutrition begins. And what's more pertinent, the per capita income of this group has declined over the last two decades while the average per capita income went up.

In Pakistan, which experienced a healthy growth rate during the 1960s, unemployment increased, real wages in the industrial sector declined by one-third, per capita income disparity between East and West Pakistan nearly doubled, and concentrations of industrial wealth became an explosive economic and political issue. And in 1968, while the international world was still applauding Pakistan as a model of development, the system exploded—not only for political reasons but because of economic unrest.

Brazil has recently achieved a growth rate close to 7 percent but persisting maldistribution of income continues to threaten the very fabric of its society.

These instances can be multiplied. There is in fact need for much more work in this field. The essential point, however, is that a high growth rate has been, and is, no guarantee against worsening poverty and economic explosions.

What has gone wrong? We were confidently told that if you take care of your GNP, poverty will take care of itself. We were often reminded to keep our eyes focused on a high GNP growth target, as it was the best guarantee for eliminating unemployment and of redistributing incomes later through fiscal means. Then what really happened? Where did the development process go astray?

WHAT WENT WRONG?

My feeling is that it went astray at least in two directions. First, we conceived our task not as the eradication of the worst forms of poverty but as the pursuit of certain high levels of per capita income. We convinced ourselves that the latter is a necessary condition for the former but we did not, in fact, give much thought to the interconnection. We development economists persuaded the developing countries that life begins at $1,000 and thereby we did them no service. They chased elusive per capita income levels, they fussed about high growth rates in GNP, they constantly worried about "how much was produced and how fast," they cared much less about "what was produced and how it was distributed."

This hot pursuit of GNP growth was not necessarily wrong; it only blurred our vision. It is no use pretending that it did not, for how else can we explain the worsening poverty in many developing countries? How else can we explain our own preoccupation as economists with endless refinements of statistical series concerning GNP, investment, saving, exports and imports; continuing fascination with growth models; and formulation of evaluation criteria primarily in terms of output increases? If eradication of poverty was the real objective, why did so little professional work go into determining the extent of unemployment, maldistribution of incomes, malnutrition, shelterless population or other forms of poverty? Why is it that even after two decades of development, we know so little about the extent of real poverty—even in such "well-planned" economies as India and Pakistan?

Besides the constant preoccupation with GNP growth, another way we went wrong was in assuming that income distribution policies could be divorced from growth policies and could be added later to obtain whatever distribution we desired. Here we displayed a misguided faith in the fiscal systems of the developing countries and a fairly naïve understanding of the interplay of economic and political institutions. We know now that the coverage of these fiscal systems is generally narrow and difficult to extend. We also know that once production has been so organized as to leave a fairly large number of people unemployed, it becomes almost impossible to redistribute incomes to those who are not even participating in the production stream. We have a better appreciation now of the evolution of modern capitalist institutions and their hold on political decision making, and hence we are more aware that the very pattern and organization of production itself dictates a pattern of consumption and distribution which is politically very difficult to change. Once you have increased your GNP by producing more luxury houses and cars, it is not very easy to convert them into low-cost housing or bus transport. A certain pattern of consumption and distribution inevitably follows.

We have a number of case studies by now which show how illusory it was to hope that the fruits of growth could be redistributed without first reorganizing the pattern of production and investment. Many fast-growing economies in Latin America illustrate this point. In my own country, Pakistan, the very institutions we created for promoting faster growth and capital accumulation later frustrated all our efforts toward better distribution and greater social justice. I am afraid that the evidence is unmistakable and the conclusion inescapable: divorce between production and distribution policies is false and dangerous. The distribution policies must be built into the very pattern and organization of production.

Where does all this lead us? It leads us to a basic re-examination of the existing theories and practice of development. It is time that we stand economic theory on its head and see if we get any better results. In a way, the current situation reminds me of the state of affairs in the developed world in the early 1930s before Keynes shook us all with his General Theory. Since existing theories fitted none of the facts in the real world, they had to be discarded. Keynes provided us with a fresh way of looking at economic and political realities. His theoretical framework was not very elegant but his ideas had a powerful impact.

The developing countries today are seeking a fresh way of looking at their problems. They are disillusioned, and somewhat chastened, by the experience of the last two decades. They are not too sure what the new perspective on development should be, but at least some of the elements are becoming increasingly clear.

A NEW PERSPECTIVE ON DEVELOPMENT

First, the objective of development must be viewed as a selective attack on the worst forms of poverty. Development goals must be defined in terms of progressive reduction and eventual elimination of malnutrition, disease, illiteracy, squalor, unemployment, and inequalities. We were taught to take care of our GNP, as this will take care of poverty. Let us reverse this and take care of poverty, as this will take care of the GNP. In other words, let us worry about the *content* of GNP even more than its rate of increase.

Second, and this follows from the first, the developing countries should define minimum (or threshold) consumption standards that they must reach in a manageable period of time, say a decade. Consumption planning should move to the center of the stage; production planning should be geared to it. And consumption planning should not be in financial terms but in physical terms, in terms of a minimum bundle of goods and services that must be provided to the common man to eliminate the worst manifestations of poverty: minimum nutritional, educational, health and housing standards, for instance. There are two major implications of this strategy.

First, we must get away from the tyranny of the demand concept and replace it by the concept of minimum needs, at least in the initial stages of development, since to weight basic needs by the ability to pay is outrageous in a poor society. It will only distort the patterns of production and consumption in favor of the "haves," as has happened in many societies.

Second, the pursuit of elusive present-day Western standards and per capita income levels, which cannot be reached even over the course of the next century, must be replaced by the concept of a threshold income which each society defines for itself and which can be reached in a manageable period of a decade or so.

Third, the concerns for more production and better distribution should be brought together in defining the pattern of development; both must be generated at the same time; the present divorce between the two concerns must end. If the pat-

tern of production (and exports and imports) is geared to satisfying minimum consumption requirements and to employing the
entire labor force, higher production will itself lead to better
distribution.

Fourth—and this is implicit in the third—employment
should become a primary objective of planning and no longer be
treated as only a secondary objective. Let a society regard its entire labor force as allocable; over this force its limited capital
resources must be spread. Let us reverse the present thinking
that, since there is only a fixed amount of capital to be allocated
at a particular time, it can employ only a certain part of the
labor force, leaving the rest unemployed, to subsist on others as
dependents or as beggars, without any personal income, often
suffering from the worst forms of malnutrition and squalor. Instead let us treat the pool of labor as given; at any particular
time it must be combined with the existing capital stock irrespective of how low the productivity of labor or capital may be.
If physical capital is short, skill formation and organization can
replace it in the short run. It is only if we proceed from the goal
of full employment, with people doing something useful, even
with little doses of capital and organization, that we can eradi-
cate some of the worst forms of poverty. With this goal, even
the character and pattern of production will change, as Dudley
Seers points out in his Colombia Report, since better income
distribution will also mean greater production of those goods
which are less import- and capital-intensive and which require
more labor.[2]

THE CHINESE EXPERIENCE

These are only a few elements in the new perspective that is
needed today on development. They are neither complete nor
carefully integrated nor perhaps very original. I offer them only
as an invitation to further thinking. And if some of this frame-

[2] Dudley Seers, *Towards Full Employment: A Programme for Colombia* (Geneva: ILO, 1970).

work sounds fairly fanciful, let me invite you to study the development experience of the largest developing country in the world, that of China. I visited it twice in the last few years and I must say that I was greatly impressed by its economic performance measured against ours in Pakistan. It was not obvious to me what the real rate of growth of China was, but it was obvious to me that they had looked at the problem of development from the point of view of eradication of poverty and not from the viewpoint of reaching a certain prescribed per capita income level. It appears that within a period of less than two decades, China has eradicated the worst forms of poverty; it has full employment, universal literacy and adequate health facilities; it suffers from no obvious malnutrition or squalor. What's more, it was my impression that China has achieved this at fairly modest rates of growth, by paying more attention to the content and distribution of GNP. In fact, China has proved that it is a fallacy that poverty can be removed and full employment achieved only at high rates of growth and only over a period of many decades.

How has it accomplished this? Of course, its political system, its isolation, its great size, its ideological mobilization, all of these have contributed to the evolution of its pattern of development. But are there any lessons to learn, even if we do not subscribe to its political system? Is there not a practical illustration here of a selective attack on the problems of poverty, pursuit of a threshold income and minimum consumption standards, merger of production and distribution policies and achievement of full employment with a meager supply of capital? It is no use insisting that these results must have been achieved at tremendous social and political costs; people in the developing countries are often undergoing these costs without any visible economic results so that they look at the experience of China with great envy and praise. It is time, especially as China's isolation ends, that there be an objective and detailed study of its experience in place of the usual rhetoric to which we have been subjected so far.

In conclusion, let me say that the search for a new perspective

on development—of which the themes of this Conference, employment and social justice, are only two facets—has already
begun in the developing countries. Many of us from these countries, who are essentially products of Western liberalism and
who returned to our countries to deliver development, have
often ended up delivering more tensions and unrest. We have
seen a progressive erosion of liberalism, both in our own countries and amongst our donor friends abroad. And we stand today
disspirited and disillusioned. It is no use offering us tired old
trade-offs and crooked-looking production functions whenever
we talk about income distribution and employment. It is no use
dusting off old theories and polishing up old ideas and asking
us to go and try them again. It is time that we take a fresh look
at the entire theory and practice of development.

                    *   *   *

My next major address on this issue was given in April 1972.
Here I tried to advance the argument a little further by outlining some of the major institutional changes a developing
country would need before launching a direct attack on mass
poverty. The text of this address is reproduced below.[3]

I have been asked to sum up the present crisis in the developing
world in the span of the next twenty minutes or so. I regard
this as a major crisis in itself since the developing world is so
diverse and the crisis in development has been building up for
so long that any summary treatment of it is likely to be challenged all around. Anyway, I am going to try, much against
my own better judgment.

NATURE OF THE DEVELOPMENT CRISIS

I believe that economic development is in serious trouble today.
And the indications are many.

[3] Address to the International Development Conference, Washington,
D.C., April 1972. It was subsequently printed in *The Washington Post,*
April 30, 1972, and in *World Development* 1, No. 7 (July 1973).

· After two decades of development, the achievements are quite meager. When you rip aside the confusing figures on growth rates, you find that for about two-thirds of humanity the increase in per capita income has been less than one dollar for the last twenty years.

· Even this increase, miserable as it may seem, has been unevenly distributed, with the poorest 40 percent of the population hopelessly squeezed in its struggle for existence and sometimes getting even less than it received twenty years ago.

· Some successful cases of development have turned into development disasters—Pakistan and Nigeria among them.

· There is "development weariness" in many developing countries today, with strident voices asking for a social and economic revolution, and there is "aid weariness" in the developed countries today, with many voices asking for an end to a partnership which was never much of a partnership.

· And to cap it all, many advocates of zero growth have sprung up in the very societies where growth had always been regarded as a sacred goddess, and who had preached to the developing countries the virtues of an undiluted commitment to growth objectives, underlining how serious the reaction really is against growth for the sake of growth.

What has really gone wrong? Why is there such disillusionment about economic development? Where are the origins of the present crisis?

I believe that the developing countries have themselves to blame for much of the present sorry mess.

Two decades ago, when the developing countries set out to accelerate their pace of economic development, they seemed to have made three basic decisions.

· Dazzled by the high living standards of the developed countries and convinced that real life begins at $1,000 or

· thereabouts, they decided to go after high growth rates in GNP in their mad chase after certain magic figures of average per capita incomes.

· They generally adopted the "mixed economy" as a style of development, convinced that they were smart enough to combine the best features of capitalism and socialism.

· They turned to the developed countries for generous assistance, hoping that this would make possible the attainment of high growth rates and living standards over a manageable period of time.

All three of these decisions turned out to be disastrous.

WIDENING DISPARITIES

The chase of the Western living standards was illusory at best. After two decades, the evidence is painfully clear. The per capita income disparity between rich and poor nations has continued to widen in the last twenty years. Today, the average per capita income of the developed world is $2,400 compared to $180 in the developing countries. The gap has widened to $2,220. It is expected to widen by another $1,100 by 1980. And all the present indications are that the gap will continue to widen and the rich nations will continue to become richer, despite all the liberalism that is generally expressed in forums like this. Just to underline how hopeless it is to expect the gap between rich and poor nations to narrow, let me mention just one comparison—the increase in the per capita GNP of the United States in one year equals the increase that India may be able to manage in about a hundred years. Therefore, to conceive the objectives of development in terms of Western living standards or to focus on the widening income gap between the rich and the poor nations is not meaningful at all, except to make the rich nations feel uncomfortable from time to time and to make the poor feel sorry for themselves. The developing countries have no choice but to turn inwards, in much the same way as China did twenty-three years ago, and to adopt a different style of life, seeking a consumption pattern more consistent with their own poverty—pots and pans and bicycles and simple consumption habits—without being seduced by the life styles of the rich. This requires a redefinition of economic and social objectives which is of truly staggering proportions, a liquidation of the privileged groups and vested interests which may well be impossible in many societies, and a redistribution of political and economic power which may only be achieved through revolution rather than through evolutionary change.

SEARCH FOR A NEW DEVELOPMENT STRATEGY

This also means that the developing countries have to search for a new development strategy. The old strategy is based on the quiet assumption that poverty can be taken care of through high growth rates, which will eventually filter down to the masses. In this strategy, high growth rates are always better than low growth rates and distribution can be taken care of after growth is achieved. Both these premises have proved bankrupt by now.

It is not true that, because high growth rates enlarge society's options, they are invariably preferable to low growth rates. It all depends on the structure of these growth rates. If a high growth rate is achieved through rising military expenditures, or through the production of luxury goods for the rich and the privileged, it is not necessarily better than a lower growth rate which is more evenly distributed. In other words, judgments about different levels of growth rates cannot be made independently of the income distribution implicit in them. It is not merely a question of how much is produced, but of what is produced and how it is distributed. GNP measurements, unfortunately, do not register social satisfaction.

Here the second part of the old strategy comes in, which argues that income distribution is a subsequent consideration. If there are more material goods and services in the system, they can always be redistributed in such a way as to create more social satisfaction. This is simply not true. And it is important that this line of reasoning be rejected, since it has done considerable damage already.

It is not true for at least the following three reasons:

· Poor societies often have very poor means of redistributing income. The coverage of the fiscal systems is generally very limited. Even when income distribution is extremely skewed, it is difficult to reach through direct taxation. To illustrate, even if 60 percent of income accrues to 20 percent of the population in India, this still implies an average per capita income level of $300 for the "rich" which is below the income tax exemption limit of $400. In other words, income transfers from one sector to the other can be arranged only to a very limited extent in poor societies through the taxation machinery.
· Income flows are not financial: they are in the form of physical goods and services. They are influenced by the initial distribution of income. If the society has increased its income in the form of luxury housing and motor cars, how do you really convert it into low-cost housing and public buses, short of their physical take-over by the poor?
· The institutions which create growth are not neutral as to its distribution. Thus if the growth institutions are characterized by wide disparities in land holdings and concentrations of industrial wealth, the process of growth will strengthen them further and they will resist and frustrate all future attempts to take away their powers and privileges through orderly reforms. This is essentially what happened in Pakistan in the 1960s.

The new development strategy, therefore, must reject the thesis that poverty can be attacked indirectly through the growth rates filtering down to the masses. It must be based on the premise that poverty must be attacked directly.

DIRECT ATTACK ON POVERTY

What are the elements in such a direct attack on mass poverty? It is difficult to say at this stage since the developing countries are only beginning to perceive this problem in a new perspective. But let me mention a few elements which are critical:

- To start with, the focus should shift to the poorest 40–50 percent in society. Who are they? How numerous are they? How have their living standards behaved over time? Let us find out a little more, even at this late stage, about the problem we set out to tackle about twenty years ago.

- In planning national production targets, the basic minimum needs of these poor should be taken into account, irrespective of whether they can express them in the market or not. In other words, market demand—which is so largely influenced by existing income distribution—should be rejected explicitly in favor of fixing national consumption and production targets on the basis of minimum human needs. We have been slaves of the concept of market demand for too long. But the concept of market demand mocks poverty or plainly ignores it, since the poor have very little purchasing power.

- It follows that the problem of development must be redefined as a selective attack on the worst forms of poverty. Development goals should be expressed in terms of the progressive reduction and eventual elimination of malnutrition, disease, illiteracy, squalor, unemployment and inequalities. Social indicators must be developed and progress of plans must be measured in terms of specific and quantitative goals in these fields and not in terms of average per capita income. We were taught to take care of our GNP, since this would take care of poverty. Let us reverse this and take care of poverty first, since GNP can take care of itself, for it is only a convenient summation, and not a motivation, for human efforts.

- It also follows that the concerns for more production and better distribution should be brought together and not treated separately. This invariably means that employment should be treated as a primary, not a secondary, objective of development since it is the most powerful means of redistributing income in a poor society. Capital should not be concentrated in a small modern sector, enjoying high productivity and savings, but spread thinly over a wide segment of the economy—through public works programs, if necessary, and even at the risk of lowering the average productivity of labor and lowering the future rate of growth. The poor societies have to face this choice squarely. They have a limited amount of capital. They can either raise substantially the productivity of a small part of the labor force in the modern sector while leaving a large part unemployed or settle for a lower average productivity but full employment. Again, it appears to me that China made the second choice and has, therefore, been able to achieve full employment and equitable income distribution at a relatively low level of per capita income.

MIXED ECONOMY

But can such a strategy of development be conceived and implemented in the present political and economic structures in the developing countries? And here we come to the second of the disastrous decisions—the choice of the mixed economy. In most cases, such a choice has combined the worst, not the best, features of capitalism and socialism. It has often prevented the developing countries from adopting honest-to-goodness economic incentives and using the free functioning of the price system to achieve efficiency in a capitalistic framework, if not equity. In reality, there have been too many inefficient administrative controls and price distortions. At the same time, the choice of the mixed economy has prevented these societies from pursuing their goals in a truly socialistic framework, since mixed economy institutions have often been more capitalistic than not. The end result, therefore, has often been that they have fallen between two stools, combining weak economic incentives with bureaucratic socialism. Neither the ends of growth nor equity are served by such confusion in social and political objectives within the framework of a mixed economy.

My own feeling is that the days of the mixed economy are numbered. The developing countries will have to become either more frankly capitalistic or more genuinely socialist. The capitalistic alternative is workable only in those situations where the society is willing to accept income inequalities over a long period of time without exploding or where extremely high growth rates (10 to 15 percent) can be financed with a generous inflow of resources from Western friends. Otherwise, the only alternative is a genuinely socialist system, based on a different ideology and a different pattern of society. But this does not mean bureaucratic socialism; it means a major change in the political balance of power within these societies and drastic economic and social reforms. Whether the developing countries can manage such a change without violent revolutions is a critical question of our time.

FOREIGN ASSISTANCE

And now let me turn briefly to the third disastrous decision—the dependence on foreign assistance. Let me make it quite clear that I am one of those who has always believed in economic liberalism and in a genuine partnership between the developed and the developing countries. But the sorry record of foreign assistance in the last two decades is beginning to convince me, as it has convinced many of my liberal colleagues, that the developing world would have been better off without such assistance. Unfortunately, I do not have the time to go into the early origins of foreign assistance, its changing motivations and its present plight, but let me offer a few observations quite baldly without elaboration.

- The level of foreign assistance that is required for a meaningful change in the developing countries over a short period of a decade or so through the growth-rate route is at least four to five times the present level of net official development assistance. The developed countries have neither the will nor the imagination to offer such assistance.
- The present levels of assistance are only of marginal significance for the developing countries and come with so many project conditions, foreign consultants, in appropriate technology, and irritating debt problems that they sap the initiative and freedom of action of the developing world.

· The developing countries must regard foreign assistance as an undependable residual in their total planning effort and turn their energies to internal institutional changes that are required for creating a different economic and social order, based on egalitarianism and a second-best standard of living.

· In the international field, the developing countries should organize their "poor power" to wring major concessions from the rich nations and to arrange for a genuine transfer of resources. Since the rich nations are going to shrink in the next few decades to less than 10 percent of the total world population with over 70 percent of world income, the poor will be numerous enough and resentful enough to organize such an effort.

· One element in such a confrontation will be to serve notice to the developed nations that the developing countries cannot pay their present foreign debt and that the world community must make arrangements for its orderly cancellation.

· Another element will be to exploit their collective bargaining power in their negotiations with the rich nations. Recently, oil negotiations by the OPEC members are expected to yield $20 billion of additional revenues to the oil producing countries by 1980.[4] Similarly, if the developing countries can exploit the current concern about the depletion of nonrenewable resources and agitate for a 10 percent tax on consumers of these minerals, they could collect as much as $30 billion over this decade for a common international development fund. Again, they can stake their claim to the commonly held resources of mankind, like oceans and space, and start demanding that at least 70 percent of the proceeds from the exploitation of such resources should go to them on the basis of world population.

What I am trying to convey here is the emerging mood in the developing countries. I am not an apostle of confrontation,

---

[4] This was written in the spring of 1972. The actual events have moved even faster than I had anticipated. (See Table 3 in the Statistical Appendix.)

nor am I prepared to forsake my own liberalism. But I think it is important to realize that liberalism cannot survive in an illiberal world. The developing countries are passing through a very dark and ugly mood. They are questioning all the assumptions on which they based their early development strategy. I cannot predict what may come out of this re-examination. But if I have to make a guess today, I would expect that economic development in the next few years will be increasingly based on a new strategy embodying a direct attack on mass poverty, a genuine turn toward socialism and a far greater degree of self-reliance. This is the new manifesto that most developing countries are trying to articulate. But there is a wide gap between articulation and implementation, between dim perception and real action. The future of the developing world may well turn on how far this gap can be bridged without violent political explosions.

·3· INTERNATIONAL ASPECTS OF NEW DEVELOPMENT STRATEGIES

W E HAVE FOCUSED SO FAR mainly on the internal aspects of new development strategies. It is time now to turn to some of the international aspects, particularly to the constant debate on inward- and outward-looking strategies and to the relevance of this entire debate to what has already been said on the need for new development styles in the Third World.

Whatever else the developing countries may be suffering from, they certainly do not suffer from any lack of advice in the field of trade policy alternatives. These days they are being offered a liberal choice between outward-looking strategies, inward-looking strategies, regional and subregional cooperation, and many shrewd combinations of all of these alternatives.

OUTWARD-LOOKING STRATEGIES

Clearly, the front-runner is the outward-looking strategy. This is the favorite prescription of most economists from the academic community. They argue, with a good deal of righteousness, that the pursuit of an outward-looking strategy would be consistent with international comparative advantage and would insure an optimum allocation of resources. Academics dismiss, with a certain degree of irritation, some of the practical difficulties in persuading the international world to become more liberal in its actual trade practices, as they believe that the world should be more rationally organized along the lines of international division of labor—and if it is not so organized at present, it ought to be changed. On the whole, they represent the voice of economic liberalism and command considerable respect and support.[1]

On the other hand, the policy-makers from the developing world generally throw up their hands in despair and frustration every time one mentions outward-looking strategies. Such practitioners typically come out with a handful of statistics and a long litany of terrible experiences they have had in gaining access to the markets of the developed countries.

With considerable justification, these policy makers point to agricultural protectionism in the developed countries. They contend that not only is the demand for their primary commodities growing slowly, but a further injury is suffered as the developed countries keep some of their primary exports out of their markets, through deliberate action to protect their own farm lobbies. For instance, the United States, Britain, Japan and the EEC (European Economic Community) spend about $21–$24 billion a year on direct and indirect support of importable primary commodities, which contrasts rather sadly with the $12 billion of net official development assistance.

In the field of manufactures, policy makers from the developing countries are apt to raise an accusing finger at the developed countries' high tariffs and restricted quotas for the import of manufactured goods from the developing countries. With considerable anger, they point to the fact that the average tariff on imports of manufactures into industrialized countries is 6.5 percent for items from developed countries, but 11.8 percent for those from developing countries, despite the Kennedy Round cuts of early 1972. The differential exists because most of the manufactured exports of developing countries are concentrated in certain groups such as textiles, leather, footwear, and other cheap consumer goods which are subject to heavier than average tariffs in the developed countries in addition to restrictive quotas.

[1] See, for instance, Harry G. Johnson, *Trade and Development: Essays in Economics* (London: Allen & Unwin, 1971); and Richard E. Caves and Harry G. Johnson, *Readings in International Economics* (Homewood, Ill.: Richard D. Irwin, 1968, for the American Economic Association).

Many policy makers in the developing countries would acknowledge that, despite all this, manufactured exports from developing countries to the developed world increased at a healthy rate of about 14 percent in the 1960s. But they are quick to point out that this was from a very small base and that much of it was accounted for by only five countries: Taiwan, Korea, Mexico, Yugoslavia, and India. Obviously, it pays to be small if one is pursuing an aggressive export policy. If India or any other large country were to try to unload, on a per capita basis, the same quantity of manufactured goods as Taiwan and Korea presently do, world markets would surely become chaotic and severely test the economic liberalism of the most ardent advocates of outward-looking trade-policy strategies.

As if this is not a sufficient list of grievances, the developing country policy makers keep pointing out, from any forum that they can get hold of, a number of other complaints which restrict their freedom of action in international competition. One of the favorite complaints is that the developing world faces unfair competition from aid tied to procurement from the country of origin, which often insures that high-priced imports available under the cover of aid from developed countries win over lower-priced imports available from developing countries without the benefit of the cover of suppliers' credits. The developing countries are also likely to point to the strength of pressure lobbies and vested interests in the developed countries which normally assure that protectionism triumphs over liberalism when the chips are down and actual policy decisions are taken.

It is difficult to decide between the liberal academics and the complaining policy makers in this case.[2] Basically, an outward-looking strategy, while attractive in principle, is still a very high-risk strategy. It assumes that developed countries are also likely to become outward-looking. But, in the international field as in any other walk of life, it takes two to tango. Since it is not quite under the control of the developing countries to make the developed world "tango," except of its own accord,

[2] In this context, see some of the recent writings of Jagdish N. Bhagwati and Anne O. Krueger, *Foreign Trade Regimes and Economic Development* (New York: NBER, distributed by Columbia University Press, 1975).

the developing countries take a tremendous risk in basing their entire future development strategy on the assumption that—to pursue the metaphor—the developed world will definitely tango. If they are denied fair access to the markets of the developed countries, they are likely to be stuck with unwanted export capacity. On the other hand, import substitution strategy carries fewer risks for the harassed policy makers; high-cost goods produced behind protective walls can still be shoved down the throats of the local populations by closing down any decent alternative. As far as the developing country policy makers are concerned, particularly in the large countries, this high element of risk is fairly decisive in their attitude toward outward-looking strategies.

INWARD-LOOKING STRATEGIES

The other alternative strategy is what is described as inward-looking, though such a description is often resented by many of its advocates. This is generally the preferred operational strategy in many developing countries, even though it is attacked with considerable vehemence by the academic community. Its advocates use all possible arguments in its favor—from export pessimism to the infant-industry argument, and from balance-of-payments crises to the need for the development of capital goods industries to sustain long-term development. If one looks around the developing world scene in the 1950s and 1960s, he would find that import substitution has generally been the basis for industrialization strategy, particularly in simple consumer goods. It is being argued by many developing countries that the 1970s should be a decade for import substitution in capital goods, as possibilities for easier consumer goods substitution are already being exhausted and as these developing countries are not likely to obtain the capital goods they require for their accelerated development through generous aid or expanding trade.[3]

[3] See, for instance, William Brian Reddaway, *The Development of the Indian Economy* (London: Allen & Unwin, 1962), p. 216.

Import substitution strategies traditionally have been the favorite target of the academic community. Many fair-minded analysts concede that import substitution is a necessary stage in the industrialization process, but they accuse the developing countries of taking import substitution to an excess and managing it behind inefficiently high protective walls, resulting in serious misallocation of resources. Often the criticism here is directed to inefficient types of import substitution rather than to import substitution strategy as such, but too often the attack is carried so far as to lose this important distinction.

It is sometimes forgotten in this debate that in most industries some part is meant for import substitution and some part becomes available for export expansion. It is clearly wrong to characterize certain industries as import substituting or as export industries because, over a period of time, one characteristic can shade into the other. Far more important, most of the debate on import substitution has unfortunately concentrated on the industrial sector, while policy makers in the developing countries view this strategy as a fairly broad-based one. For instance, considerable import substitution is possible and desirable in food production and in services. The unconscious identification of import substitution with industrialization has often meant that its critics have tended to overlook the possibilities of domestic agricultural development to replace food imports and manpower training to replace foreign consultants.

REGIONAL AND SUBREGIONAL COOPERATION

Some people, who have felt increasingly disillusioned with the debate on outward- and inward-looking strategies, have turned to regional cooperation among the developing countries as a viable alternative or, at least, a supplement. These people argue that if the developed world is not being accommodating and not opening up its markets to the developing countries, then these countries can gang up and form regional groupings wherein they can exchange their simple consumer goods and equipment with greater assurance and at better prices. The idealists in this

field think in terms of grand designs for regional markets cover-
ing large areas. The realists, however, stick to the possibility of
subregional groupings among a limited number of countries—
particularly small countries—sharing similar problems and having some natural complementarities.

Unfortunately, the developing countries have shown very
little willingness in coming together in the form of regional arrangements. The experience of subregional groupings in the
Central American Common Market, the East African Community, or the Regional Cooperation for Development (RCD) among
Turkey, Iran and Pakistan, has been fairly disappointing, quell-
ing even some of the ardent supporters of the regional cooperation alternative. There is nothing wrong with the alternative
as such, but it appears that the time for this idea has not yet arrived. It is possible that the developing countries may sink their
political differences and turn to one another if they feel sufficiently disturbed about their poor bargaining position in the
international world and about the unfair treatment that they are
getting in the markets of the developed countries. But so far, at
least, they have shown very little inclination to do so. It is my
own belief that regional cooperation on any worthwhile scale is
a matter still a decade or two away, not a practical possibility
during the 1970s.

At the same time, it is possible for the developing countries
to agree on one or two audacious actions which may protect
their interests in the international world vis-à-vis the developed
countries. One such action can be a major and uniform depre-
ciation of the exchange rates in all the developing countries,
which could help insulate them as a group and set up a natural
advantage for trading among themselves.[4] For instance, the developing countries should explore among themselves the possibility of a large devaluation, say 50 percent, particularly for
manufactured exports, which would leave their exchange rates

[4] See also, Mahbub ul Haq, Comments on Prof. Lizano's paper on "Economic Integration among Less Developed Countries," printed in the *Proceedings of the International Economic Association*, Budapest, 1974.

vis-à-vis one another the same as before but would give them a major advantage in the markets of the developed countries. Such a bold action can succeed only if there is complete uniformity in the actions of the developing countries and if the developed countries do not retaliate. At a time when the developing countries still cannot come to any agreement among themselves on a host of detailed measures which are necessary in forming regional markets, it is better to concentrate on some overall sweeping measure, preferably through the price system, which would give them a collective edge over the developed countries and an incentive to trade among themselves.

Other fields where some collective action might be possible on the part of the developing countries are the negotiation of prices of agricultural commodities or minerals and the exploitation of common-property resources of mankind, such as sea-bed resources. Many analysts point out that the recent action by the Organization of Petroleum Exporting Countries in negotiating higher prices for petroleum cannot set a precedent for other natural resources or for other developing countries as it was a fairly specialized case. This is not entirely true, as argued in Part III of this book. In fact, a number of situations are likely to arise during the 1970s where collective action on specific commodities or on specific situations may become feasible. For instance, the imposition of a uniform or varying tax on the consumption of nonrenewable resources in the developed countries and use of the proceeds for the benefit of the developing countries can become a serious possibility during the course of this decade. Again, the developing countries can argue, with considerable justification and probable success, that they should get a proportionate share from the exploitation of sea-bed resources by multinational corporations in the developed countries. We should not regard these entirely as areas of confrontation. Rather, these are areas where the natural interests of the developing countries are likely to bring them together for collective action against the developed countries who are better organized, with a far greater bargaining power, and would otherwise dictate the outcome of these neogiations unless the developing countries really get organized.

RELEVANT POLICY ALTERNATIVES

After reviewing the current heated debate on outward-looking or inward-looking strategies and on possibilities of regional cooperation, one must wonder whether these are really the relevant policy alternatives in the developing world. All these alternatives assume, implicitly or explicitly, that trade is the main engine of growth or can be the leading sector of development in the developing countries. There seems to be a certain harking back here to the experience of the developed countries a century ago when expanding trade paced economic development. However, such an approach to development strategy starts by asking the wrong question or—to repeat a trite phrase—puts the cart before the horse. In fact, the developing countries should first define a viable development strategy and regard trade merely as a derivative from such a strategy and not as a pace setter.

As pointed out in chapters 2 and 3, there is a growing consensus today that developing countries need a new development strategy, concentrating more on a direct attack on the problems of employment and mass poverty. It is increasingly apparent that it is not enough to rely on a rapid rate of growth in the Gross National Product and to hope that it eventually would filter down to the masses. What is required is specific and direct attention to the poorest sections of society through programs, projects and public services which would reach these sections. If this strategy is taken to its logical conclusion, planners in these countries will have to start with the identification of the minimum basic human needs for survival and a production program geared to satisfying these basic needs in the fields of nutrition, clothing, shelter, education, and health. This will require either a deliberate turning away from the signals given by the market, which are weighted by the current income distribution, or sweeping institutional reforms to get the income distribution right first, before defining the development strategy for the country.

Whichever way it comes out, such a development strategy would inevitably mean a greater emphasis on the production of essential commodities (such as food, clothing and housing), a much simpler second-best standard of living geared to the poverty of the country and an all-out effort to create some kind of employment for everyone participating in the labor force. An inward-looking strategy becomes, as such, part and parcel of a development strategy revamped along these lines. But this is not "inward-looking" in the same sense of the word as import substitution strategies discussed earlier. If there is substitution involved here, it is substitution for the life styles of the developed countries, which the developing countries cannot afford on a nationwide basis at the present stage of their development. The developing countries would have to define for themselves living standards or life styles that they can afford on a nationwide scale and that are consistent with their present state of overall poverty. It is inevitable that this would mean not only a much simpler standard of living, but also a much greater concentration on public services which can be distributed more equitably—public buses, public hospitals, public education, even communal housing. If developing countries really undertake such a sweeping change in their development strategies, the prestigious symbols of private ownership may also change—the familiar example being a bicycle economy instead of an automobile economy.

How important is foreign trade in the context of such a new strategy of development? It is obvious that the significance of foreign trade would diminish considerably if the developing countries were to adopt new development styles and patterns of life. For instance, it is difficult to think of many consumer goods from the developed countries which would still be imported by the developing countries. Probably they could import some essential medicines or books but, beyond that, consumer goods from the developed countries would only end up catering to the needs of the privileged few and not to the majority of the population. Again, in this context, one can think of few practical illustrations of intermediate technology which can be usefully transferred from the Western world to the developing countries. Most of this technology will have to be improvised locally. Furthermore, while machinery and raw materials would continue to figure prominently in the import budgets of the developing countries, such imports would naturally be more limited when these countries rely on their own domestic improvisations and use their local resources and talent to look after their own problems. In other words, foreign trade would become a residual in new development strategies, rather than the real basis of accelerated development as it is often regarded in traditional debates on this subject.

Let us recapitulate briefly where this quick survey of the international aspects of new development strategies really leads to:

First, we should deliberately reverse the presumed relationship between trade and development. Trade should not be regarded as a pace setter in any relevant development strategy for the developing world, but merely as a derivative. Developing countries should first define a viable strategy for attacking their problems of unemployment and mass poverty. Trade possibilities should be geared to meeting the objectives of such a strategy.

Second, if this approach is followed, trade sectors will change in character in most developing countries. The privileged minorities, which are often one of the largest consumers of imported goods, will lose their foothold.[5] These systems will also turn to a good deal of improvisation with domestic raw materials, local skills and indigenous technology. Probably, some new trade possibilities may emerge—in pots and pans, bicycles, or simple consumer goods—among developing countries themselves as these countries evolve a new and indigenous life style more consistent with their poverty.

Third, the developing countries should attempt to build a viable trading bloc by fashioning a new institutional framework for promoting trade among themselves. Most of the present in-

[5] For a succinct analysis of how the consumption patterns of a privileged minority come to dominate the composition of trade and the direction of import substitution strategies, see Celso Furtado, "The Concept of External Dependence in the Study of Underdevelopment," reprinted in Charles Wilber, ed., *The Political Economy of Development and Underdevelopment* (New York: Random House, 1973), pp. 118–23.

stitutional framework—shipping, banking, suppliers' credits, exchange rates, etc.—is geared to stimulating trade between the developing countries and the developed world.[6] The UNCTAD (UN Conference on Trade & Tariffs) can play a constructive role here by concentrating its energies on the evolution of an entirely different pattern of institutions which are more suited to the promotion of intradeveloping-countries trade. It is in this perspective that the proposal for a uniform devaluation on manufactured exports, or the various proposals regarding export refinancing for capital goods, or the demands for a review of current pattern of shipping rates should be viewed. All of these measures will help establish the infrastructure of incentives which are needed to encourage the adoption of a relevant development strategy and a sensible trading pattern in the developing world. These measures will also help increase the control of the developing countries over international trade-related services and thereby enable these countries to cut substantially into the present high profit margins enjoyed by the international middlemen, as discussed subsequently in chapter 10.

Finally, while any trade strategy should be clearly subordinated to a new development strategy, it is also important that the developing countries take advantage of the trade sector in meeting their genuine needs and not turn toward autarchy. The concept of self-reliance does not call for a rejection of trade. It is a positive concept, emphasizing greater reliance on a country's own resources, manpower, technology, ideas, institutions, and cultural values. It is consistent with a wide range of trade options. National planners everywhere must discover for themselves, through pragmatic reasoning, the reliance they can place on the trade sector without subverting their main goal of alleviation of mass poverty.

[6] See Theotonio Dos Santos, "The Structure of Dependence," in *American Economic Review* 40, no. 2 (May 1970): 231–36; also the Third World Forum, *Proposals for a New International Economic Order*, Mexico, August 1975, pp. 8–10.

·4· TOWARD A DIRECT ATTACK ON MASS POVERTY

THE THINKING ON DEVELOPMENT STRATEGIES has been in constant ferment during the first half of the 1970s. The unqualified worship of the GNP growth and production efficiency is long since over. Even the most ardent advocates of economic growth make at least a ceremonial bow to the objectives of social justice and distribution. By now, the strategy of launching a direct attack on mass poverty is generally accepted. In fact, national governments as well as the academic community are not considered respectable anymore unless the objective of poverty alleviation is woven into their development plans and their economic writings. We have undoubtedly come a long way since the 1960s. And yet, the change in our perceptions has remained largely at an intellectual level. There are not many concrete instances in the developing world where the philosophy of a direct attack on mass poverty is translated into specific development strategies and practical policy action. This is perhaps not surprising in the initial stages of a search for new development styles. The main focus of future efforts has, therefore, to be on devising practical policies for implementing the goals of poverty alleviation.

On the intellectual level at least, some new concepts have been accepted which would have been regarded as mere heresies only a decade ago. This acceptance in some cases is still very grudging, but, before we turn to considering action programs for national governments, it would be useful to summarize some of the major areas of agreement.

AREAS OF AGREEMENT

First, it is generally accepted by now that market mechanisms are neither efficient nor reliable instruments for allocating resources when the income distribution is very distorted. This does not imply a complete rejection of the price signals. In fact, appropriate price signals can be used in implementing national objectives. The confusion arises only if national goals are determined by market behavior. It is increasingly recognized that development planners should first set their targets for meeting basic human needs, irrespective of market demand, and then, only in the next phase, go on to correct the price system in such a manner as to implement these goals. A related area of agreement is the realization that institutional reforms are often more decisive for a developing country than marginal changes in the price system. There is no longer a blind faith in price corrections achieving a multiplicity of objectives. The prevailing price system is often a slave of the existing economic and political balance of power and, unless these structures are changed through far-reaching reforms regarding the ownership of the means of production, it is realized that the market mechanism can neither function efficiently nor equitably in such a situation. The emphasis has, therefore, shifted in a good deal of economic literature on subjects like land reform, public ownership of industry and key services, and setting up of new institutions to reach the poorest sections of the society.

Second, there is an increasing realization that economic growth does not filter down automatically to the masses except in the modern urban sector and at very high rates of GNP growth. This has been demonstrated by now both through empirical studies and through logical reasoning. Some quantitative analyses, which attempted to differentiate the overall growth rate of the economy from the growth rate of the poorest 40 percent of the society, have shown convincingly that the poorest sections have progressed at a much slower rate relative to the rest of the economy in many developing countries.[1] In fact,

---

[1] See Hollis B. Chenery, *Redistribution with Growth* (New York and London: Oxford University Press, 1974).

what shocked some of the analysts was the finding that, in certain cases, even the absolute level of income of the poorest majority had declined visibly in real terms over the course of the last two decades. In human affairs, nothing convinces the skeptics so much as the sheer force and volume of quantitative numbers.

At the same time, logical reasoning has convinced many academics that it is impossible to expect growth to filter down in societies where there is no equality of opportunity. If there are institutional rigidities, lack of mobility of labor, unequal levels of education, vastly unequal access to the means of production, and wide disparities in present income levels, it is inescapable that growth should get warped in favor of a privileged few, until fundamental institutional reforms are carried out. The experiences of a few countries like Korea, Taiwan, and Israel, which were cited so readily in the past as evidence that high growth rates can be combined with equity, are no longer so fashionable. It is being admitted that these experiences were unique and offer no basis for any generalizations. In these countries, a far greater equality of opportunity prevailed to begin with and it was combined with very high growth rate opportunities in certain favorable circumstances. These are conditions which do not prevail in a majority of the developing countries.

Third, most developing societies realize by now that they cannot emulate the consumption styles of the rich nations. Their present per capita income and any feasible rates of growth over the next few decades have increasingly convinced them that the consumption patterns that they can supply to their masses are entirely different from the ones presently prevailing in the developed countries. In addition, there has been a major reaction to the adverse social and cultural implications of the lifestyles of the rich nations, sparked off to some extent by the current debate in the developed world regarding the real price it has paid for its unplanned growth. Thus, there is greater interest now in the concept of basic human needs and in fashioning development strategies which are need-oriented, rather than market-demand-oriented. The concept of basic human needs, however, has remained somewhat elusive and is obviously going to be different in different societies. But it will not be an exaggeration to suggest that many development plans now start from the premise of basic needs of the poorest sections of the population and articulate specific targets and policies aimed at meeting these needs. Consumption planning has often moved to the center of the stage and many development plans are now attempting to combine production increases with distribution policies in the reallocation of investment resources.

Fourth, there is also an agreement that the economic condition of the poorest sections cannot be improved simply by distributing some purchasing power to them through short-lived welfare schemes. Any long-term improvement requires increasing the productivity of the poor by restructuring the pattern of investment through fundamental institutional reforms. Again, this is based, to some extent, on empirical evidence from the experience of a few countries which tried to stress distribution at the expense of growth—for example, Sri Lanka, Burma, and Tanzania. It was soon realized that such distribution policies could not continue for long, since the production base was not expanding fast enough to support them. It was also soon discovered, as economic realities caught up with these countries, that in poor societies there are definite limits to the redistribution of existing income and wealth and that the poor must be brought into the mainstream of economic life through the creation of meaningful employment opportunities, not welfare programs. The emphasis has, therefore, shifted to considering practical means of increasing the productivity of the poor—particularly of small farmers, landless labor, and workers in the informal urban sector. This requires new institutions which can reach these sections of the society since the existing power structures are often based on entirely different alliances between the economic elite. This also requires that the target groups for income increase have to be carefully defined in development plans and a fundamental reallocation of investment resources in favor of the poor has to be initiated.

Fifth, there is also a widespread realization that development strategies should be shaped by domestic needs and not by either export or foreign assistance requirements. It is true that foreign exchange is one of the critical bottlenecks in accelerating the pace of development in many countries, but the inference being drawn from it is increasingly different from the formulation of outward-looking development strategies. As discussed in the last chapter, the developing countries are slowly learning that trade and external resource transfers are going to remain marginal to their needs and that they must develop a pattern of production and consumption based more on their own resources, manpower, and technology. There is increasing talk, therefore, about self-reliant national development, though the framework and direction of such a self-reliant policy still remain unclear.

There are at least some of the areas of agreement which are emerging from the current debate on development strategies. Not everyone is likely to agree on them, of course. Consensus in the views of the economists, just as much as in the affairs of the politicians, is almost a delicious luxury. But the broad direction of the change in thinking is quite obvious and one can at least talk about new perceptions about development styles with a certain degree of confidence.

CHOICE OF SOFT OPTIONS

Unfortunately, the same degree of confidence cannot be expressed in the actual programs or accomplishments of the developing world. The few available examples of new development styles are those of China, Cuba, and Tanzania, which adopted these development strategies some decades back and whose experience is still neither fully digested nor objectively analyzed in much of the economic literature. For the most part, however, brave words on new development strategies have certainly not been a prelude to any meaningful action. There is a spate of seminars in the developed world on the issues of poverty, but there is still a dearth of any serious analysis in the developing world, whose problem it is to study and quantify the specific elements of a viable development strategy. There is a lack of real commitment in most developing countries to the contents of new development strategies, irrespective of their impassioned rhetoric to the contrary. And there is lack of real leverage by foreign assistance agencies to either negotiate or engineer a fundamental change in the developing countries. And here we stand, after five years of heated debate on new development styles and strategies, reviewing the actual experience in this field which does not really amount to very much. Most developing countries are still choosing soft options and are not prepared for the tough decisions required for restructuring their present development styles. And as was commented previously, the whole concern about a direct attack on mass poverty is in the imminent danger of becoming an expendable fashion. It is time, therefore, to review how in actual practice such an attack can be launched and what fundamental decisions it requires on the part of the Third World.

It must first be realized that to launch a direct attack on mass poverty is primarily a political, not a technocratic decision. It is largely a waste of time if development planners, hiding in some corridors of power, attempt to estimate quietly the extent of poverty in their country, the target income groups to be reached through development plans, the institutional reforms necessary for this purpose, and the specific sets of targets and policies required to implement their plans. This, in fact, has been done in a number of countries and the development planners have even convinced themselves that they have been formulating and implementing new development strategies. This is no more than an illusion. The new development strategies require such a basic restructuring of the political, economic and social balance of power that, unless a decision is reached at the highest political levels and the entire political movement within the country is mobilized behind it, these planning exercises will remain largely academic.

It is instructive, in this context, to look at some of the old development plans of India and the more recent plans of Pakistan, to see the sheer futility of such an exercise. Many of the technocrats and policy makers in these countries have by now persuaded themselves that there is nothing new about the objective of a direct attack on mass poverty since this has always been the cornerstone of their development planning. They also seem to believe that there is nothing more to learn about the dimensions and nature of mass poverty and they are merely amused that the rest of the world is discovering poverty at this late stage. And yet, they are tragically wrong, since they are not even at the threshold of the new policies which are required to tackle problems of poverty directly. The objective of poverty alleviation in these cases is merely a thin veneer on top of the traditional development strategies. These countries are still ruled by the same alliances between vested interests as before. They still have no institutional delivery systems to reach the poorest sections of their society, nor any political umbrella to reallocate investments in favor of the poor. The distribution of public services in these countries is often an element in aggravating the inadequacy of income distribution rather than in improving it, since most of these services (education, health, water supply, roads) are distributed in favor of the affluent sections of the society, with very limited access of the poor to the benefits of these services. India and Pakistan still insist on spending about $2.5 billion every year on defense and they send their negotiators all over the world to beg for every hundred million dollars of foreign assistance. Their development strategies are still subverted by their addiction to soft options, foreign assistance being the principal one. And yet, their development plans have adopted all the new language of a direct attack on mass poverty so that one would hardly realize, while reading these development plans, the vast gulf that separates them from reality.

The development plans of India and Pakistan are mentioned here not in any spirit of being critical of these two countries, but merely to illustrate how far we still are from any action program to attack poverty directly. These two countries also provide a good illustration because the problems of poverty are mainly concentrated in South Asia. The development thinkers and planners in these countries have generally outsmarted themselves in accepting the framework of new development strategies, without possessing any of the instruments to implement these strategies. This has done considerable damage. The politicians, who are always eager to persuade themselves that they are achieving their avowed goals, are thereby reassured that they are doing whatever is possible to remove poverty while the basic system continues to limp along in the same old fashion as ever.

NEED FOR NEW ALLIANCES

If the goal of a direct attack on mass poverty is meant seriously, it would require tough decisions in almost every walk of life. To begin with, it requires entirely new alliances to implement the new policies. At the political level, an alliance has to be fashioned between those interest groups which stand for redistribution of income and for reaching the poorer sections of society. Such an alliance, in the last analysis, must embrace the willing and enthusiastic participation of workers and peasants. Normally, a third element in this alliance is the student community, which is generally highly idealistic and provides a good deal of the initiative and drive which are needed to start a movement. Such an alliance is not easy to form. It often requires a broad-based mass movement to mobilize the energies of the people. Generally, wherever it has succeeded, the political party which embraces and symbolizes the objectives of new development is a far more formidable force than the men in government. It is ironic, therefore, that many countries in the developing world, which still rely on their traditional alliances between army, bureaucracy, landlords and industrialists, in some combination or another, adopt the slogan of poverty removal. This can only be either because of a cynical disregard for the intelligence of the masses or out of a naïve faith that an alliance of vested interests would still accommodate fundamental reforms.

Fundamental institutional reforms are, in fact, the essence of new development strategies. At the heart of these reforms is a change in the existing control over the means of production and access to key services. Normally, the rich exercise enormous economic power within these systems because they control most of the means of production in the society, such as land and capital. That is why land reforms and public ownership of major industries have become the key elements in any institutional reforms. But these reforms can easily become a whitewash, and have, in many societies.[2] Unless there is the necessary political will, it is impossible to change the established relationship between the owners of the means of production and those who have been perpetually denied these resources. What normally happens in many societies is that the governments nationalize a number of industries, banks, and some key services, like education and health, and they place these industries and public services in the hands of the bureaucrats or the same interest groups as before. It is not surprising, therefore, that these reforms amount to mere tokenism and not any real restructuring of society. This is really what has happened in a good part of South Asia, where the bureaucracy or the landlords or the industrialists have readily and enthusiastically embraced all the symbols and slogans of socialism.

Along with institutional reforms in the control over the means of production, there must also be a change in the distribution of public services to the poorest sections of the society. In the last analysis, it is the equality of opportunity, not the equality of income, which is decisive for future growth in the developing areas. The poor are denied this equality of opportunity, not only because of the prevailing income distribution but principally because they have an unequal access to education, credit system, public utilities and other services provided by the private or public sector. Their initial poverty, therefore, becomes a formidable handicap in improving their future conditions. One of the mandatory exercises which should be carried

[2] Land reforms in India, Pakistan, Bangladesh fit this description. Doreen Warriner, "Land Reform and Economic Development," in Carl Eicker and Lawrence Wilt, eds., *Agriculture in Economic Development* (New York: McGraw-Hill, 1964).

out in all national planning commissions in the Third World should be to estimate quantitatively the distribution of benefits from public services to various income groups in the society. It will often come as a major shock to many policy makers how the provision of public services, far from equalizing opportunities, actually distorts them against the interests of the poor in many societies. Such a shock is perhaps a necessary precondition to make the governments concerned redistribute their public services in a different fashion so as to improve the access of the poor to them and so as to contribute toward greater equality of opportunity.

NEED-ORIENTED STRATEGIES

One of the themes in the new development strategies, which has probably gained the most favor with development planners and policy makers, is the concept of basic human needs. It is generally accepted by now that in poor societies production planning should initially be geared to the satisfaction of basic needs. Many of the poorest countries are so short of resources that they recognize that even the target of meeting the minimum human needs in nutrition, clothing, education, health, and shelter is going to be a difficult one to achieve over the course of the next decade, if all the energies of the political system are devoted to such an objective. However, it is surprising how little quantitative work has been done so far in this field in most parts of the Third World.

There are at least three steps which are essential to formulating a need-oriented development strategy. First, the target groups (in terms of rural poor or urban poor, or small farmers, or landless laborers, etc.) must be defined with a good deal of precision, after collecting the necessary data on the profile of poverty within these countries. Second, quantitative studies must be undertaken to estimate the population which is below the minimum human needs (as defined by that society), and an estimate made regarding the production and investment targets which should be set to meet these consumption targets over a defined period of time. Third, the necessary instruments of implementation should be defined to indicate how these consumption targets are to be realized in a market where the demand signals may all be leading in a different direction. This may require a basic change in all the price signals, a number of public controls over production and investment and new delivery systems to reach the poor and to increase their long-term productivity. There is no evidence at present that these three steps are being seriously pursued by development planners in the Third World, even in countries which are officially committed to a direct attack on mass poverty.

The collection of data, of course, is the easiest one of these tasks, even though it has proved surprisingly difficult to organize in many developing countries. Although considerable work is being done in these areas, we still do not have many good surveys of income distribution, or of nutrition, or of distribution of public services. It is possible that this benign neglect is because of the political sensitivity of a lot of this information, since any such studies would lead to an intensive debate on issues of social justice within the country.[3] But if the politicians are afraid of the sensitivity that the collection of such data might raise in their countries, there can be little hope of any real commitment on their part to the essential content of the new development strategies.

Once the consumption targets have been set in relation to the satisfaction of basic human needs, the task is one of bringing production and investment planning closer to this consumption planning. It is obvious that the market signals, influenced by the prevailing income distribution, are likely to be extremely different from such specific consumption targets. There is no reason why the market should produce the kind of essential consumption goods which are required for such a strategy, if the

[3] I recall the major excitement that was caused in Pakistan when some partial information collected on the ownership of industrial assets by twenty-two family groups, collected by my wife, was released by me publicly in early 1968. See my article, "Pakistan's 22 Families," *London Times,* March 22, 1973.

poor do not have the purchasing power to influence market decisions. One of the important tasks, therefore, is to correct all the price signals and economic incentives in such a way as to weigh them in favor of the production of essential consumer goods. In the last analysis, market mechanism is a powerful force and development planners have to learn how to use it to serve their national objectives. Even in China, the price system plays a fairly significant role in the allocation of resources within the social framework, though all the price signals and economic incentives are so drastically modified that they become subordinate to the overall objectives of the country. In many developing countries, the price system often works directly against the objective of allocation of resources to essential needs. Even when the price signals are corrected, the focus of such a policy is generally to subsidize consumption goods to the poor, which often discourages their production by the private sector and, as such, vitiates the very objective which these societies wish to pursue.

The most important part of the implementation machinery, however, is the delivery system, which can allocate resources directly to the poorer groups and, thereby, lay the groundwork for a permanent increase in their productivity. These delivery systems embrace the supply of investable resources, working capital, essential infrastructure, and other public services required by the poor in order to participate in economic growth. Most developing countries have extremely poor delivery systems for reaching the poorest sections of their societies. This is no accident. This is, in fact, a reflection of the political and economic realities in these countries. Since the rich have the purchasing power and since they are the ones who are regarded as creditworthy, it is inevitable that they should control most of the institutional structures and get a major share of the services in the system. Generally, a superficial answer to this is nationalization of a whole range of services by the government. The most popular vehicle is the nationalization of banks. But the nationalization of banks, without a national credit policy, is absolutely meaningless. What is really needed is the definition of precise objectives in terms of credit—as to which income groups should get what kind of credit—rather than the symbolic ownership of the credit system. Thus, many countries have ended up nationalizing their banks, while leaving the distribution of the credit system almost unchanged.

These considerations apply even more to the rural areas which are often ruled by feudalistic power structures and where distribution of credit or other services generally ends up in the hands of the landlords and of other traditional local power groups. The developing countries still have not discovered a liberal alternative to the Chinese commune, which brings together all services within one community under the same political and economic umbrella so that it works efficiently and equitably as a delivery system for the rural areas. Many alternatives have been tried, from village cooperatives in the Asian subcontinent to *Ujjama* villages in Tanzania, but none of them have as yet provided an assured and continuous means of delivering services to the rural groups. In the last analysis, this requires a fundamental restructuring of political and economic power at the local level and that cannot happen without a mass movement or a popular revolution. This is the most formidable challenge to the policy makers of the Third World. Their adoption of new development strategies, without evolving new delivery systems, is likely to be an exercise in futility.

A DYNAMIC CONCEPT OF SELF-RELIANCE

An essential ingredient of the new development strategies is the concept of self-reliance. This concept has not been defined very adequately in most of the Western literature and still is confused with a movement toward autarchy and often interpreted very narrowly in terms of what happens to the trade of a country. In fact, the concept of self-reliance should be looked upon as a comprehensive philosophy of life. Its best expression is found generally in the writings of Mao. A good definition is also offered in the Cocoyoc Declaration:

We believe that one basic strategy of development will have to be increased national self-reliance. It does not mean autarchy. It implies mutual benefits from trade and cooperation and a fairer redistribution of resources satisfying the basic needs. It does mean self-confidence, reliance primarily on one's own resources, human and natural, and the capacity for autonomous goal-setting and decision-making. It excludes dependence on outside influences and powers that can be converted into political pressure. It excludes exploitative trade patterns depriving countries of their natural resources for their own development. There is obviously a scope for transfer of technology, but the thrust should be on adaptation and the generation of local technology. It implies decentralization of the world economy, and sometimes also of the national economy to enhance the sense of personal participation. But it also implies increased international cooperation for collective self-reliance. Above all, it means trust in people and nations, reliance on the capacity of people themselves to invent and generate new resources and techniques, to increase their capacity to absorb them, to put them to socially beneficial use, to take a measure of command over the economy, and to generate their own way of life.[4]

More specifically, there are four elements which are important in the concept of self-reliance. First, the society should not introduce any consumption goods which cannot be shared by the vast majority of the population at that particular stage of development. This essentially underlines the rationale of China's reliance on bicycles and public buses instead of introduction of automobiles, which naturally could have been owned only by a few privileged people in the country at its low level of per capita income. This means that, by deliberate action, no such consumption goods should be allowed into the society which cannot be afforded by the masses with their average per capita income.[5]

---

[4] "The Cocoyoc Declaration," *Development Dialogue,* No. 2, 1974.

[5] In the early 1960s, I was greatly impressed by the manner in which Yugoslavia was implementing this strategy. On a brief visit to Belgrade, I discovered, in my discussions with the national planners, that they were introducing an extremely small, standardized refrigerator as a first stage which the entire society could afford at that stage of development, and were deliberately planning on improving the size and quality of this refrigerator over time as the per capita income increased. Similarly, while visiting China in the latter half of the 1960s, I found that they had in-

Second, the concept of self-reliance implies the maximum use of indigenous resources and technology. In the first excited phase of development, many developing countries were in a hurry to overthrow their traditional cultural patterns or the use of their traditional skills. This often reflected a lack of confidence and pride in their own past and a mad anxiety to follow in the footsteps of the developed world. The Chinese development strategy has been one singular exception to this in blending its past heritage with its future needs. This is evident in the use of ancient Chinese skills to create new products, and the improvisation of relevant organizations and technology, from "barefoot doctors" to labor-intensive means of constructing huge buildings and dams. There is a tremendous scope today throughout the Third World to make much greater use of local resources and indigenous technology. This technology cannot be developed in international institutes outside the Third World since that would be an ironic mockery of the very concept of indigenous technology. It must be fashioned within these societies. In fact, if the emphasis of the society is on the production of simple essential goods, this reorientation in development strategy will by itself lead to an emphasis on indigenous resources and technology.

Third, the developing countries must view their reliance on foreign assistance as the minimum that the country cannot do without, not the maximum that the country can negotiate. In most parts of the Third World, there is a tremendous scope for reducing their current dependence on foreign assistance without reducing their growth rates. Unfortunately, the size of foreign assistance has become a serious political and national game in many developing countries, so that the energies of the .top pol-

---

troduced three distinct consumption goods on the communes which could be owned privately—namely, sewing machine, radio, and bicycle. These were the incentive goods which, I was informed, about 70 percent of the commune people had already acquired. There was an active debate going on as to which consumption good should be introduced next which could both serve an essential need as well as could be acquired by the majority of the commune people through increased productivity.

icy makers are often spent outside their countries in persuading reluctant donors to cough up additional assistance. It is surprising, and tragic, how soon the performance criterion for judging the success of many bureaucrats and policy makers in their own countries becomes their ability to negotiate external assistance. This generally distorts the basic signals in a society to such an extent that, in some of them, far more analysis and time are devoted to the task of negotiating assistance than to mobilizing domestic resources or to allocating them intelligently and equitably.[6]

Finally, the concept of self-reliance also implies that there must be a deliberate de-linking of the Third World from its past dependent relationships with the developed countries. Many of the developing countries have been so intimately linked with their previous colonial masters—politically, economically and socially—that any slight tremor in these mother countries can cause major earthquakes within the developing world. This was quite obvious during 1974 and 1975, when the developed world went through a period of recession and temporary interruption in oil supplies which had a major impact on the demand for raw materials from the developing countries and on the rate of growth that the Third World could maintain in the face of a slowdown of growth in the OECD countries.[7]

A self-reliant national development must be capable of protecting the essential living standards from such external shocks. For one thing, this means that a central part of such a development strategy should be the focus on food production so that the society can at least feed itself, irrespective of international

[6] From my personal experience in Pakistan in the late 1960s, I can verify that more time and energy were often spent on preparing various documents for aid consortia every year than on compiling the annual development plans.

[7] The growth in the OECD declined to 3.4 percent in 1970–74 from 4.9 percent in the previous decades but the growth rate in the poorest, primary producers fell from 4.4 percent to 1.6 percent correspondingly. (Based on information in World Bank, *Prospects for the Developing Countries, 1976–80,* July 1975).

developments. Another aspect is that the Third World countries should get together among themselves in arrangements of collective self-reliance so that they can buy some protection against the temporary disturbances in the developed countries.

ROLE OF INTERNATIONAL ASSISTANCE

What is the role that international assistance can play in the formulation or implementation of the new development strategies? Their role can at best be marginal and supportive of national development endeavors: it can never be an initiating role. External assistance can strengthen the forces working for new development strategies if the country has already set its course and has launched its own direct attack on poverty. But foreign donors are completely helpless if the necessary political will is not there in the developing countries, or if the necessary delivery systems have not been set up, or if the needed institutional reforms have not been carried out. It would be naïve to believe that donors can step into these situations with their money or with their technical assistance and fundamentally restructure these societies. It is all the more important to appreciate this fact in the present climate when it is mainly the external assistance agencies which are speaking out about new development strategies and about a direct attack on mass poverty. Such talk can be counterproductive, unless the developing countries themselves are persuaded that this is essentially their own task and no amount of foreign assistance can ever resolve or ease the tough national decisions they must make.

However, if a particular developing country is already committed to the new goals and is determined to take the necessary measures to implement them, then external assistance can help in this process. It can help primarily by linking up with the concept of basic human needs and by supporting production and investment which is geared to the satisfaction of these needs (see chapter 11). This may be shrugged off as imperialistic intervention by some of the donors, who are often criticized on this score anyway and are reluctant to get into any further controversies. But it is seldom recognized that the very act of foreign assistance is itself an act of intervention in the economic and political affairs of a country and, if one must intervene, one should at least intervene in a good cause. Whenever external assistance is introduced into a society, it strengthens some institutions, or some sections of society, or some sectors of production at the expense of others, so that intervention is a fact of life. The external agencies need not, therefore, be any more diffident or defensive if their intervention is based on the strategy of meeting basic human needs.

The debate on new development strategies stands at a critical juncture today. It can become a mere intellectual fad, with the developing countries doing nothing serious or fundamental about the restructuring of their societies. If that happens, one can foresee nothing ahead but confusion, anarchy, and political instability. On the other hand, there is also the opportunity to translate the new development strategies into practical political and economic policy action. This will not be easy. It would require a whole-hearted political commitment, mobilization of a mass political movement, fundamental institutional reforms, and some very tough decisions and choices. The intent of this chapter was to focus on some of these issues, not in order to offer a comprehensive blueprint for action—which can be prepared only by these societies themselves—but to give an overview of where we stand today in this debate. This analysis is really not very reassuring from the point of view of the Third World. Unless policies change radically in the balance of the 1970s, the internal orders in most parts of the Third World are going to be in constant turmoil. But there are enough incentives and pressures for change. We can only hope that this change occurs in time.

GLOBAL CHOICES: MYTHS AND REALITY

PART

·2·

"If the present growth trends in world population, industrialization, pollution, food production and resource depletion continue unchanged, the limits to growth on this planet will be reached sometime within the next one hundred years. The most probable result will be a rather sudden and uncontrollable decline in both population and industrial capacity."

—*Limits to Growth* study, 1972

"The failure of the world society to provide 'a safe and happy life' for all is not caused by any present lack of physical resources. The problem today is not one of absolute physical shortages but of economic and social maldistribution and misuse (of these resources). . . . We believe that ways of life and social systems can be evolved that are more respectful of the whole planetary environment. The road forward does not lie through the despair of doom watching nor through the easy optimism of successive technological fixes."

—*The Cocoyoc Declaration*, 1974

IN RETROSPECT

ONE OF THE MOST CURIOUS DEVELOPMENTS IN THE EARLY 1970s was that, while we in the developing world were struggling with the problems of economic growth and trying to understand the interaction between growth and distribution, the developed countries suddenly became concerned about the adequacy of our planet's physical resources to meet the needs of an expanding world population. This was not just a Malthusian hangover; this was a response to a serious analytical effort to study all the interrelationships between population, resources, pollution, and technology. The appearance of the Club of Rome sponsored study on the *Limits to Growth* in 1972 was a bit of a bombshell, sending shock waves all over the world.

I had only recently joined the World Bank when these exciting events were bursting upon the world scene. At first, we in the developing world viewed this new scare about physical limits to future growth with detached amusement, but this turned to feelings of apprehension since the Club of Rome study was taken fairly seriously in the industrialized nations. By sheer coincidence, I was appointed to chair a task force in the World Bank which was asked to analyze the broader policy implications of the *Limits to Growth*. The findings of this task force were contained in a 100-page report which I summarized for *Finance and Development* in December 1972. Chapter 5 draws largely on this analysis and brings it up to date in the light of subsequent developments. Our major conclusion was that the maldistribution of world resources, and not their absolute shortage, continued to be the real problem facing humanity.

At about the same time as the *Limits to Growth* thesis was dominating the intellectual scene, questions about the quality of life had begun to arise in many industrialized countries. There was a growing awareness of the serious threat that pollu-

79

tion was beginning to pose in many industrialized societies, and environmental questions were beginning to be introduced into the priority agenda of the general public and the politicians. At the same time as the developed world was passing through this phase of intense soul-searching, uncharitable questions were being raised as to why the Third World countries were relatively indifferent to the environmental problems and why they were so unwilling to learn from the past mistakes and experience of the Western world.

I must say that we in the developing countries were greatly intrigued by the sudden interest in the wider issues of quality of life, environment, and future responsibility of mankind, and our own initial thoughts on this subject were also not exactly charitable. There were suspicions that this was only a ploy to tell the developing world that they should not start consuming resources which were badly needed for the whole of mankind and which were getting depleted at a fast rate. There were suspicions that, after a century or more of accelerated development and technological progress, the Western societies were telling the majority of mankind that they must return to a simple life and try to make a virtue of it.

I raised some of these questions quite bluntly with Maurice Strong, whom I first met in late 1970 when he had just been asked to take over as Secretary General of the U.N. Conference on Human Environment, and with Barbara Ward, who had agreed to work on a background book [1] for this Conference. Over the course of the next two years, I was involved quite a bit with the preparations for the Conference on Human Environment which I attended in Stockholm in June, 1972. During this period, I came to admire the dynamism, the wisdom, the vision and the compassion of these two remarkable individuals, Maurice Strong and Barbara Ward, who did their very best to make the environmental concern equally relevant to the rich and the poor nations and who worked tirelessly for the concept of

---

[1] Subsequently published as *Only One Earth*, by Barbara Ward and René Dubos (New York: Norton, 1972).

one planet and one humanity. It was through their efforts that a group of us, from developed and developing countries, met in Founex, Switzerland, to consider the environmental concern in a developmental perspective. As chairman of the drafting committee, I had to bear a large part of the responsibility for writing this report [2] which became a rallying point for the developed and the developing countries alike. It was in this report that we first made a clear distinction between the environmental problems of the developed and the developing countries and argued for new development strategies which could combine the production of private goods with the preservation of social values. I touch upon some of these themes in chapter 6.

The Stockholm Conference on Human Environment in June 1972, was, however, a bit of a disappointment despite the most imaginative efforts of Maurice Strong and Barbara Ward to save it. The organizational parts proved the easiest to agree on: a new UN agency was created (United Nations Environment Program or UNEP) to keep the environmental concern on the agenda of mankind's normally shifting attention, and a U.N. Environment Fund was set up for a five-year period at a "generous" level of $20 million a year. But the human and political parts were far more difficult for the international community to accept since it was still not prepared to buy the concept of "one humanity" except in name. I discussed this aspect, in rather strong terms, in my keynote address to the Dag Hammarskjöld Foundation Seminar in November 1973:

> There was, in the last two or three years, again a revival of hope that man may realize the limitations of this planet and, as such, there may again be a common concern for joint development. When the concern about the environment arose in the developed countries, many of us in the developing world viewed it partly with suspicion and apprehension, but partly, at least, with some hope. The hope was that this concern could bring home to human-

---

[2] U.N., *Development and Environment* ("Founex Report"), Report of a Panel of Experts convened by the Secretary General of the United Nations Conference on the Human Environment, June 4–12, 1971 (Paris: Mouton, 1972).

ity the fact that this was a small planet and that its survival was interdependent. But I must confess that the environment concern has contributed, so far, not to uniting this world but to further dividing it. We all subscribe to the concept of one planet and one world and one humanity, but very few practical steps have been taken to translate this concept into real shape. In fact, most of the people in the Third World are acutely aware of the fact that there are two worlds, two planets, two humanities—one embarrassingly rich, and the other desperately poor, and that their concerns have drifted away gradually.

In your world, there is a concern today about the quality of life; in our world, there is a concern about life itself which is threatened by hunger and malnutrition. In your world, there is a concern today about the conservation of nonrenewable resources and learned books are written about how the world should go on to a stationary state in order to conserve these resources. In our world, anxiety is not about the depletion of resources but about the best distribution and exploitation of these resources, for the benefit of all mankind rather than for the benefit of a few nations. While you are worried about industrial pollution, we are worried about the pollution of poverty, because our problems arise not out of excess of development and technology but because of the lack of development and technology and inadequate control over natural phenomena. In the developed countries, you can afford to fuss about the adverse effects of DDT; we have to be concerned about what it means for our crops and for sustaining human lives. You can afford to be concerned about polluted beaches; we have to worry a lot about the fact that less than 10 percent of the population in the Third World has even drinkable water. I do not wish to overdraw the contrast here, but I think we must recognize something which is becoming increasingly a fact of international life—that our two worlds, while they touch and meet, they rarely communicate. And it is that process of real communication, real dialogue, that we have to encourage today in case we are to equip ourselves to deal with the problems of this world.[3]

This lack of communication also covers other fields, particularly the sensitive issue of population growth. The importance of the

[3] Mahbub ul Haq, "Development and Independence," a keynote address given to the Dag Hammarskjöld Seminar in November 1973, reprinted in *Development Dialogue,* No. 1 (1974): 5–12.

population problem is generally recognized in the developing countries but these countries often get impatient with the virtuous lectures that the rich nations try to give them on this subject. They feel that the ever rising levels of affluence in the rich nations place a far greater pressure on world resources than the increase in population in the poor lands and that it is hypocritical of the industrialized world to be so concerned about the physical limits of this planet when it is so unwilling to do anything serious about the present maldistribution of world income and resources. Some elements of this ever excited debate are covered in chapter 7.

Reviewing the last few years, it has continued to amaze me how difficult it often becomes to separate myth from reality in global debates. The concerns which have often dominated the public debate and mass media in the Western world during this period—physical limits to growth, environmental pollution, global increase of population—have been of only secondary interest to the Third World. The Third World is naturally more concerned with the national issues of poverty and development, and the international issue of the unequal relationships between the rich and the poor nations. It is only recently that these issues have begun to command the attention of the international community, as symbolized in the demand for a new international economic order. This is a theme to which I shall turn in the next part of this book.

During the early 1970s, some of us from the Third World felt increasingly frustrated by the tone and substance of the intellectual dialogue at the international level. Simplistic thinking on physical limits to growth, increased threat of environmental pollution and the Malthusian ghost of population explosion kept raising their heads in various international forums and we increasingly felt that the concerns of the developed world were drifting away from those of ours. This became forcefully clear as some of us from the Third World attended the United Nations Conference on Human Environment in Stockholm in June of 1972 and listened listlessly to anguished speeches on the unfortunate disappearance of wild life and the inconvenient pollution of beautiful beaches. We began to sense

the wide gulf which separated our thinking from those of our
friends in the Western world. We started to realize that the liberal hour in the rich nations had perhaps struck briefly in the
1960s and slipped away in a hurry.

Where were our own forums where we, from the Third
World, could discuss our own problems in a spirit of utter
frankness? What were we really doing sitting through endless
seminars and conferences where our own voice was neither solicited nor heard? Should we not establish our own institutions of
intellectual self-reliance, both at the national and the international level, which could give some form and substance to our
aimless search for appropriate development strategies at home
and to our disorganized efforts to coordinate our negotiating
positions abroad? There were uncomfortable thoughts like this
which encouraged me one evening to invite a few friends who
were present in Stockholm—Gamani Corea, Enrique Iglesias,
and Samir Amin,[4] among others. This proved to be the genesis
of the Third World Forum, an action group of about one
hundred leading intellectuals from the developing countries.
The first meeting of this group was held in Santiago, Chile, in
April, 1973, which approved the broad framework for the establishment of the Forum. The Constitution of the Third
World Forum was approved in Karachi, Pakistan, in January
1975.[5]

To my mind, the organization of the Third World Forum
was a logical step in the continuous struggle of the developing
countries for political, economic, and intellectual liberation.
From the beginning, we conceived of the Forum as a completely
independent organization with no governmental or institutional
affiliations. We agreed that its principal functions should be to:

---

[4] Respectively, currently Secretary General, UNCTAD, Executive Secretary, ECLA, and Director, United Nations Institute of Economic Development and Planning, Dakar.

[5] See Third World Forum, *Santiago Statement* (1973), *Karachi Communiqué*
(1975), and *Constitution of the Forum* (1975); obtainable from Third World
Forum Provisional Secretariat, Casilla 179-D, Santiago, Chile.

(a) provide an intellectual platform for an exchange of views on alternative development strategies and their policy implications;
(b) provide intellectual support to the Third World countries in devising their policy options and negotiating alternatives on all relevant development issues;
(c) stimulate and organize relevant socio-economic research, particularly through the regional and national research institutes, in the Third World;
(d) foster the interchange of relevant ideas and research, identify the areas of Third World interdependence and, to this end, seek to influence appropriate international, regional and national decision-making bodies to recognize and protect the legitimate rights and interests of the people of the Third World:
(e) provide support to programmes of action on all types of co-operation among developing countries by:
(i) suggesting areas, methods, and types of action that would be most effective for mutual co-operation;
(ii) defining areas in which the Third World countries could offer assistance or could benefit from assistance provided by other Third World countries;
(iii) examining and analysing mutual co-operation in all fields, including science and technology, with the purpose of facilitating the exchange of ideas, information and an efficient transfer of these between Third World countries;
(f) express views on international issues affecting the Third World and its relations with the developed world.

We were also keenly aware that the Third World Forum must work in close collaboration with liberal forces in the developed world. It could not afford to withdraw behind a self-imposed isolation. I made that clear in my opening statement to the Karachi meeting:

. . . . We come together neither in a mood of agitation nor in a spirit of protest. . . . We neither seek intellectual isolation nor needless confrontation. . . .

And the Karachi Communique made it further clear that "the Forum offers its support to all liberal elements all over the world in working towards the establishment of a more equitable world order." The Constitution of the Forum also provided for a selected number of associate members from the developed countries to build intellectual bridges for a common struggle.

The Third World Forum took its initial shape and form in the rather gloomy, despairing days of late 1972 and early 1973 when the concerns of the Third World were being summarily brushed aside from the crowded agenda of the powerful and the rich nations. We were not aware at that stage how quickly the environment would change by 1974, as a result of the OPEC action on oil prices, and how much more important it would become for the Third World to have its own forums for a serious and sensible dialogue with the rich nations on a whole range of issues concerning the restructuring of the old world economic order. In my statements in Santiago in April 1973, and later again in Karachi in January 1975, I had tried to stress the role that the Forum must play in engineering an intellectual revolution in the perceptions of mankind, particularly those in the Third World:

> History has taught us at least one lesson—that the poor and the weak always get exploited unless they get organized. Our present world order is no exception. We have often seen our poverty and our weakness exploited in the name of grand-sounding principles. . . .
>
> But it is no use wailing. No exploitation can continue for long without the tacit cooperation of the exploited. I am afraid that we have allowed a minority in the developed world to shape world opinion for too long a time. If there is any fault, the fault is clearly ours.
>
> After all, what have we done to change the realm of ideas, to fashion more relevant strategies for our societies, to equip our political negotiators in international conferences with powerful ideas and concrete briefs which could become a rallying cry for the Third World?
>
> . . . . I firmly believe that our national independence is neither complete nor meaningful unless political liberation is followed by economic and intellectual liberation.
>
> Intellectual liberation is, in particular, the more difficult to achieve since many of us are prisoners of our own past training and

somebody else's thought. But it is a vital part of the new order that the Third World seeks today.

In a broader sense, therefore, the Third World Forum constitutes a movement for intellectual self-reliance. On a national level, it marks a search for finding our own solutions within our own value systems. On an international level, it is an effort to organize the Third World intellectually to fight for its just demands in all international forums. . . .

We start today in a modest way, but this movement will inevitably grow till it becomes an irresistible force. It will spread to all our universities, to all our institutes of learning, to all our schools of thought till we achieve the intellectual revolution we are after.

This will take time. We shall first begin by providing an organized and continuing forum for our intellectual efforts. We will then go on to establish its linkages with all research and thought in our countries and commission specific studies, briefs and negotiating positions to be prepared during the current year. We may then consider the establishment of a Third World Development Center with its own publication media and its own rewards for excellence of thought, judged by the needs of our own societies.

This will all come. . . . The world can neither fight nor long resist an idea whose time has come. And if I may permit myself the luxury of a prediction, I firmly believe that this Forum will be the dominant force of the next decade.[6]

Was that a mere idle boast? A rhetorical flourish to suit the occasion? Or will history ever make a prophecy out of it? It is impossible to say. But I believe in the power of ideas. As Lord Keynes was fond of reminding us, the world is ruled by little else. I only hope that the Third World Forum does indeed generate new and relevant ideas, with professional objectivity even though in a partisan cause. It has already started organizing some serious analysis on the issues of new development styles, collective self-reliance and new international economic order—some of which I mention in the next part of the book.

[6] For the full text, see Mahbub ul Haq, "The Third World Forum: Intellectual Self-Reliance," in *International Development Review*, no. 1, 1975.

·5·   GLOBAL LIMITS TO
                         GROWTH?

IN THE BEGINNING OF THE 1970S, sudden fears began to emerge that mankind was on its way to extinction if it did not mend its ways. While the human race has got used to such dire predictions from time to time, they were taken more seriously this time around because they were neither based on prophecies of spiritual or moral decline nor on the horrors of nuclear destruction but simply on this planet's physical limits which man was allegedly trying to exceed. The final catastrophe was to be reached this time by the unchecked multiplication of human population, by the sheer exhaustion of earth's nonrenewable physical resources, and through the accumulation of threatening clouds of pollution. These were no ordinary predictions, included in the new year's messages of professional doomsday prophets: they were backed up by mathematical computer programs undertaken at a prestigious institution like the Massachusetts Institute of Technology by serious young people whose integrity and motivation were beyond dispute. The main study, entitled *The Limits to Growth,* sponsored by the Club of Rome, was published in March 1972.[1] Its central conclusion— that man is faced by ecological catastrophe unless zero growth rates in population and industrial production are attained by 1975—attracted world-wide attention and controversy. Even though some of the excitement which this book aroused has

[1] Dennis L. Meadows et al., *The Limits to Growth,* A Report for the Club of Rome's Project on the Predicament of Mankind (New York: Universe Books, 1972).

died down by now and the world is living through 1975 without any darkening shadow of ecological doom upon it—despite the current difficult economic problems—it is useful to analyze the basic thesis of *Limits to Growth* after this interval, particularly from the point of view of the Third World, since it raises some important issues of global economic and social choices.

The basic thesis in *Limits to Growth* was a simple one—and for that very reason it had a powerful appeal. It derived its conviction from the simple notion that infinite growth was impossible on a finite planet. It lent an air of frightening urgency to this notion by contending that the limits to growth were already being reached and that mankind was destined for catastrophe during the next one hundred years unless this growth was stopped right away.

The central thesis of the *Limits to Growth* model could be broken down into the following major themes:

(i) Many critical variables in our global society—particularly population and industrial production—have been growing at a constant percentage rate so that, by now, the absolute increase each year is extremely large. Such increases will become progressively unmanageable unless deliberate action is taken now to prevent this exponential growth.

(ii) However, physical resources—particularly cultivable land and nonrenewable minerals—and the earth's capacity to "absorb" pollution are finite. Sooner or later, the exponential growth in population and industrial production will bump into this physical ceiling and, instead of staying at the ceiling, will then plunge downward with a sudden and uncontrollable decline in both population and industrial capacity.

(iii) Since technological progress cannot expand all physical resources indefinitely, it would be better to establish conscious limits on our future growth rather than to let nature establish them for us in a catastrophic fashion.

The authors conceded that more optimistic alternative assumptions could be built into the model but they contended that this merely postponed the problem by a few decades so that it would be better to err on the side of action now rather than later. They were also conscious of some of the problems that zero growth rates might create for the world. They hinted at policies of income redistribution between the rich and the poor nations as well as within these nations; and they pleaded for a change in the composition of production away from industrial output and toward the social services. Unfortunately, many of the redeeming qualifications that the authors mentioned were not pursued by them and were generally lost in their anxiety to make their predictions as dramatic as possible.

THE BASIC ASSUMPTIONS

Any study of the *Limits* model clearly must start with a critical examination of the assumptions that went into the model of the world economy on which it was based; it is a truism that a model is just as good as the assumptions built into it. Careful investigations showed that many assumptions in the model were not scientifically established and that the use of data was often careless and casual. This was particularly true of the assumptions regarding nonrenewable resources and pollution. It was also discovered that, contrary to the protestations of the authors, the model was fairly sensitive to the choice of these assumptions, and that reasonable adjustments in the assumptions regarding population, nonrenewable resources, and pollution could postpone the predicted catastrophe by another one hundred to two hundred years even if one accepted the general methodology of the model. And in this context an additional one hundred years might be as vital to the human race as an extra second might be to a car driver in a traffic emergency—it could transform the whole situation.

POPULATION

The *Limits* model was right in postulating that world population had been growing exponentially in the last century and that, if the current rates of growth continued, the world's population of 3.6 billion in 1972 would double over the next thirty-five years. However, population growth in the *Limits* model was totally determined by the pace of industrial production and failed to take into account many demographic factors.

It is relatively easy to establish that the world population cannot keep increasing unchecked: there are definite limits to this growth. As Dr. Fred Singer observes, "to see that limits exist to any kind of continued growth, one need only consider that if the present world population were to be doubled 15 more times, there would be one man for each square yard on all of the land areas including Antarctica, Greenland and the Sahara Desert; and at the present rate of growth, this would require only a little more than 500 years." [2] The real question, therefore, is not whether such physical limits exist. They certainly do. The real question is how to arrest population growth in poor countries at relatively low levels of income. At the same time, we must be aware that the present population of the Third World is likely to double by the turn of the century even if family planning programs are successful, so that this must be provided for in all future economic planning exercises. These issues are discussed at considerable length in chapter 7.

NONRENEWABLE RESOURCES

A number of assumptions were made in the *Limits* model about nonrenewable resources which turned out, on closer examination, to be characterized by the same rather dramatic gloom with which the *Limits* viewed population. The figures on reserves of nonrenewable resources generally came from the U.S. Bureau of Mines, but the Bureau had warned that 80 percent of their reserve estimates had a confidence level of less than 65 percent—a reservation that the *Limits* completely ignored. Moreover, some of the reserve estimates—particularly for the Communist countries—were extremely old or incomplete; some estimates for mainland China, for example, went back to 1913!

[2] S. Fred Singer, *The Changing Global Environment* (Boston: Reidd Publishing, 1975).

Again, reserve estimates for natural resources have been revised frequently over time and are likely to change again in our own lifetime; between 1954 and 1966, the reserve estimates for one of the largest resources, iron ore, rose by about five times. It is estimated by the Bureau of Mines that even these reserves can be doubled at a price 30 to 40 percent higher than the current price. Similarly, the reserve estimates for copper today are 3.5 times their level in 1935 and it is estimated that they could be more than doubled again if the price were three times higher. Many of these reserve estimates are conservative contingency forecasts by the exploration companies *and they are related to a certain price:* if the price is higher, more resources can be exploited commercially. The authors of the *Limits* allowed for such contingencies in their model by the "generous" assumption that reserves could increase by five times over the next one hundred years, but what might appear to be an act of generosity turns out to be an unduly conservative assumption in the light of historical evidence and recent discoveries.

It can, of course, be objected that reliance on such illustrations of how the world's resource base has expanded shows an unjustified and adventuresome confidence in history. However, this can no more be faulted than the use of history in the *Limits* study which only looks at the story of irrationality, waste, and neglect.

The pessimism of the assumptions on nonrenewable resources becomes even more evident if one considers that the concept of resources itself is a dynamic one: many things *become* resources over time. The expansion of the last one hundred years could not have been sustained without the new resources of petroleum, aluminum, and atomic energy. Yet little of this was predictable in advance. And there are many more frontiers of knowledge and technology which still remain unexplored.

As an example, there exists a great potential for exploiting resources of the sea bed. Reserves of nodular materials—the most promising underwater source of minerals—distributed over the ocean floor are estimated at levels sufficient to sustain a mining rate of 400 million tons a year for virtually an unlimited period of time. If only 100 million tons of nodules are recovered every year—a target which appears to be within reach in the next ten to twenty years—it would add to the annual production of copper, nickel, manganese, and cobalt to the extent of roughly one fourth, three times, six times, and twelve times, respectively, compared to the current Western world production levels. And the present production cost estimates are a fraction of current prices—one fifth for copper, one thirteenth for nickel, one twenty-fourth for cobalt.[2] These estimates—like all such estimates—are very tentative; but there is a good deal of evidence that exploitation of sea-bed resources is fast becoming a real possibility. We should, therefore, realize that the true magnitude of resource availabilities is *uncertain* rather than proceed on the conviction that they are definably finite. Uncertainty calls for taking out reasonable insurance. The *Limits* prescription was a radical one, amounting to nothing less than telling the patient to live without exposing himself to the very risks of life.

If certain resources are likely to become scarcer—or, to use the economic jargon, if supply inelasticities are likely to develop—it is a scientific and intellectual service to humanity to draw attention to those resources and to the time period over which they may vanish, given current usage and the present state of knowledge. Research into these areas is, therefore, both useful and vital. But it is quite another thing to argue that no amount of research, no technological breakthroughs, will extend the lifetime of these resources indefinitely or to pretend that supply inelasticities will afflict all natural resources in the same manner and at the same time in an aggregate model. While identification of specific inelasticities in advance of time is a definite service, just as the many perceptive analyses on the energy crisis before the crisis actually hit the Western world in 1973,[3] sweeping generalizations about complete disappearance of all

---

[2] For a perceptive analysis of these issues, see Bension Varon, "Ocean Issues on the International Agenda," in *Beyond Dependency,* Guy F. Erb, ed., Overseas Development Council, September 1975.

[3] See, for example, Harvey Brook's article, "The Technology of Zero Growth," in the special *Daedalus* issue on "The No Growth Society," vol. 102, no. 4.

nonrenewable resources at a particular point of time in the future are mere intellectual fantasy.

It should also be remembered that the waste of natural resources is a function of both their seeming abundance and of public attitudes. It is quite possible—and indeed probable—that with either of the above factors changing, resources can be conserved without undue pain. For the major flaw of today's pattern of consumption is not really that we consume too many final goods and services, but that we use our resource inputs extremely inefficiently. If certain resources become more scarce and their relative price increases, there will be a powerful incentive for their more efficient use—a factor that the *Limits* completely ignored, as it ignored similarly potent positive factors throughout. For instance, energy can be used much more economically. There is scope for smaller cars with weaker engines, public rather than private transport, increasing efficiency in burning fuels and in generating and distributing electricity, and improved design of aircraft engines and bodies. We cannot assume that humanity would be so stupid as not to adjust if threatened with its physical extinction.

Looking at the problem, as *Limits to Growth* had done, in terms of quantifying the life expectancy of resources as presently constituted, it can be safely concluded, on the basis of more complete and scientific analysis, that these resources are sufficient to last very much longer than stipulated. It is not a question of expecting natural resources to accommodate forever our current patterns of growth, production, and consumption; clearly, they will not. But natural resources will last long enough to allow us time to make deliberate adjustments in the way we use them so that resource needs can be met indefinitely. We have seen no convincing evidence to suggest that mankind faces a final curtain about one hundred years from now through depletion of nonrenewable resources.

POLLUTION

The assumptions regarding pollution were the weakest part of the model of world economic activity on which the *Limits* was based. In many instances, they were not established on any scientific basis. We still know so little about the generation and absorption of pollution, and about the effects of pollution, that definite functions are very hard to establish.

Although little is known about the generation of pollution, it was claimed in the *World Dynamics* model,[4] on which *The Limits to Growth* model completely relied, that it increases at the same speed as the growth in capital stock per capita. As natural resources are used, progressively more capital must be applied to extract a given amount of final output—because of the necessity of using increasing amounts of energy in production as resources are either consumed or disposed of. Hence pollution grows to increasingly higher levels. In fact, the prediction of a pollution catastrophe depends on the value of the ratio assumed in the model between the pollution level and capital stock per capita. Just to demonstrate how tenuous assumptions underlie major conclusions on world disaster: if the assumed value in the *Limits* model could be reduced by five eighths—an adjustment well within the error range of the data—the prediction of catastrophe would be completely erased. Since data on actual relationships between pollution and capital stock are sparse, there is no particular reason to favor one value for the ratio rather than another.

Again, in discussing the earth's capacity to absorb pollutants, the *World Dynamics* model assumed, entirely arbitrarily, that the world's overall capacity to absorb pollution was four times the present annual level and that pollution levels beyond certain limits would start affecting human mortality. While it may be true that accumulating pollution levels may destroy present concepts of living during the next one hundred years, there is little evidence that life itself will be destroyed.

Furthermore, the authors do not fully consider that higher levels of industrial development will allow societies to devote additional resources to taking care of the pollution problem, without sacrificing continued economic growth. It has been estimated, for example, that the United States could spend $16

[4] Jay Wright Forrester, *World Dynamics* (Cambridge, Mass.: Wright-Allen Press, 1971).

billion a year, or about one third of the annual increase in its Gross National Product, and achieve a substantial reduction in pollution over the next six years. Despite this, the United States could still increase its per capita consumption by another $900 over this period. Similarly, it has been calculated that about 80–90 percent of the present pollution can be removed at a relatively low cost: the cost increases would be about 5 percent for industrial waste; 2 percent for thermal electricity; and 10 percent for automobiles.

Despite such objections to the *Limits* model, our intention is not to contend that pollution is of little global concern or that it is unrelated to economic growth. It is simply that information of the kind given above—which is extremely pertinent to the limits projections—illustrates that pollution buildup and world collapse is not necessarily inevitable even with continued economic growth.

NATURE OF THE MODEL

As we turn from an analysis of the basic assumptions of the *Limits* model to its essential nature and methodology, we are greatly handicapped by its extreme aggregation. The whole world is treated as one and homogeneous even when it is clear that the real world is characterized by vast differences in income and consumption patterns; for instance, the per capita income levels in developed countries are fourteen times those in the developing countries; an average American "consumes" twenty-five times the physical resources that an average Indian does, due to vast differences in income and consumption habits; the United States consumes about 40 percent of the world's energy resources with only 6 percent of the world population; and the style of development, the patterns of growth, and the composition of consumption demand vary widely in different parts of the world.

The highly aggregate nature of the model, therefore, raised a number of difficulties in a more serious analysis.[5] For one thing,

---

[5] This aspect of the *Limits* model has been considerably refined in the sequel brought out by the Club of Rome in 1975: See Mihajito Mesarovic and

it was not clear how seriously one could take averages of various variables which were widely dissimilar. For another, it made any plausible interpretation of the model very difficult. There was only one aggregate natural resource or one aggregate pollutant, keeping one guessing as to how representative its behavior was of the real world which was marked by much greater diversity, complexity, and substitutability.

More important, it was not possible to get any useful policy guidance from an aggregate view of the world. The real world was divided politically into a number of nation states and economically into developed and developing countries. They did not all behave similarly nor were they all affected in the same manner by the dire predictions made in the model. Thus, if natural resources were being progressively depleted, this would raise their price and benefit the producing countries which were mostly in the developing world. The transfer of resources from the rich to the poor nations in such a situation would by itself alter the overall pattern of growth rates and initiate some of the badly needed adjustments. This is, in a way, one of the implications of the recent increase in oil prices. Such natural checks and balances arise in the real world but they are not allowed for in the *Limits* aggregate world model which moves only in one direction—toward disaster.

Before we can arrive at any useful or relevant conclusion, a minimum condition is to construct at least a "two-world" model, distinguishing between the developed and the developing world. Without a greater degree of disaggregation, there is every danger that such a model would become a caricature of the real world rather than a mere abstraction.

The methodology used in the *Limits* model further reinforced the unrealistic assumptions that it started from. It did not allow for economic costs and prices nor for conscious choices made by society; there were no real corrective mechanisms—only physical engineering relationships. The world kept on proceeding in its merry way—frittering away its resources, populating itself

---

Edward Pestel, *Mankind at the Turning Point: The Second Report to the Club of Rome* (New York: Dutton, 1974).

endlessly, accumulating pollution—until one fine morning it hit disaster.

Is this a realistic abstraction from the world as we know it? In the real world, there is not one nonrenewable resource but many. They do not suddenly disappear collectively but become more and more scarce individually. As each resource becomes more scarce, price signals flash and alarm bells ring all over the world. This directs technological research into them; possibilities of substitution are explored; conscious choices are made by society to economize on them, to do without them, or to enlarge their exploitation by using marginal reserves or by recycling them at a higher price. In other words, corrective mechanisms start working. Similarly, it is hard to believe that a pollution crisis can sneak upon humanity as insidiously as the model implied. Even a modest level of pollution would mean that while the world average of persistent pollutants was still quite low and not yet obnoxious to human health, some particular localities would be suffering to a point at which corrective action would have to be taken—London, for example, introduced legislation in the 1950s to help purify its air and eliminate the deadly "pea soup" fogs.

Since the authors of the *Limits* model were interested in long-term projections, they should also have used a longer-term historical perspective. They would have found it interesting and educational if they had stepped back about one hundred years in historical time and fed the data, state of knowledge, technology, etc., of that time into their computer to see what kind of predictions followed. And if the computer showed that we all met final disaster a few years ago—or, at least, should have—they should then have examined the corrective mechanisms which came into play to save humanity from such a disaster. Was it because population growth in the developed world did not behave in the manner predicted at the time of Malthus? Was it because technology always kept ahead of man's physical problems? Was it because human society made a few conscious and sensible choices? Such a study could be quite educative. It would have shown how the corrective mechanisms—which were completely absent in the *Limits* model—worked in real life.

And it would have obliged the authors to show us why these corrective mechanisms are supposed not to work in the future.

Humanity faces these problems one by one, every year in every era, and keeps making its quiet adjustments. It does not keep accumulating them indefinitely until they make catastrophe inevitable. One does not have to believe in the invisible hand to subscribe to such a view of society. One has merely to believe in human sanity and its instinct for self-preservation. While the model itself contained hardly any mention of conscious corrective mechanisms, in a larger sense its very appearance could be regarded as part of the corrective mechanisms which societies devise in response to major problems. We return later to this aspect and to the larger message of *The Limits to Growth*.

One of the most curious parts of the model is its treatment of the role of technology. In an age of the most dramatic technological progress, the authors contended that there could not be a continuation of such rapid progress in the future. And this was merely an assumption, not a proven thesis. The model *assumed* that certain things in this world—population, capital stock, pollution—would grow at exponential rates; but it *assumed* that certain other things—specifically technology to enlarge the resource base and to fight pollution—would not grow exponentially. Any such model was inherently unstable and it was no surprise that it led to inevitable disaster.

The authors' assumptions were, however, scarcely realistic since man so far has continuously proved his ability to extend the physical limits of this planet through constant innovations and technological progress. There is no reason to think that technological innovations in conserving, recycling, and discovering new resources, and in combating pollution would stop simply because, by their very nature, we cannot predict them in advance.

POLICY IMPLICATIONS

The policy implications which flow from the *Limits* model were the least stressed and the least developed part of the book. Yet, these policy implications have attracted the greatest attention since the book appeared. The major policy conclusion from the model was the prescription of a zero growth rate, both in population and in material production. But that prescription was not logically derived from the model. Even if one accepted some of the premises of the authors about certain physical limits to further unchecked growth, it was not clear from their work why the world must immediately move in 1975 to zero growth rates. Since the model was excessively aggregated, the authors were in no position to discuss various alternative choices which were still open to society even if physical limits to growth were conceded.

There is first the choice between development and defense. Presently, about $250 billion are being spent on defense, which is one of the major users of world resources and generators of pollution. If society is really concerned about resource constraints, could it not consciously choose to devote less resources to defense and more to development? Again, there is the choice of patterns of growth. If natural resources become more scarce, could society not decide to have a different pattern of consumption—based on more social services and leisure—which is less resource-consuming? Finally, if the rich nations were to stop growing, the growth of the developing world could well proceed without putting major pressures on global physical limits, whatever these may be. These are some of the real choices that humanity faces at present and a good deal of debate is centering on them. But these choices could hardly be considered in the context of the *Limits* model which was sweeping in its overall policy prescriptions.

Another area of policy concern is world income distribution. If we were to accept, as the authors did, the thesis that the world could not be "saved" except through zero growth rates, we must also demonstrate that world income redistribution on a massive scale was possible. Otherwise, freezing the present world income distribution would not "save" the world; it would only bring about a confrontation between the haves and the have-nots. The *Limits* recognized this but skipped the issue

rather lightly as if it were a mere irritant. It did not address itself to the basic issue: How was such a massive redistribution of
income to be brought about in a stagnant world? Through negative growth rates in the developed world and positive growth
rates in the developing countries? Through a mass immigration
of the populations of the developing countries into the developed world? Through a massive transfer of resources under a
world income tax? And what was the realism of all this in a
world that was rather reluctant to transfer even 1 percent of its
Gross National Product in the form of development assistance?
While income redistribution is a desirable objective and, as
argued in Part 3 of this book, it is an important element in the
search for a new international economic order, we must recognize that it is going to be even more difficult to achieve—both
within and between nations—if there is no prospect of future
growth and various interest groups fight to keep their share in a
stagnant world.

The policy implications of the *Limits* model about population
growth seemed to be more valid than about future growth in
production. Even when one rejected the notion of zero growth
rate in industrial and agricultural production and in capital
stock, one could appreciate the advantages of stabilizing world
populations. This would release much energy and effort from
catering to ever increasing numbers and divert it to improving
the well-being of the existing population levels. It is increasingly true that the absolute increment in world population
every year is becoming uncomfortably large and we are fast
becoming an overcrowded planet. It is also true that slower
population growth would reduce the urgency of technological
solutions to resource shortages and pollution crises: there is no
reason why humanity should be under constant pressure to seek
or accept technological fixes in desperation, without considering
the full environmental implications of new technology. But the
Limits model performed no real service by linking population
growth rate only with per capita industrial production levels.

In the last analysis, we may well find that social and political
limits on future growth turn out to be far more important than

mere physical limits. It may be possible to overcome some of the physical limits through continued technological progress, as has happened during the last century, but it might become increasingly more difficult to cope with the complex political and social problems that an overcrowded planet creates. We are already witnessing a growing feeling in many societies that individuals are becoming an impersonal part of the total society and can no longer relate to it meaningfully, either in the social field or through the political forums. The question we may well have to debate is whether the world is growing too large to govern itself while maintaining any decent political order or social cohesion. But this is a much larger question, and a much more relevant one, than the *Limits* model raised or could even begin to cope with.

There are many areas of potential disaster that humanity faces, irrespective of the sterile dialogue on whether physical limits to human survival exist or not. These disasters may arise because of the inadequacy of national or international institutions to deal with the problems of a large planet and the inability of these institutions, both public and private, to recognize and react to potential crises. Issues of nuclear war and income disparity between rich and poor nations fall within this category and have rightly engaged a good deal of the attention of mankind. While the sweeping conclusions of *Limits to Growth* and the publicity which accompanied the appearance of the book created enough shock waves to start some serious work on issues of global survival, the main danger was that the debate might get dragged into the wrong channels—that is, in fighting some of the false issues that the *Limits* had raised rather than into more constructive fields. Carl Kaysen reached a very apt conclusion on this point:

Finally, therefore, how much does "crying wolf" help to direct social energies toward improving our responses to these problems? In principle, it is not only useful, but indispensable. The social mechanism is made up of human beings moved by passion far more than by reason. The mobilization of feeling that is the necessary prelude to all but the most routine social action required some stimulus stronger than a sound argument. But to be effective, the cry must be well-directed: the wolves must be imminent and they must indeed be wolves. On this score we can give only a moderate grade to "Limits," or, more properly, to its sponsors in The Club of Rome. The problems they call us to attend are real and pressing. But none are of the degree of immediacy that can rightly command the urgency they feel. Indeed, at least two problems of worldwide consequence outside the scope of this world seem to be more urgent than any it deals with: the creation of an international order stable enough to remove the threat of nuclear war, and the diminution of the staggering inequalities in the international distribution of wealth. A good sentry does not cry up tomorrow's wolves and ignore today's tigers.[6]

The basic weakness of the *Limits to Growth* thesis, therefore, was not so much that it was alarmist but that it was complacent. It was alarmist about the physical limits which might in practice be extended by continued technological progress, but complacent about the social and political problems which its own prescriptions would only exacerbate. Yet it is such problems which are probably the most serious obstacles in the way of enjoyment of the earth's resources by all its population. The industrialized countries may be able to accept a target of zero growth as a disagreeable, yet perhaps morally bracing, regimen for their own citizens. For the developing world, however, zero growth offers only a prospect of despair.

REAL MESSAGE OF THE *LIMITS* MODEL

It was unfortunate that much of the real message of the *Limits to Growth* got buried under the heated controversies that the book excited in 1972 since the authors had chosen to dramatize their findings, which led them to many inappropriate and unnecessary conclusions. Yet issues of global physical limits and the long-term choices that humanity faces are hardly irrelevant and should be an important part of man's concerns. Reviewing the excitement that the book generated after the safe distance of three years now, my own conclusions are that there were at least

[6] Carl Kaysen, "The Computer That Printed Out W*O*L*F," *Foreign Affairs,* July 1972.

four messages that the *Limits* model delivered, or at least should have, which deserve serious debate and analysis.

First, how can we focus human response on longer-term issues of global survival and adjustment when the policy attention of most politicians and the general public everywhere is consumed by short-term, day-to-day concerns? Who is going to do the global planning at a time when the gestation period for taking corrective actions is lengthening so that diagnosis and analysis must proceed far ahead of actual adjustments? In a way, the analysis of the global energy problems before 1973 illustrates this dilemma. Not much attention was paid to this analysis, particularly in the United States, and it was only the actual oil crisis of 1973–74 which forced the policy makers to consider issues of energy production and conservation. Similarly, pollution is another issue which needs to be looked at in a longer-term perspective: yet the attention it gets from the policy makers depends on the shifting public mood. The central question, therefore, is how to think, plan, and execute longer-term adjustments in our global society when the attention of the governments is often taken up by the short-run, urgent problems, irrespective of whether or not they are the most important issues that humanity faces. In a world becoming increasingly interdependent and often requiring adjustments which should be anticipated by decades, the needs and dimensions of international planning become probably just as important as those of national planning. In the last analysis, therefore, *Limits to Growth* was a forceful plea for such longer-term analysis and global planning. Since it would be idealistic to expect that the governments elected only for a specific time period will normally extend their own time horizon of what they consider as their legitimate concerns, the only alternative is to educate the public opinion about these longer-term issues and this is where serious analysis of the *Limits* type can be useful if it does not provoke unnecessary controversies.

Second, while we have firmly rejected the thesis of global physical limits, at least one particular implication of the increased pressures on the physical resources of this planet needs to be underlined. Even when technological innovations keep extending the lifetime of many physical resources, it is quite apparent that the cost at which the marginal reserves are exploited keeps rising quite sharply. This is likely to make the late development start of the poor nations quite costly, since the more easily accessible resources would have been exhausted by the rich nations. There is a logical case, therefore, for the poor nations demanding a higher price for their nonrenewable resources both because of their progressive depletion and, *in addition,* to cover the higher costs of development inflicted on them by the earlier exploitation of these resources by the rich nations.

Third, the *Limits* model unfortunately focused on the overall scarcity of resources, without pointing out that the existing maldistribution of income is one of the most important factors in these scarcities. For instance, there is enough food in the world today to feed everyone: the current food problem is not a problem of overall scarcity but that of gross maldistribution of food supplies between the poor and the rich nations.[7] An important message of the *Limits* model should, therefore, have been that some of the present intense pressures on physical resources can be eased by a major redistribution of world income. In fact, if we concede that the planet has some physical limits, it becomes imperative that the existing physical resources should be more equitably distributed. The *Limits* model could not deal with this issue since it insisted on regarding the world as one aggregative entity.

Finally, the *Limits* model carried major implications for readjusting life styles both in the developed and the developing countries. The developed countries must search for less resource-using styles of consumption, implying a major shift from durable consumer goods to social services and leisure. The developing countries must find their own patterns of consumption, as an extension of their own cultural values and their particular stage of development, rather than a mindless pursuit of the material standards of the Western countries. As discussed in Part 1 and in the next chapter, this search for new development styles has already begun in earnest.

[7] See Mahbub ul Haq, "The Triumph of Sanity," in *CERES* 8, no. 3 (May–June 1975), Rome.

·6· THE ENVIRONMENTAL THREAT

THE RISING CONCERN about physical limits to global growth in the early 1970s was also accompanied by an increasing anxiety about environmental degradation, primarily in the industrialized world. Public opinion in the developed countries in this case was far ahead of their governments and often forced the policy makers to consider action on defining minimum environmental standards and on legislating environmental safeguards. Suddenly, there was an open and often excited debate about the various threats to the quality of life in the developed world.[1] Partly, this was a reaction against unbridled materialism; partly, a certain nervousness that man may be losing control over the side effects of technological progress;[2] partly, a belated demand that individuals and groups should assume their broader social responsibilities, particularly for the social costs of their own actions. In the last analysis, however, it was probably a genuine search for a new development style which could integrate the quantity of goods and services with certain qualitative objectives, particularly with greater availability of social services and leisure.

CRITICAL DIFFERENCES

After some initial skirmishes, the developing countries have also begun to appreciate the relevance of the environmental concern

---

[1] See, for instance, W. Beckerman, "Why We Need Economic Growth," *Lloyds Bank Review*, no. 102 (October 1971); and H. J. Barnett, *Scarcity and Growth* (Baltimore: Johns Hopkins University Press, 1973).

[2] M. Taghi Farvar, ed. *The Careless Technology: Ecology and International Development* (New York: Natural History Press, 1972).

to their own situations, but there are some fundamental differences between their concerns and those of the developed countries.

The first and most important difference is that the Third World is not merely worried about the quality of life, it is worried about life itself. In many parts of the developing world, life itself is endangered by poor water, poor sanitation, crowded housing, sickness, disease and natural disasters. The essential difference is that the environmental problems of these poor societies arise not because of excessive technology or development but from the lack of control of man over nature. So, unlike the developed countries, development is often a cure, not a cause for environmental problems. For instance, environmental problems are those of open drains, poor water supply, and prevalence of disease so that development of good water supply and sewerage facilities and extension of health services is a prerequisite to overcome these problems.[3] This often requires a fast rate of growth and application of modern technology. Not many developing countries can afford the luxury of turning their back on more goods and services since they start with so few.

The second major difference is that, in a good part of the developing world, there is planned development and a fair amount of government control over what is done even in the private sector. So unlike the classic American experience, where private capitalism during the last few decades flourished with a minimum of social controls, one often finds an excessive degree of social and administrative controls over every walk of life in many developing countries. As such, the patterns of development which are currently being adopted in these countries cannot completely ignore social costs or callously disregard the larger implications of economic growth.

However, when conflicts arise between a higher rate of growth in national production and greater protection of environment and conservation of resources, these poor societies gen-

---

[3] For a good discussion of the infrastructure requirements of the poor countries, see Otto H. Koenigsberger et al., *Infrastructural Problems of the Cities of Developing Countries* (New York: Ford Foundation, 1971).

erally face very cruel choices. For instance, the choice often is whether to put in the chemical fertilizers and risk the adverse environmental effects of the new agricultural technology, or not to do so and endanger the very sustenance of life in these societies. These are not really choices at the margin—whether these societies grow a little more or a little less while protecting their environment—since many of these countries are surviving on $5–$6 monthly income per person. Whenever a choice has to be made between present survival or future well-being, it is inevitable that the choice would be made in favor of the present generation. The developed countries must have much greater sympathy and understanding for such choices by now since their own concern for environmental protection considerably weakened as soon as their rates of growth slowed down in 1974–75 in the wake of the increase in the oil price (e.g., relaxation in the introduction of stringent environmental standards in new cars, greater permissiveness in allowing strip mining for coal). And these choices in the developed world were made at a much higher level of per capita income where the choice was hardly between environmental protection and starvation.

Finally, as we see it in the developing world, the choice is not so much between present and future, between development and environment, but it is essentially the choice of a certain pattern and style of development. As discussed in Part I of this book, it is increasingly being recognized that the previous patterns of development, which concentrated exclusively on high rates of growth in the Gross National Product, irrespective of what was being produced and how it was being distributed, are no longer valid or relevant. They do not satisfy the aspirations of the people. New development strategies must be fashioned which cater to the basic human needs and which are a logical extension of the cultural patterns of these societies (see chapter 4). The main question is whether, in this quest for new development styles, the developing countries can learn from the mistakes of the Western societies: for instance, they have a fresh opportunity to decide whether they want to promote an "auto culture" for a few or public transport for the many.

Let us discuss here briefly how various trade-offs between present and future are considered and actual choices made between development and environment concerns in the developing world. There are two types of choices. First, the society faces a choice when certain natural resources or environment are going to be destroyed in the pursuit of economic growth. In this case, greater knowledge about what the future damage is going to be can enable these societies to make more rational choices now. This is the kind of choice that was recently faced in a steel plant project in Turkey and in an ore-mining project in Brazil, where the analysis showed that the original design of these projects would damage some of the other natural resources which would endanger future productivity of these projects themselves. Some cost calculations showed that by spending about 2 percent more in the case of the Turkish steel plant and 3 percent more in the case of the Brazil ore-mining project, the future danger to the other productive assets could be eliminated. In this case, after the World Bank had made its own analysis and brought it to the attention of the governments concerned, they were willing to accept the costs because they regarded such a trade-off between present and future entirely reasonable and well within their capacity to afford. But in those cases where the cost may turn out to be much higher, say 25 percent to 50 percent, these societies would be hard pressed to make the choice in favor of present growth, which is what they need for mere survival, rather than for future environmental protection. Such cases also raise the general policy question of who should pay for such environmental costs, to which we return later in this chapter.

The second type of choice that these societies face is between satisfying the essential needs of the masses and between preserving certain natural assets which constitute the so-called quality of life. In this case, the choice is quite clear for many of the developing countries. Confronted with the preservation of wildlife or human life, they have to opt for the latter. If, for instance, an irrigation project is being contemplated in a certain country—this, in fact, is an actual example—which is going to destroy one of the famous national parks, this is a cost that the society has to cheerfully bear if there are no other economical alternatives. And the society has neither the time nor the option to quibble too much about whether it is a reversible or irreversible damage, a debate which often warms the hearts of the conservationists in the developed countries.

The developing countries face these difficult choices not only at the national level but also in international trade and in the transfer of resources and technology. Some of these issues are raising awkward questions for the developing world, particularly the choices that the developed countries are likely to make under the influence of environmental concern in their future relations with the developing world.

INTERNATIONAL TRADE

Many developing countries are viewing the possible impact of environmental issues on international trade with considerable apprehension. They fear that some of their raw material exports may be displaced by the development of less-polluting technology. The demand for some others may be reduced by the recycling of raw materials. There is also a fear that non-tariff barriers may go up in the developed countries on such exports of the developing countries as they do not meet the stringent environmental standards imposed by the developed countries. Dairy products and fruits and vegetables may suffer in particular. The banning of import of certain vegetables and fruits carrying traces of DDT by some European countries has strengthened these fears. There is an unarticulated assumption here that some of this action is likely to become quite arbitrary and discriminatory. In fact, there is a fear that many protectionists may jump at the chance to question not only the quality of the imported products but the environmental conditions under which the products were produced. Since economic liberalism is not particularly strong these days, it is feared that the argument of "sweated environment," like the equally fallacious argument of "sweated labor," may be skilfully exploited by protectionist lobbies in the industrialized countries.

In analyzing these fears, it is useful to distinguish between various kinds of trade disruption that can arise from environmental action since international response may have to be different in each case. It is also useful to remind ourselves that changes in the pattern of trade are a normal feature of international developments: we should be concerned only if trade disruptions are likely to be of major dimensions or if they arise out of actions which are arbitrary and not subject to international monitoring.

First, trade may be disrupted because some products are found to be contaminated or to carry definite health hazards. In such cases, international controls on the movement of such products must be invoked in the larger interests of all countries. However, most cases are not likely to be so extreme. A more common variation will be quality control through higher environmental standards for those products which carry some health risks: this may particularly apply to agricultural products. In such cases, the scope for discriminatory and arbitrary action is fairly wide and it is necessary that some international safeguards should be established.[4] For one thing, an effort should be made to agree upon uniform, environmentally acceptable standards for various products. This means that the same standards should always be applied to imports as to the corresponding domestic products. This also means that same or similar standards should be invoked by all nations so that there is no rise in non-tariff barriers against imports. Agreement on uniform environmental standards for products which are most likely to be affected in international trade will also help ensure that there is enough time given for adjustment to trading nations and that there is some international mechanism to monitor the enforcement of these standards in a nondiscriminatory fashion.

[4] One good example of restrictive practices is in the trade of citrus fruits, in which less developed countries now have a comparative advantage. The standards set for imports into the developed countries, based on sugar content of the fruit, seemed to have been kept high to exclude imports from the developing countries. For a detailed discussion, see John McPhee, *Oranges* (New York: Farrar, Strauss and Giroux, 1971).

Second, trade disruption may arise because less-polluting technology displaces some imports or reduces their need. Since developing countries depend more heavily on primary exports,[5] they are likely to be affected to a much greater extent by such developments. One of the first things to establish here is the likely order of magnitude of such a problem: otherwise we may all be chasing ghosts. It is unlikely that this will be a sizable threat for many developing countries as only a very few items are being mentioned at the moment (such as lead) for which developing countries are not the principal suppliers. In any case, the prospect of reduced use per unit of future output for some raw materials may still not mean greatly reduced imports by developed countries as output itself expands. If there is any major impact, it may be in the case of some raw materials which suddenly become the victim of technological progress (in this case, less-polluting technology) and on which some developing country was particularly dependent. While one cannot readily think of any significant examples at this stage, it is important that such a possibility should be recognized and the international community should accept the principle of compensatory financing in such eventualties to reassure developing countries that their development prospects will not be jeopardized by some sudden technological development. This assurance is necessary for two reasons. One, it is politically explosive if people in the developing countries come to believe that their bread and butter is being seriously threatened by the efforts of the developed countries to improve their environment and quality of life. Two, the principle of compensatory financing is already accepted for any major shortfalls in export proceeds of the developing countries. Its extension to cover major trade disruptions arising out of environmental action will only be a logical step.

Third, it is quite possible that many vested interests in the developed countries would like to see uniform environmental standards apply not only to the final products but also to the in-

[5] During 1970–72, primary exports accounted for 52 percent of the total exports of the developing countries. This share will decline to only 48 percent by 1980.

dustries producing those products. If industries in the developed countries have to adopt stringent environmental standards which make their products more expensive and less competitive than imports from the developing countries, they may start arguing for tariffs or quotas against such imports on the ground that these are products of a "sweated environment." They may allege that it constitutes unfair competition if industries in the developing countries are allowed to pollute their environment whereas they cannot do so with impunity. Such thinking will be both fallacious and dangerous, and this is what is feared most by the developing countries as they have experienced trade discrimination against their manufactured exports on a host of grounds, including the equally fallacious "sweated labor" argument. It should be realized that many social costs were ignored or postponed by the developed countries in their phase of rapid industrialization so that enforcement of high environmental standards at this stage is an acknowledgment of this reality and not an argument for enforcing similar standards in the developing countries. If anything, it is an argument for international redistribution of industry, as discussed later. It would be ironic if this argument is used to put up tariff or non-tariff barriers against the competing imports from the developing countries.

While some of the exaggerated fears of the developing countries about trade disruption should be put in their proper perspective through careful analysis and more factual information, it is also necessary that some international agreements should be arrived at which provide these countries with adequate safeguards. Developing countries have generally a weak bargaining position and nothing can reassure them more than an expressed willingness on the part of the developed countries to reach an understanding with them that their growing concern with environment will not detract from their commitment to international development. Furthermore, some concrete action should be initiated in the trade field to reduce the possibilities of adverse impact on the developing countries.

First and foremost, all countries should agree not to invoke environmental concern as a pretext for discriminatory trade policies or reduction of access to markets or encouragement of protectionist tendencies. Second, in order to reduce the scope for arbitrary action by individual countries, the United Nations family of organizations, particularly UNEP, should assist governments in negotiating mutually acceptable international environmental standards of products in as many areas as possible. Third, it should be agreed by all the countries that uniform environmental standards cannot, and will not, apply to processes or industries producing the product. Fourth, it would be helpful if an early warning system is established whereby developed countries can inform their trading partners in the developing countries in advance about the actions they propose to take on environmental grounds which have trade implications and to consult with them about trade alternatives and even to assist them in meeting the higher environmental standards by extending credits. A useful role can be played here by the UNCTAD (United Nations Conference for Trade and Development) in identifying the major threats to exports which may arise from the environmental concern and the remedial action that may be possible. Finally, in those cases where legitimate environmental concern results in a "major" disruption in the exports of a particular developing country, the international community should accept the principle of compensation to sustain the country's development in the short run.

The suggestions offered above are only illustrative of the kind of international arrangements which should be made to minimize the adverse impact of environmental concern on international trade. The main point is that there are certain areas where the interests of the developing countries can conceivably suffer by the growing environmental concern and it would be proper, indeed necessary, to identify such areas and to strive for international agreements which can reduce the risk of serious trade disruptions. At the same time, it should be recognized that the growing environmental concern can also give rise to certain new opportunities. It is possible, for instance, that the current concern with the polluting implications of some synthetics (e.g., plastics and detergents) may encourage a return to certain natural fibers.[6] Again, the recycling of raw materials may also help more efficient resource use—in particular, use of waste materials from the developing countries as well. Some of these positive opportunities should be carefully analyzed and their implications for international trade and development identified. One of the principal areas of such opportunities—viz., geographical redistribution of industry—is analyzed later in this chapter.

TECHNOLOGY TRANSFER

There is considerable confusion at present as to the direction in which environmental concern is likely to influence the transfer of technology from the rich to the poor nations. On the one hand, there is a view that the technology that is transferred will become even more inappropriate than it is at present, as it will be geared to the pollution control requirements of the developed countries and may contain features which the developing countries do not require at the present stage of their development. As such, it will not only become more capital-intensive but also more expensive, with estimates of additional cost ranging between 5 percent and 20 percent. It is further alleged that many developing countries will have little choice but to import some of the less-polluting technology under tied credits and, thereby, accept a real reduction in the volume of their foreign assistance. On the other hand, there is a view that less-polluting technology may well turn out to be less, rather than more, expensive in terms of the real use of resources. It is also argued that the developed countries are presently getting ready to make considerable investments in developing new technology to fight environmental degradation, and this can only be beneficial to the developing countries which can, at a later stage, pick and choose various elements out of this technology suitable to their conditions, without having to make a sizable investment in its development.

[6] For an interesting analysis of the possible outcome for developing countries of environmental restrictions in the developed countries, see Norman McCrae, "The Year 2000," *The Economist,* November 1973.

It is surprising how little concrete information is presently available on the cost of new less-polluting technology. The only way to put this problem in somewhat better perspective is to encourage a good deal of research into the type of technology that ought to be developed to fight various environmental hazards, the suitability of such technology for different societies at different stages of development, and additional cost that the development or use of such technology will impose. While research of this kind should be encouraged in many national and international forums, it would be useful to organize some of it under the auspices of the U.N. Committee for Science and Technology, particularly such research as is of most direct interest to the developing countries. Some firm facts must be established before any overall judgments can be made.

Meanwhile, we should attempt to reach agreement on a few basic propositions. First, it should be agreed that the same kind of less-polluting technology will not be appropriate for developed and developing countries alike and room should be provided for considerable adaptation and improvisation. Second, and this flows from the first, the temptation to apply uniform environmental standards or guidelines in project appraisal should be firmly resisted. Nothing is going to cause so much resentment as the tendency by some donors to judge the development projects of the developing world by the standards applicable to their own countries. And third, there should be an agreement in principle that if the adoption of less-polluting technology significantly raises the costs of development in the developing countries, some arrangement will be made for sharing these additional costs between the developed and the developing countries. The environmental concern should not lead to a reduction in the real flow of assistance to the developing nations: it must be utilized to increase these flows since the resources required for taking car of both developmental and environmental objectives are likely to be much higher.[7]

---

[7] For a more detailed reflection of the Third World point of view, see United Nations, *Development and Environment* (New York, 1971).

REDISTRIBUTION OF INDUSTRIES

One of the major issues that is likely to arise from the growing environmental concern is the international specialization in the so-called "polluting" industries. It is quite likely that the additional cost of less-polluting technology, or very stringent controls over pollution, will tend to drive out several industries from the developed countries, such as petroleum refining, chemicals, metal extracting and processing, paper and pulp. A major controversy has already arisen whether the developing countries should move in and accommodate some of these industries. There is a school of thought arguing that the developing countries should not become "pollution havens" for the benefit of the developed countries; that they should impose their own stringent pollution controls and keep these industries out as far as possible. There is another school of thought arguing that a tremendous opportunity has arisen for the developing countries to move in quickly into such industries, irrespective of any environmental hazards, since rapid growth must take precedence over environment at this stage of their development.

Much of this controversy is way off the mark. There is absolutely no reason why the developing countries should not increasingly concentrate on some of the industries which the developed countries find too "pollutive" or too costly in their context. This, after all, is the basic principle of international division of labor and the shifting comparative advantage. The developing countries, on the whole, have imposed a relatively low demand on their environmental resources in the past so that they can accommodate a greater volume of waste products, or residuals, at this stage of their development. At the same time, there is no reason why they should not put in some safeguards against major environmental degradation arising out of these industries. These safeguards are obviously going to be much less stringent and, in many cases, relatively less expensive than in the developed countries. As such, the developing countries do not have to give up their concern with environment while specializing in some of these so-called pollutive industries. In fact, an historic opportunity has opened up for them. The developed countries, in their anxiety to grow fast, ignored some of the social costs of their industrialization and these postponed costs have accumulated by now to pose difficult choices for their present generation. If this contributes to slow down the growth of some of these industries in the developed countries and to encourage a move toward a better geographical redistribution of industries toward the developing countries, which were left behind in the race for development, it would only be a just redressing of the international economic balance. In fact, this is one case where the interests of the developed and the developing nations are mutually compatible rather than conflicting so that everybody gains by a sensible redistribution of industries.

One of the issues which is mentioned frequently in this connection is the role of the multinational corporations.[8] It is feared that these corporations will try to get away from the stringent environmental controls in their home countries by exploiting the environment of the developing countries and then remitting huge profits back home. This kind of reasoning mixes up two entirely different arguments. What policy the developing countries adopt regarding the role of the multinational corporations is their exclusive prerogative: they can decide it in the light of what investment, growth, employment, technology, etc., these corporations bring in and what they are allowed to take out, besides, of course, the political and social environment within which the multinational corporations have to function. They can curtail the role of these corporations or modify the rules of the game as they desire. But this is no argument against going into the so-called pollutive industries where comparative advantage may increasingly favor the developing countries.

ENVIRONMENTAL COST SHARING

As mentioned earlier, one of the principal issues that the developed and the developing countries must debate is: who pays for

[8] For a discussion, see Carnegie Endowment for International Peace, *FOUNEX Report* (New York, 1972).

the higher costs in the developing countries arising out of either international or domestic actions for environmental improvement? The developing countries argue, with a good deal of justification, that these costs should be borne largely by the developed world, which has grown rapidly and without much social planning in the past, is responsible for a major part of the past environmental degradation, and has the resources and the capability to bear these costs. Obviously, the developed countries are somewhat impatient with environmental concern becoming yet one more argument for coughing up additional funds for the developing countries. But the question is a decisive one and must be faced, especially if the environmental concern is to be viewed in the perspective of global responsibility.[9]

Why should the developed countries pay a major part of the costs of environmental improvement in the developing countries? One can offer various arguments but, in the last analysis, they all link up with the principal issue of our time: the increasing gap between the rich and the poor nations and the need for international redistribution of incomes, themes which are discussed at some length in Part 3 of this book. The developed countries have by now the means to fight their environmental pollution while continuing to increase their per capita incomes at a satisfactory rate, but the developing countries possess neither the means for reaching satisfactory levels of living in the near future nor the resources for environmental improvement. For developed countries, it is often a trade-off between possession of ever more material goods in a more polluted environment or a somewhat lower increase in goods and services in a less polluted environment: in either case, they do not face the cruel choice between sheer survival and better environment that most developing countries face. For instance, it is estimated that even a "substantial" reduction in environmental pollution in the United States will cost about $16 billion a year during 1970–76, or about one-third of the expected *increase* in GNP during this period. In other words, the United States can look after its environmental pollution and yet *increase* its per capita

[9] Barbara Ward and René Dubos, *Only One Earth* (New York: Norton, 1972).

income by another $900 during this period. The basic issue, therefore, is the present capability of the developed world to tackle both development and environment problems at a time when the developing countries lack the means to do so.

There is another reason why the concept of international responsibility of the developed countries must be stressed in this field. The exploitation of the common-property resources of mankind (like ocean beds) is just beginning and may accelerate in coming years, spurred by the feared depletion of nonrenewable resources. These common-property resources belong to the whole of mankind and not to any particular nation, but only the developed countries have the capacity to exploit them at this stage. It is vital that some international agreement be reached on this question if the rights of over 70 percent of the world population living in the developing countries are to be safeguarded. Otherwise, some advanced nations will enrich themselves further by exploiting mankind's common-property resources for their own benefit.

It is for these reasons that the developed countries ought to be persuaded to bear the major part of the costs of environmental improvement. One indication of this would be a declaration by the developed world that their growing environmental concern would be accompanied by an increase, not a reduction, in their assistance for development. Another would be their willingness to set up a Special Fund for environmental improvement for which they contribute the major part of the resources (the present fund of $20 million a year is hardly sufficient for even the necessary research on environmental issues or for international monitoring and control). Such a Fund should not be raised by government contributions, which tend to be unreliable and inflexible, but by taxing major international pollutants, with safeguards that the burden does not fall on the developing countries. For instance, even a 1 percent levy on the freight charged by oil tankers can raise as much as $200 million a year. Other users of international environment can be similarly taxed. The basic idea should be to build in some automaticity in the resources for such a Fund.

The Fund can be utilized for a variety of purposes including environmental research and information, compensation for major trade dislocations resulting from environmental action, financing of additional costs of development projects arising from more stringent environmental standards, and development of various environmental resources, such as ocean beds which are the common property of mankind, mainly for the benefit of the developing countries. The precise manner in which the resources for this Special Fund are raised or the purposes for which the Fund should be utilized are matters which require careful analysis and discussion, but such a concept of international responsibility is only a logical culmination of the growing concern with environmental issues in the developed world and the principal way that the interests of the developing countries can be safeguarded. When all is said and done, the basic question boils down to this: Will the growing perception of the concept of "only one earth" and "only one environment" also lead to the nobler concept of "only one humanity" and to the grander vision of a greater international responsibility for the accelerated development of the developing countries and a more equitable sharing of environmental costs? Or will it become a narrower concern of the developed world, leading to many awkward confrontations with the developing countries rather than to a new era of international cooperation?

Even more important is the perspective in which the debate on development and environment, which dominated the international scene in the early 1970s, must be placed now. Much of this debate strayed into many side issues and blind alleys when the real emphasis should have been on the relationship betwen the rich and the poor nations in a fast shrinking planet. The debate has recently returned once again to this central theme which is the major focus of the next part of this book.

THE POPULATION BURDEN

THE VERY RAPID INCREASE in the population of the developing countries in the last three decades has once again raised the Malthusian specter. When viewed along with the rate at which man is exploiting some of the nonrenewable resources of this planet, the specter of Malthus, this time around, seems very real to many analysts. According to them, the dire predictions of that nineteenth-century Cassandra, forgotten for some time because of the extraordinary technological advances which brought new resources to surface, seem near fulfillment. There is, therefore, a tremendous urgency in the appeals that are being made to the developing countries to control their population growth and thereby reduce the burden on the world's resources.

STERILE DEBATES

The population problem, by what is more a happenstance, has thus gotten linked with the problem of resource depletion and environmental pollution. This unfortunate, and as we shall presently see, untenable connection, has had some serious consequences. The most important of these is the needless apportioning of blame between the developed and the developing countries. Facts, of course, can always be picked up to support contending positions. The developing countries allege that it is the affluence of the developed countries which is placing an enormous pressure on the world's natural resources, not the population growth in the Third World. For instance, the total energy consumption in the developed countries has in the last

two decades increased at the rate of over 5 percent per annum.[1]
The developed countries point accusingly at the rate of population growth in the developing countries which touched an un-
precedented level of 2.3 percent per annum during the same
period.[2]

This type of polarization has plagued the discussions on most
of the issues of global importance. For instance, at the United
Nations Conference on Human Environment in Stockholm in
1972, the countries of the Third World accused the industrial
nations of a careless and irresponsible use of man's common
heritage, thus making the process of development not only
more difficult but also increasingly costly. At the United Nations Conference on Population in Bucharest in 1974, the developed countries seemed to turn the tables on the Third World,
holding it responsible for an equally careless and irresponsible
use of man's fertility potential. At Stockholm, the developing
countries interpreted the industrial countries' concern with environmental problems as an alibi for not meeting the Second
Development Decade's targets for concessionary assistance. At
Bucharest, the developed countries saw Third World's reluc-
tance to bestow the status of a global problem on the high rate
of population growth in many less developed countries as an excuse for continuing with "soft options." While at Stockholm,
the developing countries introduced the concept of "addi-
tionality," claiming that there should be suitable compensation
for any reduction that environmental considerations may bring
about in the quantum of real resources flowing to them; at
Bucharest, the developed countries brought forward the criterion of population-resource balance, suggesting that all those
countries which were out of step in this respect should first
adopt immediate measures to restore equilibrium.

It is unfortunate that the highly charged atmosphere of the
Bucharest Conference prevented those people, who have taken a

[1] Joel Darmstadter and Hans H. Landsberg, "The Economic Background of
Oil Crisis," *Daedalus* 104, no. 4 (Fall 1975), p. 16.
[2] World Bank, *Population Policies and Economic Development* (Baltimore:
Johns Hopkins University Press, 1974), p. 8.

sober view of the population problem, from influencing the policy makers in both the developed and the developing countries. To brush aside the problem of population is as wrong as to suggest that it can be solved within a short period of time. No group of people, no matter where they come from, can claim that the addition of a very large number of people to the world's already large population does not pose a problem; similarly, no one should proclaim that the problem can be met merely through an appropriate use of resources.

In this chapter, some facts about the population situation are presented first. A straightforward presentation of information about demographic developments, past and future, can help dispel a number of myths about the population problem. Then the current knowledge about family formation is used to suggest a set of constructive approaches to this problem. Finally, we discuss how the developed and the developing countries can get together in controlling the exponential growth of the world's population.

NATIONAL, NOT GLOBAL, PROBLEM

Before starting this analysis, however, one point must be made clearly since confusion on this score vitiates many demographic debates. Population growth in the developing countries is a national, not a global problem. It is a national problem because the economic progress of these societies is being considerably handicapped by their increasing numbers and because the meager resources of these countries could have had provided a more satisfactory increase in their living standards but for the major and continuing increase in their population. No national planner can, therefore, dismiss lightly the existing population problem and various feasible approaches to contain future increases in population.

But the population growth in the developing countries is not a *global* problem. It could have been described as a global problem only if it was responsible for putting the major part of the pressure on the world's resources. That it clearly does not do.

When it comes to the pressure on the world's natural resources, it is not only the sheer numbers which are relevant but also their income and their consumption demand. The Third World (excluding OPEC) contains about 70 percent of the total world population but enjoys only 11 percent of the world's Gross National Product (see Table 1 in the Statistical Appendix). By definition, therefore, it consumes only about one tenth of the world's resources. In fact, its consumption of nonrenewable resources may be even less because its general pattern of consumption is based on simple goods which are much less resource-using than the life styles in the rich nations. This also means that the present annual increment in population in the developed countries (even though it is less than 1 percent per annum) poses far more of a global problem in relation to world's resources than the 2.3 percent annual growth in the population of the Third World, because of the considerable disparity in incomes at present between the rich and the poor nations. In quantitative terms, the current increase in the population of the developed countries places at least eight times as much pressure on the world's natural resources as the population growth in the Third World simply because each new member of the rich nations enjoys about twenty times the income of the poor nations. Unfortunately, in this world of ours, an American and an Indian are not born equal in economic terms since it costs our planet earth about thirty times as many resources to feed the former than the latter.

This is the heart of the dialogue: the essential distinction between numbers and affluence. The poor nations resent the fact that their population growth is held responsible for creating global pressures. They point out, quite justifiably, that these pressures arise from the consumption styles of the rich nations, not from their population "explosion." In the next few decades at least, no conceivable slowdown in the population of the Third World can help ease the major part of the pressure on global resources. The developing countries also are quite mystified that there is so little analysis of the current population growth in the developed countries and so much preoccupation with the population increase in the Third World when the former consumes eight times more global resources than the latter. They rightly point out that even a slight redistribution of world's income can help ease the pressure on the world's resources far more than any possible reduction in the population growth of the Third World. This conflict in perceptions can be resolved only by admitting frankly that the population growth in the developing countries is not a *global* problem but a *national* one. And it is certainly a serious national concern to which the developing countries must devote their full attention, without having to fight shadow battles with the rich nations. It is in this perspective that we turn to its analysis.

SOME BASIC FACTS

The first demographic fact is not so much the present size of the Third World population or its rate of growth in the next few decades, but that the fertility behavior of individuals is governed to a considerable extent by the environment in which they reproduce. It is now well known that environment may considerably modify the timing of reproductive processes.[3] The rate of fertility is high in the developing countries compared with that in the developed nations for the reason that family formation in the former is taking place in an environment that is conducive to a higher rate of reproduction. The fertility rates in the developing world are not much different from those experienced a century and a half ago by the developed nations of today. There is, therefore, little reason to imply that there exists in the developing countries an extraordinary urge to procreate. The urge to multiply seems to overtake all the threatened species. It is no more unique to *Homo sapiens* of today's developing nations than it was to those who a hundred and fifty years ago inhabited the presently developed parts of the world. This compensatory mechanism worked in Europe to restore the demographic equi-

[3] R. L. Holmes, *Reproduction and Environment* (New York: Norton, 1968), has an excellent and highly readable account of the interaction of environment and human reproduction.

librium after the Black Plague.[4] It also works in today's developing countries to retain a balance between a family's requirement of "child services"[5] and its capacity to provide its members with a bare level of subsistence.

The remarkable demographic difference between the developed and the developing countries is not in their historical and present rates of fertility but in their rates of mortality. Whereas in eighteenth-century Europe the fertility rate was only marginally higher than the death rate, in the developing countries it is often three times as high. Therefore, whereas the population of Europe grew at a very slight rate in the pre-Industrial Revolution period, it is "exploding" in the developing countries.

It is interesting to note that this basic demographic difference generally gets reflected only in the world population models. In most discussions, the focus is on the rates of population growth rather than on the demographic factors responsible for bringing it to its present level. When we reflect somewhat more deeply on the nature of this problem, it is obvious that most of the developing countries are faced with a situation for which they cannot supply an immediate solution. This point is so crucial to an understanding of the nature of the problem that it deserves some emphasis.

The population model incorporated in *Limits of Growth* took proper cognizance of these factors. The world population was set to "explode" not so much because of excessive high rates of fertility in the developing countries but because of a continuation in the trend of mortality decline. With no significant changes in fertility (an unwarranted assumption to which we shall return presently), the gap between birth and death rates was likely to grow, resulting in exponential, and hence explosive, rates of population growth.

[4] For an interesting discussion of this phenomenon, see Paul R. Ehrlich and Anne H. Ehrlich, *Population, Resources and Environment: Issues in Human Ecology* (San Francisco: Freeman, 1972).

[5] The term is that of G. Becker. See his "An Economic Analysis of Fertility" in National Bureau of Economic Research, *Demographic and Economic Changes in Developed Countries* (Princeton, N.J.: Princeton University Press, 1960), pp. 209–40.

Some of the recent population models have moved away from the more conservative fertility assumptions in the *Limits* forecast. The World Bank model, after making some downward adjustment in the present fertility rate in the developing countries, projects the rate of growth to decline from the present level of 2.3 percent to just over 2 percent for the last decade of this century. According to this projection, the world population by the turn of this century would be 6.4 billion, with 5 billion in the developing countries. If these estimates turn out to be correct, the Third World's share in the world population would increase from 70 percent in 1970 to 79 percent in the year 2000.[6]

The demographic helplessness of the developing countries can be perceived more graphically in the Mesarovic-Pestel population model incorporated in their report to the Club of Rome.[7] The model, using four very different fertility assumptions, predicted population equilibrium rates for the developing countries. Under the constant fertility assumption, the Third World population would amount to 10 billion in only fifty years from now. The population figures thereafter are so astronomical as to be almost ridiculous to consider. The model then goes on to make three different assumptions about fertility declines. The most optimistic, and of course the least practical, assumption sees fertility declining to the replacement level in 1975. If this were to happen, the population of the developing countries would stabilize at 6.3 billion. With fertility reaching replacement levels in 1985 and 1995, the equilibrium population would be of the order of 8 billion and 10.2 billion respectively. Therefore, even under the most optimistic circumstances, the less developed countries will still have a population twice as large as their present one; under the more feasible assumptions, this population could increase about threefold. What this and other dynamic models suggest is that, in the current demographic situation of the Third World, there is a built-in momentum that would carry it through a period of rapid popula-

[6] World Bank, *Population Policies and Economic Development*, p. 8.
[7] Mihajilo Mesarovic and Eduard Pestel, *Mankind at the Turning Point*, (New York: Dutton, 1974), pp. 70–82.

tion growth. This period of demographic transition is with us and there is not much that can be done about it.

This does not mean that there is no solution to the problem of population growth. What the foregoing analysis underscores is that we have to learn to accommodate at least an additional three to four billion people in the developing countries of today. The solution to the problem is both in preparing ourselves for this eventuality as well as planning to reduce the number of people which would be added to the Third World population. Estimates of future increment range from three to six billion. It would be a major triumph if the Third World can keep down the rate of population growth to the lesser part of this range.

APPROACHES TO THE PROBLEM

No one will deny that continued population growth at the present rate is a serious matter which should engage the urgent attention of humanity. The question is not whether population growth can continue unchecked forever; it simply cannot. The real issue is how to arrest it through deliberate policies of population planning.

It was in the early 1960s that the problem of population began to receive the serious attention of the development community and, as in so many other cases, the impulse was to rush in with the latest technology and generous resources. The activity in the early and mid-sixties produced a tremendous amount of euphoria. It was widely believed that the use of the latest contraceptive devices would produce dramatic reductions in the fertility rates. The assumption behind this approach was, of course, naïve. Families were large in the developing countries not so much because the poor people did not know, nor have the means, to separate sex from reproduction. The rate of fertility was high mainly because of many social and economic factors, one of the most important being that the families needed a certain quantum of child services.[8]

In the sixties, more than a dozen population control pro-

[8] For an analysis of the demand of child services and its impact on family size, see Michael C. Keeley, "A Comment on 'An Interpretation of the

grams were launched in the developing countries of Asia. These countries, with a population of nearly a billion, spent on an average $100 million per year on public and private initiatives of family-planning programs. With per capita incomes of no more than $100, this amounted to an expenditure of nearly a dollar per head of the fertile population—not an insignificant amount considering the fact that the per capita expenditure on education was not much more than that.

It is a sobering thought that the countries with the largest political and economic commitment to family planning often produced about the poorest results with regard to reducing fertility. For instance, the available evidence from Pakistan suggests that the rate of fertility, as shown by the census of 1972, was not appreciably lower than that in 1961, this despite a massive family-planning program that claimed 1.4 percent of the total development expenditure during most of the 1960s. India also spent large sums in support of fertility-control programs but the impact of these programs was not much better than that in Pakistan.[9]

Notwithstanding the failure of large family-planning programs in more densely populated parts of the Third World to reduce fertility rates in any significant manner, there has been a small but steady decline in the overall fertility rate in the developing countries since about 1960. The birth rate for all developing nations declined from 43.9 during 1950–55 to 42.0 during 1960–65. The rate for the 1965–70 period is estimated at 40.6 births per thousand population.[10] These rates are still high but at least the trend is hopeful.

The decline in the birth rates has been generally more pro-

Economic Theory of Fertility,' "*Journal of Economic Literature* 13, no. 2 (June 1975):461–67.

[9] For an analysis of Pakistan's family-planning effort, see Shahid Javed Burki (ed.), *Development Policy and Population Policy: The Pakistan Experience* (Washington, D.C.: Smithsonian Institution, 1975); for a very critical account of the Indian experience, see Mahmood Mandani, *The Myth of Population Control: Family Caste and Class in Indian Village* (New York: Monthly Review Press, 1972).

[10] World Bank, *Population Policies . . . ,* p. 13.

nounced in those countries that have experienced high rates of economic growth, suggesting a close relationship between economic development and population growth. This has led some Third World analysts to claim that development is the best contraceptive. It is in this relationship between household incomes and fertility rates that we can expect to find the germs of a solution to the problem of population growth.[11]

This relationship masks a number of other linkages. The inability of official family planning programs in several developing countries to bring down the rate of fertility suggests that fertility, as a dependent variable, can be explained only in relationship to a large number of social and economic variables.[12] For a population policy to succeed, some of the more important variables should be taken into account. For example, evidence from countries with family-planning program failures, as well as data from those fewer developing nations that have succeeded in curbing rapid growth, lend support to the conclusion that two of the variables with which fertility is closely related are level of literacy and extent of medical services.

A number of recent studies also point to a link between infant and child mortality and the rate of fertility [13] primarily because a couple's desire for a family of optimum size takes into account anticipated wastage through infant and child mortality. In a comparison of birth rates in families living within the same socioeconomic environment but having experienced different infant and child death rates, it has been found that those with higher death rates had higher rates of fertility.[14] In addition, a

[11] William Rich, *Smaller Families Through Social and Economic Progress* (Washington, D.C.: Overseas Development Council Monograph No. 7, 1973).

[12] Dudley Kirk, "A New Demographic Transition," in *Rapid Population Growth: Consequences and Policy Implications.* National Academy of Sciences. (Baltimore: Johns Hopkins University Press, 1971).

[13] ICP Staff, *The Policy Relevance of Recent Social Research on Fertility* (Washington, D.C.: Smithsonian Institution: Occasional Monograph Series No. 2, 1974).

[14] Judith A. Harrington, *The Effect of High Infant and Childhood Mortality on Fertility: The West African Case,* Department of Population Planning, School of Public Health (Ann Arbor: University of Michigan, n.d.).

lower infant and child death rate is not immediately reflected in the birth rate, because it takes time for parents to become convinced that mortality has indeed been permanently reduced to a point that justifies a change in their expectations of the number of surviving children.[15] In many developing countries, rates of infant mortality remain high despite advances in medical science and health coverage in the last four decades. The death rate of infants less than one year of age is currently estimated to average 140 per 1,000 live births, compared with 27 per 1,000 in the developed world. Of 111 countries for which such data are available, forty-five have rates higher than 100 per 1,000; not one of these countries is in the industrial world.[16]

While the fertility rate and the infant and child mortality rate are a function of each other, important areas for public policy intervention, both in terms of economic planning and population planning, should be nutrition, food production, and income distribution. Indeed, the programs aimed at increasing food output have a better chance of reducing population growth and alleviating poverty than traditional family-planning programs. The trade-off between these programs must be recognized since they both claim financial funds and, even more important, scarce administrative resources.

There are some other important determinants of fertility in addition to child and infant mortality rate and the participation of females in the labor force that should also be taken into account. In most developing countries the incidence of female marriage is well over 90 percent while the average age of marriage is less than twenty years. In the developed countries, on the other hand, the incidence of marriage is as low as 60 percent while the average age of marriage is twenty-four years.[17] The

[15] Paul T. Schultz, "An Economic Perspective on Population Growth" in *Rapid Population Growth: Consequences and Policy Implications.* National Academy of Sciences. (Baltimore: Johns Hopkins University Press, 1971).

[16] World Bank, *Population Policies. . . .*

[17] *National Bureau of Economic Research, Demographic and Economic Changes in Developed Countries* (Princeton, N.J.: Princeton University Press, 1960), *passim.*

most significant example of the impact of these variables is the case of the People's Republic of China where the female age of marriage increased by nearly a third in less than a decade.[18] Similarly, there is a high correlation between rates of fertility on the one hand and female literacy and participation of females in the labor force on the other. The most dramatic examples of the contribution of these determinants of fertility are to be found among the island communities of Taiwan, Singapore, and Mauritius.

In other words, there are other ways of bringing down the birth rate than those tried through the family-planning programs in the sixties. All of these can be included in a development program that places a strong emphasis on income distribution and a general change in the economic and social environment.[19]

SOME ELEMENTS OF POLICY ACTION

With nearly two decades of work in the population area behind them, the countries of the developing world have now a considerably better perception of the problems they face. They are deep in a demographic trap; dissemination of the latest family-planning technology will not bring them out of it. Nor would the numbers game be of much help to them. By now, most of them are well aware of the consequences of rapid deterioration of man-land ratio in agriculture and ever increasing crowding of the already crowded urban sector. Stamp-size plots in the countryside, producing just enough food to keep the human reproductive system working, are constant reminders to these countries that they cannot afford to add many more people to their

[18] Leo A. Orleans, "China's Experience in Population Growth: The Elusive Model," *World Development* 3, nos. 7 and 8 (July–August 1975).

[19] For two approaches to this model, see James Kocher, *Rural Development, Income Distribution and Fertility Decline* (New York: Population Council, 1973); and William Rich, *Smaller Families Through Social and Economic Progress* (Washington, D. C.: Overseas Development Council, Monograph No. 7, 1973).

134 · GLOBAL CHOICES: MYTHS AND REALITY ·

already large populations. Tens of thousands of shelterless pavement dwellers in the cities, which are already exploding with millions of inhabitants, serve further notice that these countries are fast running out of living space. There is, therefore, little additional information or notice that population models can provide to the people of the Third World.

They know that the problem has to be solved, they are aware that it cannot be solved quickly, and they are suspicious that the pressure that is sometimes exerted on them by the developed nations to take their population problem seriously merely serves to ease the collective conscience of the developed world. New contraceptives and ever new, even ingenious, ways of distributing them are not entirely without value. Their usefulness is limited by the fact that a very large number of people are just not ready to use them. To make full use of the latest techniques in family planning, we have to change the social and economic environment in which families are formed. As we have already indicated, this is a complex process and much more expensive than family-planning programs. But this is the only approach that is likely to succeed. It is much more judicious for the resource-poor developing countries to adopt measures which have been proven to produce results than to go in for programs that have worked only in the dehumanized environment of laboratories.

The sure solution to the problem of population is to be found in the solution to the problem of poverty. For instance, only a sharp reduction in the rate of infant and child mortality will convince parents that they do not have to introduce a high element of wastage in their calculations. However, reducing infant and child mortality has proved to be a much more difficult task than reducing adult mortality. One reason for this is that malnutrition poses a major threat to children. In many cases, it is the primary cause of death in children under five years of age. Therefore, the problem of high child mortality cannot be solved by advances in medical science alone; medicine has to be assisted by nutrition. Increasing nutrition involves not only producing more food but making its distribution within the family less skewed in the favor of adults. A population program that takes note of the powerful relationship between infant and child mortality on the one hand, and fertility on the other, would have an agricultural component so as to increase the availability of food; an income distribution component in order to make it possible for the poor to obtain a part of the increased supply of food; an educational component to emphasize children's need for food; a health component to protect the young from the diseases to which they are most susceptible and, eventually, a family-planning component to provide information and material to those families who now know that their children have a reasonable chance of surviving to adulthood. Such a program would be expensive. It may cost perhaps four times as much per fertile couple as traditional family-planning programs. But it is the only sure approach to population control.

The developing nations will, therefore, have to add more components to their family-planning programs than the traditional stress on mechanical devices. For instance, plans to increase female literacy would delay marriages, reduce incidence of marriage, increase female participation in the labor force, increase family income, make families more receptive to children's nutritional requirement, and, finally, make parents more willing to practice family planning. The fact that the high-fertility countries of Asia have very low rates of female literacy, female participation in the labor force and female contribution to family income, indicates not only a relationship between birth rate and a number of socioeconomic variables but also suggests a relatively unused instrument for reducing population growth.

In other words, the solution to the population problem does not lie in new technology (time-releasing contraceptive capsules implanted in the skin), or in new ways for technological dissemination (cash awards to those who present themselves as "adopters"), or in making the Third World leadership aware of the consequences of population growth (the Bucharest Conference). The solution is much less dramatic but considerably more resource-intensive. It is only by solving the problem of economic and social deprivation that the countries of the Third World can expect to reduce their population growth. This is a tall order but, in keeping with the theme of this book, the only plausible solution. It is plausible because the population problem is imbedded deep within the cultural, social, and economic heritage and institutions of these countries. It simply cannot be isolated and treated separately as an artificial entity that will respond to modern technology. It will require the same kind of fundamental institutional reforms, the same kind of restructuring of economic and social values, the same kind of direct attack on mass poverty as we have discussed before. The discussion in this chapter makes clear once again the connection that the Third World sees between the burden of population and the burden of poverty, and between the burden of poverty and the maldistribution of world's resources. Part 3 of the book spells out in more detail the choices available to all countries, of the Third World as well as the First and the Second. Part 2 has served to show why we should not allow excessive concern about resource depletion, environmental degradation, and population growth to unnecessarily limit the choices available to mankind. Mankind is indeed at the turning point. But it cannot steer past it with its hands tied at its back.

A NEW INTERNATIONAL ECONOMIC ORDER

PART

·3·

"We have a proud foundation on which to build. . . . Our economic support helped our major allies regain their strength; we contributed to a global trading and monetary system which has sustained and spread prosperity throughout the world. . . . Thirty years after the founding of the United Nations, its achievements have been substantial and its promise is great."

—Henry Kissinger, 1975

"Thirty years have passed since the signing of the United Nations Charter launched the effort to establish a new international order . . . [yet] more people are hungry, sick, shelterless and illiterate today than when the United Nations was first set up. . . . To this day, at least three quarters of the world income, investment and services, and most of the world's research, are in the hands of one quarter of its people. . . . Now and in the immediate future, mankind's predicament will be rooted above all in the structures, policies and behaviour within and between the nations of this world."

—Barbara Ward, 1975

IN RETROSPECT

DURING THE LAST EIGHTEEN YEARS, WHILE I WAS ALTER-
nately practicing the art of economic planning and voicing my
heresies about development strategies, I also got an opportunity
to observe the workings of the international economic order at
fairly close range. From 1960 to 1970, I was a member of the
Pakistan's official delegation to the aid consortia, organized
under the chairmanship of the World Bank, which met every
year to consider Pakistan's economic performance and to pledge
external assistance funds. This ritual was carried out with such
deadly seriousness, with the donors and the recipients antici-
pating each others' moves and making uncanny adjustments in
negotiating tactics, that it was to leave a lasting impression on
my mind of the inner workings of aid diplomacy. My association with the World Bank during the last five years has further
added to these insights. But these are subjects too recent and
too delicate to be explored here.

I must say that I started off as a believer in foreign assistance
and the critical difference that it could make to the growth
prospects of the developing countries. The subsequent years
were to bring many disillusionments with the actual workings
of foreign assistance,[1] just as much as with the workings of the
political, economic and social orders within the developing
countries. I was particularly concerned that the availability of
foreign assistance was leading to the adoption of soft options

---

[1] See, for instance, some of my articles on this subject: "Tied Credits—A
Quantitative Analysis," printed in *Capital Movements and Economic Development*, Proceedings of the International Economic Association, John Adler,
ed. (New York: Macmillan, 1967); and "Foreign Assistance—Some Critical Issues," presented to the *UN Second Inter-Regional Seminar on Development Planning*, Amsterdam, Netherlands, September 1966.

and permanent dependency,[2] even though such assistance was often so small as to make only a marginal difference to the long-term growth prospects of the developing countries. I was also increasingly convinced, as argued in chapter 2, that "the developed countries have neither the will nor the imagination" to offer "the level of foreign assistance that is required for a meaningful change in the developing countries over the short period of a decade or so."

I expressed some of my growing cynicism about foreign assistance in a lighthearted vein when I was asked by Barbara Ward to comment on the Pearson Commission's Report [3] in a conference she organized in February 1970:

> Mr. Polanski's Dilemma
> One of the major deficiencies of the Pearson Commission Report is that, although it is titled "Partners in Development," it does not really define the emerging relationship between the developing countries and the developed world. I had quite an argument about this with my friend Mr. Polanski. It all started when Mr. Polanski made a very provocative statement that there never has been, and there never will be, any meaningful partnership or aid relationship between the developed world and the developing countries. Now I simply could not let such a statement go unchallenged, and I argued that this partnership is nothing new and has always existed and will always exist. It existed in the last two centuries in the form of a colonial relationship between equal partners; it exists today in the form of an aid relationship between independent states. Even the terminology has changed only slightly: it was known as "White man's burden" previously; it is known as "debt burden" today. The only thing that might have changed, I conceded, is some impatience in the developed world to terminate this partnership, and this was entirely natural and understandable. When the developed world was on the receiving end of the partnership with its colonies, there was no unseemly haste to end a

[2] This was particularly true of the availability of food grain assistance under PL 480 in Pakistan which made the country neglect the full and speedy development of its considerable food grain production potential.

[3] Lester B. Pearson et al., *Partners in Development,* Report of the Commission on International Development (New York: Praeger, 1969).

mutually beneficial relationship. But today, when it is at the giving end, it is naturally slightly impatient that we in the developing countries should grow up and assume our own burdens.

I also did a neat little exercise to convince Mr. Polanski that this relationship greatly promoted international growth and cooperation. I argued from the experience of India and Pakistan that, when we were associated with Britain in a partnership in the nineteenth century and the British had this slight problem about financing their industrial revolution and their structural transformation, we willingly brought out our gold and our diamonds and our agricultural produce for nominal prices and told them to go ahead and not lose the opportunity for a technological breakthrough. We cheerfully stayed on as an agrarian economy and applauded the industrial strides of our partner. In the modern terminology, such a thing will be called a transfer of resources, but the world was such a happy community at that time that we never even dreamed of such terms or asked for performance audits.

Mr. Polanski, unreasonable as he is, wanted to know the magnitude of the transfer and I mentioned an off-the-cuff figure of $100 million—a modest estimate for which I may be disowned by my fellow economists in the subcontinent. I could not confirm to him whether this amount was 1 percent of our GNP at that time. Anyway, I argued that this amount could be treated as a voluntary loan, at 6 percent interest, which has been happily multiplying over the years so that it stands at $410 billion today. I also explained to him that, since the amount is doubling every twelve years, at this stage it is an advantage to leave it with Britain, as it will be $820 billion by 1982. We can always draw on this amount whenever we need to finance a bit of our own delayed structural transformation. But Polanski, who does not understand the basic principles of sound international finance, kept on insisting that we must call up the loan immediately. I tried to reason that Britain is in no position to pay, and, being equal partners, we are in no position to collect. If we insist on quick repayment, the international community may have to do a bailing-out operation. I also told him that in matters like this we ought to be more generous and, at the very least, undertake the standard debt rescheduling exercise—for instance, we could forget the $10 billion and only ask for the remaining $400 billion.

But Polanski, I am afraid, remains unconvinced and I am at a loss how to explain to him the inherent logic and strength of our partnership in development. And, much to my annoyance, I discovered that, when I was not looking, Polanski had taken away my copy of the Pearson Commission Report and, after the title "Partners in Development," had added a big question mark(?).[4]

Since I expressed the above sentiments five years ago, I have had the time to reflect on the whole range of international economic relations between the rich and the poor nations. I have felt increasingly disturbed that the so-called international market mechanism is weighted heavily against the interests of the poor nations and that they are often denied an equality of opportunity, much the same way as the poorest sections of society are within the national order. Much of my own thinking on the international economic order has been, in fact, an extension of my ideas, expressed in Part 1, on the need for restructuring of national orders.

My own thinking on the relations between the industrialized countries and the Third World has gone through many vicissitudes. I have often wavered uncertainly between confrontation and cooperation, depending on how world events have moved, and generally found myself clutching onto a curious mixture of both since the tactical realities are complex. By temperament, I believe in evolving a new framework of global cooperation through a sensible, serious dialogue that does not treat the past balance of power as sacred. But I often despair of the prospects for such a dialogue. At times, it appears that confrontation is a necessary prelude even for a cooperative dialogue. Many of my friends in the Third World seem to share the same mood.

In the early 1970s, it appeared to many of us that the Third World will need to withdraw into itself and fashion its own policies, irrespective of the pressures from the rich nations.[5] The curtain of poverty which separated our two worlds seemed to extend far beyond mere economic considerations. There were

[4] Reproduced in Barbara Ward, *The Widening Gap,* (New York: Columbia University Press, 1971), pp. 278–79.
[5] Mahbub ul Haq, "The Third World Crisis," *The Washington Post,* April 30, 1972, which is also reflected in chapter 2 of this book.

cultural, racial and political factors isolating us from the Western societies, besides our common heritage of suffering. The example of China, which had done much the same thing two decades earlier and which was now emerging from its self-imposed isolation to the awed applause of even the conservative elements in the American society, offered a great temptation to try the experiment even on a wider scale. On deeper reflection, however, this proved to be a treacherous course. It required the kind of political and economic discipline and adoption of national and collective self-reliance policies which could perhaps be managed in a few countries but were certainly idealistic to hope for in all countries of the Third World at the same time. There may yet be compulsions for such a course in the future. But the Third World does not seem to be ready for it at this stage.

By 1972, I was becoming convinced, however, that the rich nations were mistaking the short-run weaknesses in the bargaining power of the Third World for permanent impotence. It was at that stage that I started arguing that the poor nations should "organize their poor power to wring major concessions from the rich nations and to arrange for a genuine transfer of resources." [6] I advocated the use of collective bargaining techniques by the Third World for raising the prices of nonrenewable resources, negotiating a settlement of past debts, staking out a claim for the exploitation of common-property resources of mankind like oceans and space, and levying international taxes on the consumption of the rich nations.

While these views spread some shock waves in the Western world at that time, they were, on the whole, taken quite lightly. After all, where was the real collective bargaining power of the Third World that I was advocating so passionately? It was partly in self-defense that I took up the basic theme again in another address in 1973 [7] when I argued that if the rich nations were not so hopelessly complacent about short-

[6] *Ibid.*
[7] A keynote address to the Dag Hammarskjöld Foundation Seminar in November 1973 on "Development and Independence," subsequently printed in *Development Dialogue,* no. 1, 1974.

run developments and if they were only prepared to view the situation in a longer-term perspective, they would realize that "there is going to be a dramatic shift in the balance of power between the developed and the developing nations over the course of the next few decades." I cited many arguments in support of this, from demographic trends to nuclear spread to control over natural resources; many of these arguments are reproduced in chapter 9. In my anxiety to drive home the basic point, I also indulged in the luxury of some exaggeration: "I think that most people in the developed countries look at these problems from the wrong end of the telescope. They keep arguing that, even though international order may be unjust, the Third World has to reconcile itself to it and find its place in it. I do not think that they realize that the Third World *is* the future international order and that the developed countries have to start thinking today in terms of fashioning policies to come to some reasonable accommodation with [it]." The speech was delivered in early November 1973, just a few weeks before the OPEC members raised the price of oil about four times through collective action. By April of 1974, the Third World nations had already taken up the battle cry of a New International Economic Order.

It was interesting to watch the reaction of the industrialized nations to the demand for a new order. At first, they dismissed it casually as mere rhetoric. They felt that the Third World had lost its head, emboldened by the success of the OPEC and without realizing that oil was a unique case. Some of their spokesmen [8] tried to ridicule the demand for greater social justice at the international level as the hangover of "British Socialism" and a not too clever device by the Third World nations to turn world attention away from their own domestic mismanagement to external issues. The developing countries did not help their cause either by giving the impression at times that they were out to wring only a few concessions from the rich nations, and by setting no concrete order of priority in

[8] Daniel P. Moynihan, "The United States in Opposition," *Commentary*, February 1975.

their own discussion agenda.[9] But these were the early days of
their new trade unionism. The first task was to shout, to raise
slogans, to smash a few windows. More serious dialogue could
only have come later.

A number of promising developments took place between the
Sixth and the Seventh Special Sessions of the United Nations
General Assembly in April 1974, and September 1975, respectively. The rich nations began to realize that the international market mechanism had not worked equally well for all
nations—rich and poor, large and small, strong and weak. They
were also impressed by the political unity and the reasoned elo-
quence of the Third World within the United Nations forums.
European countries were in any case more willing to come to
terms with the Third World nations,[10] realizing their own vul-
nerability and dependence on the raw materials of the developing countries and having a greater sense of history. The United
States came around, reluctantly but surely, to the prospects of
serious negotiations with the Third World, both because of the
lack of any decent alternatives and because of the fear of losing
the support of its European allies if its negative attitude had
persisted. The culmination of this process came with a skillful address by the U.S. Secretary of State, Henry Kissinger, to
the September 1975, Special Session of the United Nations,[11]
where he unveiled a number of specific proposals to redress
world economic imbalances and indicated a willingness on the
part of the industrialized nations to enter a new era of serious
negotiations with the Third World to restructure world institu-

[9] U.N. General Assembly, Sixth Special Session, *Declaration and Programme
of Action on the Establishment of a New International Economic Order*, Resolutions No. 3201 and 3202, May 1974.

[10] This was evident in the Lomé Agreement which helped stabilize export
earnings of forty-six associated developing countries (see Marion Bywater,
"The Lomé Convention," in *European Community*, March 1975), and in
their more accommodating attitude in the Paris Conference on International Economic Cooperation in April 1975 and January 1976.

[11] Henry Kissinger, "Global Consensus and Economic Development,"
Address to the Seventh Special Session of the U.N. General Assembly,
September 1, 1975.

tions in a step-by-step approach. Indeed, the specific proposals in the speech were not its most important part since many were kept deliberately vague and came with little assurance of additional financing. What was really important was the fact that the United States was slowly coming to the conclusion that an orderly dialogue with the poor nations on a new order could not be avoided for long.

During this phase, when the rich nations were gradually making up their own mind, we in the Third World were concerned that the movement for a new international economic order should not be diverted into the wrong channels. We largely viewed this movement as the birth of a new international trade unionism of the poor nations where the Third World was serving notice that it would negotiate with the developed countries in the future through the instrument of collective bargaining. However, it was extremely important to define fairly early what was to be negotiated and through what specific means. We realized, of course, that it was basically a political struggle. But at some stage, the trade unions have to send in their negotiators to the back rooms to hammer out tough agreements and delicate compromises. The Third World had to be prepared for that.

In particular, it was necessary to restore a proper perspective on some of the main issues. The demand for a new order was still being regarded as a set of specific concessions which the rich had to make to the poor. To our minds, this was a complete misunderstanding of both the inherent nature of the demand for a fundamental restructuring of past relations of dependency as well as a misreading of historical forces. What was at stake, we felt, was equality of opportunity, not equality of income. Institutional reforms were needed, not charity. The parallel with the reform of national orders was so obvious—and so well accepted by the rich nations—that I could not resist the temptation of drawing attention to it:

> If history is to be our guide, I believe that we may well be on the threshold of an historical turning point. On the national level, such a turning point was reached in the United States in the 1930s

when the New Deal elevated the working classes to partners in development and accepted them as an essential part of the consuming society. On the international level, we still have not arrived at that philosophic breakthrough when the development of the poor nations is considered an essential element in the sustained development of the rich nations and their interests are regarded as complementary and compatible, not conflicting and irreconcilable. And yet we may be nearing that philosophic bridge. . . .

It is important that the current demand of the developing countries for a New International Economic Order is perceived in its correct perspective:

First, the basic objective of the emerging trade union of the poor nations is to negotiate a new deal with the rich nations through the instrument of collective bargaining. The essence of this new deal lies in their obtaining greater equality of opportunity and in securing the right to sit as equals around the bargaining tables of the world. No massive redistribution of past income and wealth is being demanded: in fact, even if all the demands are added up, they do not exceed about 1 per cent of the GNP of the rich nations. What is really required, however, is a redistribution of future growth opportunities.

Second, the demand for a New International Economic Order should be regarded as a movement, a part of an historical process, to be achieved over time, rather than in any single negotiation. Like the political liberation movement of the 1940s and the 1950s, the movement for a new economic order is likely to dominate the next few decades and cannot be dismissed casually by the rich nations.

Third, whatever deals are eventually negotiated must balance the interests of the rich and the poor nations. The rich nations have to carefully weigh the costs of disruption against the costs of accommodation and to consider the fact that any conceivable cost of a new deal will be a very small proportion of their future growth in an orderly, cooperative framework. The poor nations have to recognize that, in an interdependent world, they cannot hurt the growth prospects of the rich nations without hurting their own chances of negotiating a better deal.[12]

[12] See Mahbub ul Haq, "Towards a New Planetary Bargain," in Richard N. Gardner, ed., New Structures for Economic Interdependence, (Rensselaerville, N.Y.: The Institute on Man and Science, September 1975).

At the same time as we were trying to restore a correct perspective on the demand for a new order, we were concerned in the Third World that a longer-term negotiating strategy be devised, focusing on a few priority areas and balancing the interests of both the rich and the poor nations so as to have a reasonable chance of acceptance and implementation. I stressed this theme in a number of forums—in a conference at Rensselaerville, New York, in May 1975; [13] as a participant in a twentyman expert group compiling the Tinbergen report on the new economic order in June 1975; [14] and as chairman of the Special Task Force of the Third World Forum on the same subject.

> Establishment of a new international economic order should be seen as part of an historical process, which will go on for years, and not something that can be achieved through a single set of negotiations. . . .
>
> We believe that it is possible to evolve proposals which balance the longer-term interests of the developed countries and the Third World and which, as such, are acceptable to the entire international community. For instance, security of earnings to the producing countries can be counterbalanced by security of supplies to the consuming countries. Greater share in benefits to the host governments can be matched by longer-term assurances to the transnationals for the protection of their investments. The democratization of the international financial institutions can be carried out in such a way as to increase the voice of the Third World without losing the interest of the rich nations. . . .
>
> . . . We believe that the longer-term interests of the rich and the poor nations are mutually compatible in a fast shrinking planet. But this mutuality of interests must be established on new concepts of a creative partnership, not on old patterns of dependency: on a dynamic view of future interdependence, not a revarnished image of past relationships. [15]

One of the most delicate questions concerned the movitation and attitude of our own societies. We were even more concerned

[13] *Ibid.*

[14] Jan Tinbergen, *Reviewing the International Order,* Interim Report, Rotterdam, June 1975.

[15] The Third World Forum, Special Task Force, *Proposals for a New International Economic Order,* Mexico/New York, August–September 1975.

than our friends in the developed world that the Third World nations should not use the slogan of a new international economic order to evade tough political and economic decisions at the domestic level. After all, the real task of development lay back home. No degree of international agitation can ever obscure that fact; no amount of international resource transfers can ever substitute for national decisions on fundamental reforms. The intellectuals from the Third World face a cruel dilemma here. If they stress the issue of reform of national orders ahead of the international order, they run the risk of providing a convenient excuse to the rich nations to postpone serious discussions on the reform of the present world order as well as of losing the support of their own national governments. Yet what can possibly be gained by greater equality of opportunity internationally if it is denied to the vast majority within the national orders? And how much credibility the demand for a new international order is likely to have if serious imbalances persist in the national orders? It was with this in view that we tried to place this issue in some perspective in the report of the Third World Forum:

> We remain convinced that the task of developing our societies is essentially our own responsibility. We must carry out ourselves the internal institutional reforms which are necessary for this purpose. We do not advocate to our societies that they find a convenient alibi in the international order for every lack of progress on the domestic front. Nor do we expect the outside world to assume our burdens. We believe in a policy of self-reliance for the Third World which extends to every field of economic activity, not only trade. In fact, reforms in the international order will be meaningless, and often impossible to attain, without corresponding reforms in the national orders.
>
> At the same time, however, the present international institutional structures must be thoroughly re-examined since they systematically discriminate against our societies and deny them the basic equality of opportunity to which they are entitled.[16]

It was against this backdrop of evolution of ideas that the Seventh Special Session of the United Nations General Assembly

[16] *Ibid.,* pp. 3–4.

met in New York in September 1975 to debate the establishment of a new international economic order. The mood on both sides of the fence was more accommodating this time than in the earlier discussion in April 1974. No final solutions were reached. No major breakthroughs were either attempted or achieved. But at least a few areas of negotiation were narrowed down and agreed upon. An orderly dialogue had just begun between the rich and the poor nations. Among the somewhat more specific agreements to come out of this Session were:

—adequate international financing facilities for buffer stocks to secure stable, remunerative and equitable prices;

—substantially improved facilities for compensatory financing of export revenue fluctuations;

—reduction or removal of non-tariff barriers and continuation of Generalized Scheme of Preferences;

—concessional financial assistance to be increased substantially and its flow made predictable, continuous and increasingly assured;

—developed countries to confirm their continued commitment to 0.7 percent ODA target and to agree to implement it by 1980;

—establishment of a link between special drawing rights and developmental assistance;

—endorsement of a substantial increase in the capital of the World Bank Group and in the resources of IDA;

—UNCTAD to consider the need for, and the possibility of, convening as soon as possible a conference of major donor, creditor and debtor countries to devise ways and means to mitigate debt burden;

—Development Committee to formulate proposals on increased access on favorable terms to international capital market;

—role of national reserve currencies to be reduced and special drawing rights to become the central reserve asset of the international monetary system in order to provide for greater international control over the creation and equitable distribution of liquidity;

—endorsement of the proposed International Fund for Agricultural Development with initial resources of one billion SDR;

—acceptance of the principle of a minimum food aid target and establishment of a target of 10 million tons for 1975–76 season.[17]

These were not particularly breathtaking agreements. Many of these proposals have been reiterated in earlier conferences. But the spirit of accommodation on both sides was remarkable. A vague negotiating umbrella was often accepted in order to start off the process of dialogue, rather than risk a serious breakdown in communications. Only the events of the next few years will show how far action follows intentions and whether the spirit of accommodation lasts or evaporates into mutual recriminations and confrontation again.

This part of the book has been written under the shadow of fast-breaking developments. When events are moving so rapidly, all one can do is to focus on some of the medium and longer-term objectives and analysis, while realizing that the pace of events may date them more quickly than one anticipates. Some of this analysis has been attempted in the next few chapters.[18] Chapter 8 reviews the workings of the existing world economic order and analyzes the basis of the accusation by the poor nations that the present international institutions systematically discriminate against their interests. In the next chapter, I try to analyze whether the poor nations have the necessary bargaining power to bring about fundamental changes in the international economic order. Chapter 10 explores the major changes in the rules of the game that the developing countries should seek and alternative strategies for negotiation. Since a crucial aspect of the new international economic order must be a new framework for resource transfers from the rich to the poor nations, this is the theme of chapter 11.[18]

[17] U.N. Seventh Special Session, Resolution No. A/RES/3362 (S-VII) on *Development and International Economic Cooperation,* September 1975.

[18] Some of the ideas in these chapters were also presented in a series of lectures I gave in Georgetown, Guyana, in November 1975. See *Third World and the International Economic Order,* Georgetown, Guyana, April 1976.

The debate on a new international economic order has begun only recently. Many issues are still undefined. The outlines of the debate are often quite hazy. We are probably too close to actual events to look at them with the necessary objectivity and detachment. But I remain convinced that the revolution in thinking which has swept the world in the last five years on the issues of national development strategies—and which was commented on in Part 1 of this book—is already on its way and will change our perceptions on the international economic order quite dramatically in the next few years.

·8·   A LINGERING LOOK AT
THE OLD ECONOMIC ORDER

THE VASTLY UNEQUAL RELATIONSHIP between the rich and the poor nations is fast becoming the central issue of our time. The poor nations are beginning to question the basic premises of an international order which leads to ever widening disparities between the rich and the poor countries and to a persistent denial of equality of opportunity to many poor nations. They are, in fact, arguing that in international order—just as much as within national orders—all distribution of benefits, credit, services, and decision-making becomes warped in favor of a privileged minority and that this situation cannot be changed except through fundamental institutional reforms. This thinking appears to underlie their demand for a "New International Economic Order." [1]

When this is pointed out to the rich nations, they dismiss it casually as empty rhetoric of the poor nations. Their standard answer is that the international market mechanism works, even though not too perfectly, and that the poor nations are always out to wring concessions from the rich nations in the name of past exploitation. They believe that the poor nations are demanding a massive redistribution of income and wealth which is simply not in the cards. Their general attitude seems to be that the poor nations must earn their economic development, much the same way as the rich nations had to over the last two centuries, through patient hard work and gradual capital forma-

---

[1] U.N., *Declaration and Program of Action on the Establishment of a New International Economic Order*, A/RES/3201 and 3202 (S-VI), May 1, 1974.

tion, and that there are no short cuts to this process and no rhetorical substitutes. The rich, however, are generous enough to offer some help to the poor nations to accelerate their economic development if the poor are only willing to behave themselves.

In reviewing this controversy, we must face up to the blunt question: Does the present world order systematically discriminate against the interests of the Third World, as the poor nations contend? Or is the demand for a new order mere empty rhetoric against imagined grievances, as the rich nations allege?

FAILURES OF MARKET SYSTEM

There is sufficient concrete evidence to show that the poor nations cannot get an equitable deal from the present international economic structures—much the same way as the poorest sections of the society within a country and for much the same reasons. Once there are major disparities in income distribution within a country, the market mechanism ceases to function either efficiently or equitably since it is weighted heavily in favor of the purchasing power in the hands of the rich. Those who have the money can make the market bend to their own will. This is even more true at the international level since there is no world government and none of the usual mechanisms existing within countries which create pressures for redistribution of income and wealth. Barbara Ward quite succinctly summarized the case against the workings of the international market mechanism in a situation of gross inequalities in world income:

To rely solely on the market system [in such a situation] has wider consequences for society in general and for resource use in particular. The capacity to sell, to have responsive buyers, becomes the overriding criterion for producing goods. This raises a number of problems. Production is geared to those who can effectively buy. Internationally, that means richer countries rather than poorer countries, and nationally it means middle and high income groups rather than the poorer people. Within most developed societies, social mechanisms—public ownership, redistributive income tax, welfare schemes, social insurance—try to offset this trend. No such institutions are at work at the world level, nor in a number of developing countries. In such conditions, market mechanisms are linked, by their own logic, to the affluent, making resources available to those who can buy them and not necessarily to those who need them. This fact generates a series of backward linkages. It determines the nature of the technology needed to maintain the consumption of the more affluent. It guides the allocation of resources in research and development. This in itself creates a demand for certain types of professional know-how, rather than for others.[2]

As was discussed in Part 1 of this book, it is only recently that new perceptions on development strategies are beginning to be accepted within national orders. It is being increasingly realized that economic growth does not automatically filter down to the poorest sections of the society; that the distribution of all credit, investment resources and public and private services gravitates towards the richest sectors unless there is a conscious intervention in the market by the government; that equality of opportunity cannot automatically be ensured when vast inequalities in the distribution of income and wealth prevail; that the essence of new development strategies in such a situation is to make resources and opportunities available to increase the productivity of the poor on a permanent basis, not to place the poorest people on a short-term dole; that fundamental institutional reforms are required to remedy the situation, not marginal adjustments in the price system; and, finally, that a restructuring of political and economic power takes place either through revolutions or when the rich realize that the political risks of rebellion far outweigh the economic costs of reform.

Evolution of thinking at the international level generally follows that at the national level, though with a time lag of several decades. This is likely to be true in the case of the thinking on the new international economic order as well. There is a remarkable parallelism between the situation of the poorest sections within a society and that of the poorest nations (particularly those below $200 per capita income currently, containing

[2] Barbara Ward, Report on the UNEP-UNCTAD Symposium on *Patterns of Resource Use, Environment and Development Strategies,* Cocoyoc, Mexico, May 1975.

over one billion people) within the international community. This parallelism has been only dimly perceived at present. It is ironic at times to witness that some of the developed countries, which so eagerly advocate the new development strategies to the developing countries, suddenly develop a case of schizophrenia when it comes to a discussion of a new economic order at the international level.

And yet the poorest nations within the international community face many of the same crippling handicaps as do the poorest people within a nation. The world economic growth does not automatically filter down to these nations. Their initial poverty becomes a major handicap in obtaining either short-term credit or long-term investment resources as they are regarded, in the fashionable parlance of international life, simply "uncreditworthy." All international mechanisms, structures and decision making get mortgaged to the interests of the rich nations. The income disparities between the poor and the rich nations, in such a situation, are bound to increase unless a conscious attempt is made by the international community to reduce them.[3] The heart of such an attempt lies in increasing the productivity of the poor nations—through their own efforts and through an automatic transfer of resources to them—rather than in any marginal adjustments in the present flow of foreign assistance. This requires the evolution of many of the same institutions and mechanisms which have been gradually accepted at the national level—including the acceptance of the concept of international taxation and establishment of an international central bank. And just as in national orders, the short-term costs of reform to the rich nations are likely to be outweighed by the long-term benefits to the entire international community in

---

[3] This is as true of the income gap between the developed and the developing countries as between the poorest and the richer developing countries. For instance, the absolute disparity in per capita income (in constant U.S. dollars) increased from $2,700 to $4,000 between developed and developing countries during 1960 to 1974 while the income disparity between the poorest (below $200) and other developing countries (above $200) also went up during the same period from $330 to $625.

terms of more harmonious economic growth and greater political stability.

But this is still a case at a level of generality which is neither convincing nor helpful unless it is backed up by concrete evidence. It is here that the Third World has not helped its cause much since it did not undertake the detailed homework that was necessary to demonstrate that the poorest nations were being consistently denied equality of opportunity. It is time, in fact, that the research institutions of the Third World should do some serious work in documenting specific instances of inequities in the world order.

In undertaking such a serious analysis, the two staple diets that the Third World has used so often in the past must be discarded. First, the poor nations cannot keep the rich nations feeling either guilty or uncomfortable by simply pointing out that three-quarters of income, investment, and wealth are in the hands of one-quarter of its population. The rich nations are increasingly turning around and saying: "So what? We worked for it and so should you." The world income disparities are not an issue, *per se.* It must also be demonstrated that the prevailing disparities are creating major hurdles for the poor nations in carrying out their own development programs and are denying them the basic equality of opportunity to which they ought to be entitled.

Second, the Third World has often used the argument of instability of commodity prices and worsening terms of trade to illustrate their uncertain plight in the present world order. This argument has been overdone and is certainly not the heart of the matter. As discussed in chapter 11, if low earnings are stabilized, they would still remain low. The Third World needs higher earnings, not only more stable earnings. In any case, worsening terms of trade and commodity price instability are mere symptoms, not the root cause of the problem of unequal relationships. Ultimately, the reasons for this inequality in relationships must be sought in international economic structures and mechanisms which put the Third World at a considerable disadvantage and which require thorough-going institutional reforms. It is worthwhile to explore some of these areas in a more concrete fashion, even though the necessary background research work is not fully available at present.

EVIDENCE OF INEQUITIES

First, there is a tremendous imbalance today in the distribution of international reserves. The poor nations, with 70 percent of the world population, received less than 4 percent of the international reserves of $131 billion during 1970–74,[4] simply because the rich nations controlled the creation and distribution of international reserves through the expansion of their own national reserve currencies (mainly dollars and sterling) and through their decisive control over the International Monetary Fund. For all practical purposes, the United States has been the central banker of the world in the post-World War II period and it could easily finance its balance-of-payments deficits by the simple device of expanding its own currency. In other words, the richest nation in the world has had an unlimited access to international credit facilities since it could create such credit through its own decisions. This has been less true of other developed countries, though Britain and Germany have enjoyed some of this privilege at various times. This has certainly not been true of the developing countries which could neither create international credit through their own deficit financing operations nor obtain an easy access to this credit because of the absence of any genuine international currency and because of their limited quotas in the Fund.[5] The heart of any economic system is its credit structure. This is controlled entirely by the rich nations at the international level. The poor nations merely stand at the periphery of international monetary decisions. This is nothing unusual. Like in any normal national banking system, the poor get very little credit unless a concerned government chooses to intervene on their behalf.

[4] See Table 10 in the Statistical Appendix.

[5] For a very perceptive analysis of the international monetary system, see Robert Triffin, *New Structures for Economic Interdependence*, Richard N. Gardner, ed., Rensselaerville, N.Y., Institute on Man and Science, September 1975.

Second, the distribution of value-added in the products traded between the developing and the developed countries is heavily weighted in favor of the latter. The developing countries, unlike the developed ones, receive back only a small fraction of the final price that the consumers in the international market are already paying for their produce,[6] simply because many of them are too poor or too weak to exercise any meaningful control over the processing, shipping, and marketing of their primary exports. As a very rough estimate, the final consumers pay over $200 billion (excluding taxes) for the major primary exports (excluding oil) of the developing countries (in a more processed, packaged, and advertised form) but these countries receive back only $30 billion, with the middlemen and the international service sector—mostly in the hands of the rich nations—enjoying the difference. On the other hand, the rich nations have the resources and the necessary bargaining power to control the various phases of their production, export and distribution—often including their own subsidiaries to handle even internal distribution within importing countries. In fact, if the poor nations had been able to exercise the same degree of control over the processing and distribution of their exports as the rich nations presently do and if they were to get back a similar proportion of the final consumer price, their export earnings from their primary commodities would be closer to $150 billion. Again, there is a parallel here between national and international orders: within national orders as well, the poor receive only a fraction of the rewards for their labor and a high proportion of the value-added is appropriated by the organized, en-

---

[6] Unfortunately, few detailed studies have been undertaken so far on individual commodities to document the margins between producer's return and the consumer's price. One of these studies is on bananas (see Jean Paul Valles, *The World Market for Bananas: 1964–1972* (New York: Praeger, 1974), where the empirical evidence shows that the producers obtain less than 10 percent of the final price. A detailed commodity-by-commodity study of the margins between producer's and consumer's price can illuminate concretely the areas where policy action is most needed and could yield the most promising results. The U.N. Special Session in September 1975 has directed UNCTAD to carry out such a study.

trenched middlemen unless the national governments intervene.

Third, the protective wall erected by the developed countries prevents the developing world from receiving its due share of the global wealth. The rich nations are making it increasingly impossible for the "free" international market mechanism to work. In the classical framework of Adam Smith, the cornerstone of the free market mechanism is the free movement of labor and capital as well as of goods and services so that rewards to factors of production are equalized all over the world. In fact, world inequalities can simply not persist in such a framework. Yet immigration laws in almost all rich nations make it impossible for any large-scale movement of unskilled labor in a worldwide search for economic opportunities (except for a limited "brain drain" of skilled labor); not much capital has crossed international boundaries, both because of poor nations' sensitivities and the rich nations' own needs; and additional barriers have gone up against the free movement of goods and services—e.g., over $20 billion in farm subsidies alone in the rich nations to protect their agriculture and progressively higher tariffs and quotas against the simple consumer goods exports of the developing countries, like textiles and leather goods (see chapter 4). The rich, in other words, are drawing a protective wall around their life styles, telling the poor nations that they can neither compete with their labor nor with their goods, while paying handsome tribute at the same time to the "free" workings of the international market mechanism. Unfortunately, while the rich can show such discrimination, the poor cannot by the very fact of their poverty. They need their current foreign exchange earnings desperately, just in order to survive and to carry on a minimum development effort, and they can hardly afford to put up discriminatory restrictions against the capital good imports and technology of the Western world. There is again a parallel here between national and international orders. Within national orders as well, the poor generally have very little choice but to sell their services to the rich at considerable disadvantage just in order to earn the means of their survival.

Fourth, another area in which the unequal bargaining power

of the poor and the rich nations shows up quite dramatically is the relationship between multinational corporations and the developing countries. Most of the contracts, leases, and concessions that the multinational corporations have negotiated in the past with the developing countries reflect a fairly inequitable sharing of benefits. In many cases, the host government is getting only a fraction of the benefits from the exploitation of its own natural resources by the multinational corporations. For instance, Mauritania gets about 15 percent of the profits that the multinational corporations make from extracting and exporting the iron ore deposits in the country. Similarly, in Liberia the foreign investors export nearly one fourth of the total GNP of the country in terms of their profit remittances. Such examples can be multiplied.[7] In fact, it would be useful to tabulate all the concessions, contracts, and leases which have been negotiated between the multinational corporations and the developing countries and to present to the world an idea of what the present sharing of benefits is between host governments and multinational corporations in case after case. Such a factual background will not only illustrate the concrete and specific fashion in which the poor nations are now discriminated against but could also be a very useful prelude to the necessary reforms.

Fifth, the poor nations have only a *pro forma* participation in the economic decision making of the world. Their advice is hardly solicited when the big ten industralized nations get together to take key decisions on the world's economic future; their voting strength in the Bretton Woods institutions (World Bank and International Monetary Fund) is less than one third of the total; and their numerical majority in the General Assembly has meant no real influence so far on international economic decisions. In fact, it may well be an indicator of the sense of accommodation that the rich nations are willing to show that they have started protesting against the "tyranny of the majority" at a time when the majority resolutions of the poor nations within

[7] See, for intance, Richard J. Barnett and Ronald E. Muller, *Global Reach: The Power of the Multinational Corporations* (New York: Simon & Schuster, 1974).

the United Nations carry no effective force and when the Third World countries are not being allowed to sit even as equals around the bargaining tables of the world.

Finally, to take an example from the world of ideas, these unequal relationships pervade the intellectual world and the mass media as well. The developing countries have often been subjected to concepts of development and value systems which were largely fashioned abroad. While economic development was the primary concern of the developing countries, so far it has been written about and discussed largely by outsiders. The mass media, which greatly shape world opinion, are primarily under the control of the rich nations. The Nobel Prize, which is presumably given for excellence of thought, is given to so few in the Third World, even in nontechnical fields such as literature. Is it because the poor nations are not only poor in income but also poor in thought? Or is it because their thought is being judged by standards totally alien to their spirit and they have no organized forums for either projection or dissemination of their thinking? [8] The answer is quite obvious. There is no international structure, including intellectual endeavor, which is not influenced by the same inequality between rich and poor nations.

HISTORICAL PERSPECTIVE

The basic reasons for this inequality between the presently developed and developing nations lie fairly deep in their history. In most parts of the Third World, centuries of colonial rule have left their legacy of dependency. Political independence has often not succeeded in eliminating either economic dependence or intellectual slavery. On the contrary, the big powers have sometimes cultivated their spheres of political and economic influence with ruthless determination in the mistaken notion that it is in their long-term interest. They have at times purchased the shifting alliance of various leaders and governments in the Third World, confusing this with an alliance with

[8] Mahbub ul Haq, "The Third World Forum: Intellectual Self-Reliance" in *International Development Review*, 1 (1975):8–11.

their people and often ignoring the strong underlying forces of nationalism within these countries. Many Third World countries have been willing victims in this game because of a complex of motives, ranging from the narrow, personal self-interest of a few individuals to the inferiority complex of new nationhood, from hopes of temporary gains to fears of national survival. The international scene has often been dominated by relationships based on outmoded concepts of feudalism, where political or economic assertions of independence were met by swift retribution by the super-powers so as to prevent any further insubordination in the ranks.

The international economic life in such a situation became organized around principles which man had learnt from tribal days onwards. The industrialized countries, with their enormous economic and political power, stood at the center of this world order. The developing countries stood at the periphery, supplying their raw materials and services to the metropolitan center and being grateful for whatever little return they could get from the benevolence of the rich. It is not that the rich deliberately exploited the poor. It is merely that this pattern was based on concepts of feudalism, not democracy; on unequal relationships, not equality of opportunity. As such, it was inherently unstable. The first dent came with the movements for political liberation. The second stage—for economic liberation—is being set by the demand for a new international economic order. And accompanying it all is an intellectual ferment in the Third World, sweeping aside the cobwebs of inferiority complex and bringing into power a new generation of people, confident of themselves and their countries, believing in their own culture and their manifest destiny, and willing to deal with the industrialized world only on a basis of equality.

In this context, a net bilateral transfer of about $12 billion of official development assistance to the poor nations every year is neither adequate nor to the point: the quantitative "loss" implicit in the previously quoted examples of maldistribution of international credit, inadequate sharing of benefits from the export of their natural resources, and artificial restrictions on the movement of their goods and services (not to speak of labor) would easily amount to $50–100 billion a year. More pertinently, the poor nations are seeking greater equality of opportunity, not charity from the uncertain generosity of the rich.

The demand for economic equality must be seen, however, in its proper historical perspective. It is a natural evolution of the philosophy already accepted at the national level: that the governments must actively intervene on behalf of the poorest segments of their populations ("the bottom 40 percent") who will otherwise be bypassed by economic development. In a fast-shrinking planet, it was inevitable that this "new" philosophy would not stop at national borders; and, since there is no world government, the poor nations are bringing this concern to its closest substitute, the United Nations.

At the same time, the developing countries must recognize the intimate link between the reform of the national and international orders. If national economic orders in the poor nations remain unresponsive to the needs of their own poor and if they continue to benefit only a privileged few, much of the argument for a fundamental reform in the international order would disappear, as any benefits flowing from such a reform would go only to a handful of people who currently wield political and economic authority. Moreover, when the international and national orders are dominated by privileged minorities, the possibilities of a tacit collusion between their natural interests are quite unlimited. The developing countries have to learn, therefore, that reforms in their own national orders are often the critical bargaining chip that they need in pressing for similar reforms at the international level.

The reforms in the national orders of the poor nations, however, are a necessary but not a sufficient condition for a major improvement in the economic conditions of their masses. According to a recent World Bank study,[9] if the present internal and external policies continue unchanged, the poorest developing countries, below a per capita income of $200, face the prospect of virtually no increase in this low level of income during 1975–80.[10] A major change will be required in the internal

[9] World Bank, *Prospects for Developing Countries: 1976–80*, July 1975.

policies (in saving and investment policies and in the distribution of rewards of economic growth) if such a grim prospect is to be averted. But a good part of this effort will be frustrated if these countries cannot import the needed machinery and technology and if critical foreign exchange shortages persist because of their limited access to the international market either through trade or through international resource transfers. The solution for this is not piecemeal reforms—via selective trade "concessions" or somewhat larger foreign assistance—since these achieve exactly the same purpose, and provide as temporary a relief, as limited social security payments to the poor within a national system. The long-term solution is to change the institutional system in such a way as to improve the access of the poor to economic opportunities and to increase their long-term productivity, not their temporary income. (See chapter 10.)

PRINCIPLES FOR CHANGE

The basic principles for such a change can be easily established and follow logically from the analysis of institutional imbalances cited above. For instance, any long-term negotiating package should include:

—revamping of the present international credit system by phasing out national reserve currencies and replacing them by an international currency;

—gradual dismantling of restrictions in the rich nations on the movement of goods and services as well as labor from the poor nations;

—enabling the developing countries to obtain more benefit from the exploitation of their own natural resources through a greater control over various stages of primary production, processing, and distribution of their commodities;

[10] The developing countries above $200, because of their better opportunities in the export of manufactured goods and their better access to the international capital market, are expected to pull away further from the poorest less developed countries by experiencing a per capita growth of about 3 percent per annum during the same period.

—introduction of an element of automaticity in international resource transfers by linking them to some form of international taxation or royalties from the commercial exploitation of international commons or international reserve creation;

—negotiation of agreed principles between the principal creditors and debtors for an orderly settlement of past external debts;

—renegotiation of all past leases and contracts given by the developing countries to the multinational corporations under a new code of conduct to be established and enforced within the United Nations framework; and

—restructuring of the United Nations to give it greater operational powers for economic decisions and a significant increase in the voting strength of the poor nations within the World Bank and the International Monetary Fund.

In fact, some of these negotiating principles can be left deliberately vague in the first instance to gain general acceptance for them and to give both sides sufficient room to maneuver during the actual negotiations. This has already happened to some extent in the Seventh U.N. Special Session, as mentioned on page 150. But no amount of adroit drafting or skillful negotiations can hide the fact that whenever such fundamental reforms in the international order are attempted, they are likely to change the world balance of power in no uncertain terms. The existing power structures may not accept that without a major fight.

The debate on the establishment of a new international economic order has only recently begun. The battle lines are still being drawn; the battle plans of the rich and the poor nations are hardly clear at present. Our world may well be "poised uneasily between an era of great enterprise and creativity or an age of chaos and despair," [11] between a grand new global part-

---

[11] Henry A. Kissinger, "Global Challenge and International Cooperation," a speech delivered to the Institute of World Affairs, University of Wisconsin, July 14, 1975.

nership or a disorderly confrontation. Unfortunately, there are very few examples in history of the rich surrendering their power willingly or peacefully. Whenever and wherever the rich have made any accommodation, they did so because it had become inevitable since the poor had become organized and would have taken away power in any case. The basic question today, therefore, is not whether the poor nations are in a grossly unfavorable position in the present world order. They are, and they will continue to be, unless they can negotiate a new world order. The basic question really is whether they have the necessary bargaining power to arrange any fundamental changes in the present political, economic, and social balance of power in the world. This is the question to which I will turn in the next chapter.

Let me conclude this part of the discussion with three main observations.

First, a tremendous responsibility rests on the universities, research institutions and various intellectual forums of the Third World. It is for them to work out carefully concrete instances of systematic discrimination built into the existing economic order—whether it be the inadequate return from raw material exports, or inequitable sharing of gains from multinational corporations, or unequal distribution of world liquidity. This should be done in a spirit of serious, objective analysis so that there is concrete documentation available to the negotiators from the Third World to press this point in international forums. There is no excuse for the Third World not to produce a sufficient number of factual and convincing studies on this subject since they have a legitimate case and since, in the last analysis, facts are always more powerful than words.

Second, the Third World must keep stressing, as often as it can, that the basic struggle is for equality of opportunity, not equality of income. The Third World is not chasing the income levels of the rich nations. It does not wish to imitate their life styles. The Third World is only suggesting that it must have a decent chance to develop, on an equal basis, without systematic discrimination against it, according to its own value systems and in line with its own cultural traditions. The Third World is not asking for a few more crumbs from the grand table of the rich. It is asking for a fair chance to make it on its own.

Finally, the Third World has to make it quite clear in its future negotiations that what is at stake is not a few marginal adjustments in the international system: it is its complete overhaul. The Third World should also make it clear that it is not foolish enough to think that a new international order can be established overnight. It is willing to wait. And it is willing to proceed in a step-by-step manner. But it is not willing to settle for some inadequate, piecemeal concessions in the name of a step-by-step approach. Short-term tactics can vary so long as they do not mortgage the long-term goals.

·9· THE BARGAINING POWER OF THE POOR NATIONS

O NE OF THE MOST COMMON FALLACIES of the rich is that the poor have little bargaining power and can be conveniently ignored. This is a mistake that the rich no longer make within national orders since they have witnessed too often in history the violent overthrow of the privileged minority whenever the poor masses became desperate and organized. Moreover, national governments, however much they may depend on their alliance with vested interest groups, always keep looking over their shoulders to appease the poor majority lest their economic and social conditions become intolerable. With the gradual evolution of national orders, the poor have got themselves organized in many countries into a formidable countervailing power to the entrenched interests of the rich, mainly through the formation of trade unions. Yet, at the international level, we see the same skepticism about the real bargaining power of the poor at a time when we are probably witnessing the establishment of a trade union of the poor nations.

The reasons for this skepticism are obvious. First, the rich nations are analyzing mainly the economic bargaining power of the poor nations while their real power, as argued later, is political. Most of the analysis proceeds in terms of the control that the poor nations presently exercise over natural resources or their current importance in international trade and commerce [1] and it is concluded, quite wrongly, that unlike the OPEC members, other poor nations are in no position to challenge the

[1] See, for instance, Ernest Stern and Wouter Tims, "The Relative Bargaining Strengths of the Developing Countries" in Ronald Ricker, ed., *The Changing Resource Problem of the Fourth World* (Washington, D.C.: Re-

overwhelming control of the rich nations over the present world economic order. Second, such analysis is often conceived in a short-term perspective, mistaking the current poverty of a majority of mankind for permanent impotence. As soon as we take a broader, longer-term perspective, it becomes obvious that the Third World *is* the future international order and that the developed countries have to start thinking today in terms of fashioning policies to come to some reasonable accommodation with this future order.[2]

This is not the result of any wishful thinking: this follows automatically if we view the entire issue in its proper historical perspective. It is true that the Third World is not important enough today—financially, economically, or politically—to figure in the calculations of the developed countries. But, in the longer run, there is likely to be a dramatic shift in the balance of power between the rich nations and the Third World.

SHIFTING BALANCE OF POWER

First, if we look at the demographic trends, we find that the rich nations are a shrinking minority of the world. Today they are about 30 percent of the total population of the world; by the turn of this century, they will have dwindled to 20 percent, and by the middle of the next century to about 10 percent. There is a real question whether such a shrinking minority will be able to control the economic, financial, and political destiny of the world—and what means it may have to employ to do that. It is inevitable that the dependence of the rich nations on the poor nations will greatly increase over time—for their natural resources, the use of their space and oceans, even for their labor and effective demand. This is likely to create "a reverse dependency" where the life styles of the rich will come to depend on the continued goodwill of the poor.

---

sources for the Future, 1976); and Fred Bergsten, "The Threat from the Third World," in *Foreign Policy,* no. 11.

[2] Mahbub ul Haq, "Development and Independence," *Development Dialogue,* no. 1 (1974):5–12.

Second, there is no way that this shrinking minority could continue to draw a protective wall around its life styles or withdraw behind a fortress and keep commanding the world's resources on its own terms. There is likely to be another development during the next few decades which is going to reduce greatly the room for maneuver of this privileged minority—viz., the spread of nuclear weapons. It seems inevitable now that the nuclear monopoly will not remain in the hands of a few nations by the turn of this century but a number of poor nations—particularly the more populous ones like China, India, Pakistan, Brazil, Egypt, with a combined population of over three billion by then—will not only command nuclear weapons but also possess delivery systems. However regrettable such a development may be from a world point of view—and there are many chances of its becoming quite catastrophic in a world as unjust as ours—an important implication of this development for the international balance of power would be that the sheer size of numbers would begin to tell as the threat of nuclear terror by a few super powers is neutralized. Throughout history, the only way a small minority has continued to exercise a dominant control over human affairs is through its monopoly over some forms of human destruction. Once this advantage is neutralized, the minority begins to realize how dependent it is on the goodwill of the majority for its continued existence.

Third, we do not have to indulge in such morbid speculation to recognize that even the balance of economic power is likely to change fairly decisively in the next few decades. Take, for example, the control over natural resources. Most of the agricultural raw materials for industrial use and mineral resources are produced in, or controlled by, the Third World: this should be quite obvious from a glance at Table 4 in the Statistical Appendix. The developed countries, particularly outside the United States, are going to be increasingly dependent on the natural resources imported from the developing countries. Initially, these resources were obtained by many developed countries on the basis of a colonial pattern of exploitation of the developing world. Later, the availability of cheap oil enabled the developed countries to replace many of the natural fibers by synthetics and to create new resources for continued industrialization. But this created a major and increasing dependence on oil which made the developed countries more vulnerable to the inevitable increase in the price of oil. It is already apparent that the price of oil in the future would be determined by the availability of viable substitutes rather then by the previous unequal bargaining power of the producing and the consuming nations. It is true that there is hardly any other raw material where the producers can exercise such decisive control over supply, where the consumers' demand is so inelastic, where the substitutes will take so long to develop and at so high a cost, and where the natural resource is a wasting asset over time. But while these features are not there in other raw material exports of the developing countries, comparison with the oil situation also misses two basic points: (i) The rich consumers are bound to become ever more dependent on natural resources in the future as per capita incomes increase further in the industrialized world. There is no way that the developed countries can overcome the trend toward an increasing demand for natural fibers from abroad without either becoming even more dependent on imported oil or incurring a prohibitively high cost because of the alternative uses of their capital and labor. The future advantage is likely to belong more to the producers of raw material than to the innovators of technology. (ii) It is true that most raw material exports of the developing countries (such as tea, coffee, cocoa, rubber, etc.) are not priority items for the developed world but, as argued in chapter 8, the rich nations are getting a substantial value-added through the processing, shipping, advertising, and distribution of these commodities (over $150 billion) and it is not going to be an economically painless process to substitute for them.

Fourth, the developed countries are likely to need the Third World in the future even to sustain the effective demand for their expanding production. Although the poor nations are not really important today in the economic calculations of the rich nations, a realization may come over the next few decades that the prosperity of the developed world cannot be sustained with the continued impoverishment of the Third World. The Western societies learned a useful lesson through the depression of the 1930s, that every extra dollar going to labor was not a dollar taken away from profits but would come back twice over through effective demand and really grease the wheels of prosperity. This led to the birth of enlightened capitalism—the New Deal at the national level—where as much attention was paid to sustaining the purchasing power of the workers as to worrying about the profits of the capitalists. Today we have a situation where the capital of the world is getting concentrated within a handful of nations but its labor is mainly crowded in the Third World. Taking a fairly long-term view, it is just not possible to keep this capital and labor apart through immigration laws or through restrictions on capital transfers and yet have the basis of continued world prosperity. The evolution of a New Deal at the international level is, therefore, only a question of time. In fact, this also shows how intimately interlinked and mutually compatible the concerns of the rich and the poor nations may prove to be if both sides are prepared to look sufficiently ahead in the spirit of enlightened self-interest.

Fifth, we must also recognize that, in an interdependent world, the common property resources of mankind—like ocean beds and space—are going to acquire ever greater importance in a crowded planet. Only the rich nations today have the capital, technology, and political power to exploit these resources but it is impossible to colonize the pattern of their exploitation in the same fashion as happened to the resources on land. And as the majority of mankind acquires greater political and nuclear power in the next few decades, it is inevitable that it would demand a greater control over these international commons which belong to all humanity. The rich nations cannot, therefore, extend their technological options by turning to the resources of the international commons, except by international agreement; otherwise they may well be risking territorial battles for the right to the future use of these international commons.

Sixth, while we are discussing the relative economic power and options of the rich and the poor nations in the future, one of the most important elements that must be analyzed is the prospect of an economic collaboration between the OPEC and other countries of the Third World. The OPEC member countries have been able to arrange a fairly substantial increase in their total financial earnings (see Table 3 in the Statistical Appendix), about 90 percent of it from the industrialized world (about $100 billion a year in 1975, projected to increase to nearly $200 billion by 1980 in current prices). Though the future projections vary a good deal, it is reasonable to assume that the accumulated foreign exchange reserves of the OPEC (particularly Saudi Arabia, Kuwait, United Arab Emirates and Libya) will account for a major proportion of the total world reserves in another decade. The economic clout that these OPEC members will be able to wield over time would, therefore, be considerable. The acquisition of such vast financial resources by the OPEC is too recent a phenomenon for them to have realized its full potential: but money is a great teacher and it is evident that the OPEC will soon discover the inevitable power that goes with money.

RULE OF OPEC

How would this newly acquired economic power be exercised in the last analysis? Will the new rich join the old rich, as the history has often told us, in preserving the old economic order or will they join forces with the poor nations in changing this order both to their own liking and to that of the poor nations? This is the key question.

There are a number of reasons why the new rich may defy history and refuse to join the old rich. To begin with, the new rich are receiving a considerable proportion (about 90 percent) of their higher income from the old rich, unlike the historical pattern wherein the rich mainly receive their surplus from the labor of the poor. It is, therefore, not very easy or convenient for the new rich to join forces with the old rich, without losing a good part of their new income and economic power. Furthermore, the OPEC member countries are a small part of the world population (7 percent), often with underdeveloped economies and poor defense arrangements, so that they may be well aware that their best protection is the continued political support of the Third World, for which they will be willing to pay a substantial price.[3] This is all the more true when it is recalled that the four countries which are likely to enjoy continued financial surpluses into the 1980s—viz. Saudi Arabia, Kuwait, United Arab Emirates and Libya—have a combined population of less than 10 million which is about 0.2 percent of total world population. Also, many of the OPEC member nations are more aligned with the Third World countries—racially, religiously, linguistically, culturally—than with the developed world. Finally, the OPEC members can play the role of leaders in the councils of the Third World: in the councils of the industrialized nations, they are still regarded as second-class powers. If one must speculate, there is considerable weight of evidence that the OPEC will view their future world role in close collaboration with the Third World. Concrete evidence of this emerged in April 1975, when the OPEC members refused to negotiate with the industrialized countries on the question of energy unless other raw materials of the developing countries were also added to the agenda and when they asked for a Special Session of the U.N. General Assembly in April 1974, and again in September 1975, to discuss the establishment of a new international economic order. Their concern for the Third World support is also evident from the pace of their assistance to the developing countries. The OPEC members are already committing [4] over 5 percent of their combined GNP in ODA (Official Development Assistance), or about fifteen times as much proportionately as the industrialized countries although under no compulsion to do so since their average per capita income is still around $1600 (excluding Indonesia and Nigeria) or about one-third of that in the developed world.

If the OPEC members choose to strengthen the bargaining

[3] Since most of these countries require such political support also for their continuing struggle against Israel, it underlines the importance of this factor in their calculations.

[4] Of course, the disbursements are much lower, as they would naturally be in the first few years till they catch up with the commitment levels provided these commitment levels are maintained.

position of the poor nations, a number of options immediately open up.[5] The international monetary system can be restructured simply through the device of OPEC members insisting on payments for their oil exports in SDRs (Special Drawing Rights) rather than in national reserve currencies of the rich nations. This can give them a decisive leverage in the creation and distribution of international liquidity, particularly as they use their new financial strength to change the present control over the International Monetary Fund. Again, in the trade field, the current bargaining position of the poor nations in the primary commodity markets can be greatly transformed if the OPEC were to finance commodity buffer stocks, or even a commodity bank along the lines suggested by Lord Keynes in the 1940s.[6] Moreover, new trade channels can open up in many fields between the OPEC and the Third World countries, particularly in food, where the OPEC can provide fertilizer and finance to some promising food producers in the Third World in exchange for future repayments in food. Another field where the OPEC can pass on greater bargaining strength to the poor nations is the renegotiation of past external debt and past contracts and leases given to the multinationals: the disruption this might cause in the flow of resources to the poor nations can be smoothed over by the OPEC standing ready to provide alternative financial flows. Taking yet another illustration, the new financial strength of the OPEC is likely to lead to a major change in their voting power within the international financial institutions which is a lever they can use to get a greater say in the eco-

---

[5] See Mahbub ul Haq, "An Eight-Point Action Program for the New Economic Order," a paper presented to the Third World Forum meeting, Karachi, January 1975.

[6] See Lal Jayawardena, "Annex on Background Material in the Fields of Trade, International Monetary Reform and Development Financing," in *A New United Nations Structure for Global Economic Cooperation* (New York: United Nations, 1975), pp. 69–75. The proposals for UNCTAD IV Conference, scheduled in May 1976, regarding an integrated commodity stabilization program and establishment of a common financing fund come fairly close to the spirit of the Keynesian idea.

nomic decision-making councils of the world, not only for themselves but for other members of the Third World.

It is not our intention to sketch out various possible scenarios that the OPEC members can choose in collaboration with the Third World. The main point is that the growing financial strength of the OPEC introduces an important element in the world balance of power which will not only increase uncertainty on the part of the old rich but could also directly and materially strengthen the bargaining position of the poor nations.

Besides exploring concrete possibilities of economic and political collaboration with the OPEC members, there is another area of bargaining power which the poor nations have not yet exploited fully in their tactical battles ahead. An impression has been created that a new international economic order is needed only by the Third World. This is wrong, both factually and tactically. The European nations should have a vital stake in the emergence of a new order as the post-World War II structures took shape when Europe had only a fraction of the political and economic power they have acquired by now and, as such, they have much to gain vis-à-vis the United States in any structural readjustments that take place. Similarly, the socialist bloc had opted out of international economic and financial structures in the cold war era of the 1950s and 1960s and gone the route of barter trade and bilateral aid relationships. The trade and external economic relations of this bloc have increased tremendously by now and it is only a matter of time that it should seek a full integration with the international monetary system and try to influence the new world economic structures which emerge. The OPEC members have a stake of their own in the evolution of new structures, particularly in the monetary field, since they are at present confronted with a world situation where they have no national reserve currency of their own, where they lose control over even the recycling of their own financial surpluses since they have no choice but to deposit them in the currencies and central banks of the rich nations under the present arrangements, and where they have a nominal voice (less than 5 percent vote) in the affairs of the Bretton Woods institutions. A major change in their present position can come only with the creation of a reserve currency of their own or with the establishment of an international central bank and creation of an international currency over which they can seek and exercise a sizable influence. Thus, the United States is probably the only major power which may feel that its short-term interests are threatened by a real adjustment in the balance of world economic and political power. Its opposition to any fundamental restructuring is both natural and obvious unless it chooses to see the problem in historical perspective or unless it is convinced it will be isolated in its lone struggle against the emergence of a new order.

Since the Third World has fairly limited economic bargaining power in the short run, it is tactically important that it should carefully cultivate the underlying interests of other political and economic blocs in a fundamental change in the world economic order. And since the evolution of new economic structures is bound to take time, it is necessary that the Third World uses its limited economic bargaining power in the short-run in a negative sense at least—to block all such piecemeal reforms and limited arrangements as the developed countries are currently seeking for their own benefit through various forums (e.g. Interim Committee, Paris Conference, *ad hoc* consultations with OPEC) till they obtain a commitment to consider more fundamental reforms for the benefit of the developing countries. The poor nations may not have the economic bargaining power today to establish new arrangements of their own liking. But they certainly have enough votes, if they stand together, to prevent any modifications that the rich may like to make in the international monetary and financial system to keep running things a bit more smoothly for themselves. In any unequal struggle, the power of a filibuster is an important and time-honored protection for the weak.

POLITICAL POWER

In the last analysis, however, the real bargaining power of the poor nations is political, not economic. The Third World contains the overwhelming majority of mankind. It increasingly enjoys a decisive control over the United Nations General Assembly. Its vast population can be disregarded at present; its U.N. resolutions can be ignored; its demands can be brushed away as mere rhetoric. This is nothing unusual in the initial phases of a trade union movement. But if the new trade union of the poor nations holds together—and its unattended grievances are likely to keep uniting it—it is only a matter of time before the management is forced to enter into serious negotiations and the public posturing on both sides ceases as they send their chosen representatives into the backrooms to hammer out hard, tough compromises.

Whether it is national orders, or the international order, the real bargaining power of the poor lies in their ability and their willingness to disrupt the life styles of the rich. In any such confrontation, the rich have far more to lose and are generally far more willing to come to a workable compromise.

As the rhetoric cools down on both sides, the rich nations are likely to weigh carefully the costs of disruption against the costs of accommodation and to consider the fact that any conceivable cost of a new deal will be a very small proportion of their future growth in an orderly, cooperative framework. In fact, any such new international order would ultimately promote the self-interest of both sides—much the same way as the New Deal did within the United States in the 1930s—by leading to a more harmonious world with expanding markets and a booming international economy. The short-run cost of a New Deal at the international level (probably $50–100 billion a year), while heavy, would still be quite manageable as it would constitute 1 to 2 percent of the GNP of the rich nations and could easily come out of the consequent higher growth possibilities. Moreover, even the costs of a temporary disruption in growth can be very high. For instance, it is estimated that, during 1974–80, the OECD countries could "lose" $300 billion in unachieved growth and potential asset formation.[7]

While one hopes for such a cooperative framework for negoti-

[7] Hollis B. Chenery, "Restructuring the World Economy," *Foreign Affairs* 53, no. 2, January 1975.

ations, it is good to remember that, in history, vast changes in the existing power structures have rarely taken place voluntarily, as acts of vision and foresight. As Barbara Ward observed:

From history we know that such vast changes of purpose have sometimes been achieved by cooperation and dialogue, sometimes by direct and even bloody confrontation, perhaps most often by a confused and uncertain mixture of both confrontation and cooperation. The reason for the uncertainty is obvious. Those who profit by a system can become obsessed by their determination to change nothing. . . . Those who suffer can, on the contrary, come to believe that nothing short of total disruption will genuinely affect anything. . . . At this level of polarization, dialogue is impossible and violence inevitable. . . . The task is, therefore, to discover the . . . basic common interests for the whole human species and the workable mixture of dialogue and confrontation that will permit the nations, both the weak and the strong, to discover those interests together and do so in time.[8]

Unfortunately, the rich often make their accommodation only when it becomes inevitable, either through an actual conflict or in anticipation of it by shrewdly calculating the costs of accommodation against the costs of disruption. Whether or not there is an actual confrontation, it is obvious that the increasing despair of the majority of mankind can become one of the most disruptive forces in the smooth workings of the present world order. What Robert S. McNamara had to say about the national orders is perhaps equally valid for the international order:

When the highly privileged are few and the desperately poor are many—and when the gap between them is worsening rather than improving—it is only a question of time before a decisive choice must be made between the political costs of reform and the political risks of rebellion.[9]

All sane people must surely hope that an ugly confrontation

---

[8] Barbara Ward, Report on the UNEP-UNCTAD Symposium on *Patterns of Resource Use, Environment and Development Strategies,* Cocoyoc, Mexico, May 1975.

[9] Robert S. McNamara, *Annual Speech to the Board of Governors,* September 1972.

can be avoided between the rich and the poor nations and a genuine era of global cooperation ushered in, but this can hardly be achieved without all countries agreeing on the need for a fundamental restructuring of international economic relations. There is no substitute for that—neither the reasoned but empty appeals of the rich in the name of global interdependence nor the impassioned rhetoric of the poor in the name of social justice. What is needed is a new deal at the international level, as discussed in the next chapter, which bases the future relations between the rich and the poor nations on new concepts of equality of opportunity, not on the old patterns of dependency.

CHOICE OF TACTICS

We have discussed in this chapter the various components in the bargaining power of the poor nations. Two observations are necessary to place this discussion in some perspective. First, the existence of bargaining power does not necessarily mean that it should be used. In fact, the more bargaining chips you acquire, the less you may need to use them so long as the other side knows and respects the chips you have. Emphasis on relative bargaining power does not, therefore, mean an advocacy of confrontation. It may well be a prelude to meaningful negotiations. In the negotiating phase that the Third World is now entering, it cannot only rely on appeals to international morality and fair play. It must acquire additional bargaining power and forge tactical alliances.

Second, its bargaining power in the short-run is going to remain limited under the best of circumstances. The Third World must learn to husband this limited bargaining strength to its best tactical advantage. Several steps are essential:

(i) A major part of the bargaining strength of the Third World lies in its political unity. This unity is going to be even more important in the struggle ahead and far more difficult to keep as the ranks of the Third World may be divided by the lure of short-term gains and separate deals with the rich nations. If that happens, the Third World would deserve the perpetuation of an inequitable economic order as it would have demonstrated that it is not yet ready to challenge the existing balance of power. Deliberate disruptions in the ranks of the trade union of the poor are nothing new. It will be for the Third World to demonstrate that its political maturity is a perfect foil to such tactics.

(ii) One of the essential tactics of the Third World should be to proceed through the process of collective bargaining so that whatever bargaining strength its individual members possess is pooled together. This means resisting a case-by-case approach at the initial policy level while accepting it as an operational necessity once the overall policy decisions are reached. Concretely speaking, if the guiding principles for commodity stabilization or debt rescheduling or monetary reform are to be agreed upon, this must follow from a process of collective bargaining. Once a satisfactory umbrella is established, specific agreements can always be reached commodity-by-commodity, case-by-case and country-by-country. Collective bargaining is necessary for establishing policy guidelines while a case-by-case approach is required to reach specific, operational agreements. If the process is reversed, the bargaining power of the Third World will be further weakened and it is easier for the rich nations to take advantage of their diverse circumstances and interests.

(iii) Serious analysis must be undertaken in the institutes of the Third World on the major components of political and economic power in the world today; how they have developed historically and how they are likely to change over time; and how the Third World can adopt a coherent and purposeful strategy for engineering a change in world power relationships. While their politicians fight in the vanguard, academicians of the Third World must supply them with relevant analysis.

(iv) The Third World can help its cause a great deal by establishing a substantive secretariat to serve the needs of its own forums (like the Group of 77, the Group of 24, the Non-Aligned Conference) and to develop negotiating positions for discussion with the rich nations in international forums such as the UNCTAD, the Interim and Development Committees, the four commissions being set up by the Paris Conference etc. Such a substantive secretariat should help coordinate the diverse interests of over one hundred members of the Third World, which would be quite a challenge in itself and which is badly needed for any serious negotiations with the well-organized Group of 10 on the side of the industrialized nations. A central secretariat of this kind should be manned by the best people from the Third World and its main task should be to produce well-researched, well-documented, specific proposals which harmonize the political and economic interests of the Third World and which can become their main negotiating agenda.[10]

(v) The best tactic for the Third World is to proceed through the present United Nations structure, while seeking reforms in this structure as well. The Third World is developing a major political voice, and some organization, within the United Nations forums and it is important to build upon and consolidate this advantage. Tactically, it may be wise to accept small, more manageable negotiating forums at times to advance the dialogue in a quieter, less polemical fashion so long as the links of any such negotiation are maintained with the United Nations and the advantage of collective bargaining is not lost.

(vi) Finally, the Third World must keep stressing in its negotiations that a new order is needed not only by and for the Third World but by other economic and political blocs as well which wish to see a readjustment in the present balance of world economic power—Europe, which has fully recovered by now from the battering it took in World War II; Socialist bloc, whose current economic and financial isolation is bound to end; and OPEC members which have just acquired a significant proportion of world's financial reserves. Because of its own limited bargaining power in the short-run, it would be entirely appropriate if the Third World counts on—and deliberately encourages—the vested interests of other powerful blocs in the emergence of a new international economic order.

---

[10] It is important to create only one central secretariat which serves all the various groupings of the Third World rather than separate secretariats for each group, both to achieve maximum degree of coordination and to use the scarce Third World expertise to best advantage. In fact, the Third World Forum, discussed in Part 2, can well become the nucleus of such a secretariat facility if the Forum is properly organized.

·10·
TOWARD A NEW INTERNATIONAL ORDER

T HE DIALOGUE BETWEEN the rich and the poor nations on a new international economic order has accomplished at least a few limited objectives so far. There has been a grudging acceptance by the rich nations that serious negotiations are inevitable; some broad areas of negotiation and a few negotiating principles have emerged out of the resolutions of the Seventh Special Session of the U.N. General Assembly; and there is a search now for appropriate negotiating forums to discuss these issues a little further. This is a good start. But there still is great confusion as to what institutional reforms are at stake and what is the shape of the new world of the next few decades that both sides are trying to negotiate.

There are at least two distinct schools of thought. One believes in marginal changes in the present institutional structures to make the international system work somewhat more efficiently and more equitably (discussed in chapter 11). Accordingly, the strategy of this school of thought is that specific improvements should be sought on a large number of fronts —from commodity price stabilization schemes to transfer of technology—and that these should be negotiated and implemented in a step-by-step approach. The other contends that the existing institutional structures reflect past and present imbalances in political and economic power, and that they should not be reformed only in a marginal fashion but must be replaced by new institutional arrangements. This debate is nothing new. At the national level, it has emerged in the form of those who believe in the effectiveness of corrections in the price system against those who believe in fundamental institutional reforms. Whenever existing power structures are challenged, there will always be a split on appropriate tactics between conservatives and radicals even when they are both agreed on the ultimate objective—which is not often the case.

Leaving tactics aside, what is the ultimate objective? If it is equality of opportunity at the international level, as discussed in chapter 8, how is it to be achieved? What institutional setup will make it possible? The tactics and the strategy of negotiations will, of course, be dictated largely by the realities of the international situation but, looking for a while beyond immediate discussions, what is the grand design that the Third World—and, indeed, the world as a whole—should seek? It is difficult to say at the moment, since adequate intellectual and analytical work has not been done so far, but at least the search should begin.

POSTWAR RESTRUCTURING

The last time such a grand design was conceived was in the mid-1940s when the Second World War was ending and when a new world structure of political and economic power had to be constructed. The result was the establishment of the United Nations and the Bretton Woods institutions of the International Monetary Fund and the World Bank. The shape of these structures was necessarily influenced by the balance of power existing at that time even though there was some attempt to anticipate longer-term needs. In the 1940s, many of the Third World countries were still colonies, bound in a relationship of political and economic dependency with the colonial powers. The communist countries chose to stay outside some of this institutional framework, particularly the Bretton Woods institutions, as they regarded them as a Western contrivance at a time when the cold war between the two blocs was just getting under way. As such, while these institutional structures were meant to serve larger world interests, the Western interests naturally took precedence whenever a conflict arose. Perhaps Lord Keynes would contest even this reconstruction of the situation of those times since he learned, in his frequent duels with the American representative, Mr. White, on the actual blueprint of the Bretton Woods institutions, that it was primarily American interests which prevailed, since America had emerged by then as the predominant political and economic power in the Western world in the wake of a battered Europe. Keynes tried valiantly, but in vain, to replace gold and national reserve currencies with an international currency ("bancor"); to place the temporary liquidity of the balance-of-payments-surplus countries automatically at the disposal of the deficit countries; to set up a commodity bank for the stabilization of primary commodity prices; and to suggest a structure of control of international financial institutions which was less dominated by the United States. But Keynes did not succeed in carrying through his ideas. He was far ahead of his time and the prevailing balance of power was against him. It is perhaps not surprising, therefore, that many of the current ideas on institutional reforms bear some kinship to Keynes's original conception.

Another grand design must be constructed today in line with the changes which have taken place in the last thirty years and the shifts in the balance of power which are likely in the next few decades (see chapter 9). The Third World countries have already achieved their political independence—with a few remaining colonies ready to be liberated. These countries naturally seek a relationship of greater equality and self-respect with the Western world, both in their political and economic dealings. They are also impatient to eliminate mass poverty and to accelerate their economic development and they expect the international structures to help in this process. At the same time, the socialist bloc—with one third of the world population—is gradually coming out of its isolation and seeking greater integration with the world trade and payments system. The world financial balance of power has also been changed drastically by the collective action of the OPEC members. And within the Western alliance, West Germany and Japan have arisen from their helpless condition of the 1940s and are posing a strong challenge to the predominance of the U.S. economic power. A new grand design is needed, therefore, not only by the poor nations. It is required by a world that has changed and which is likely to change even more drastically in the coming decades.

The search for such a grand design must begin at several levels. For instance, at the political level, there is a real question how new political alliances must be created to preserve a structure of peace. What should be the role of the United Nations in this? Should the veto system in the Security Council, which reflects the old balance of power, be changed in favor of a more democratic system of arriving at international political consensus? How should the voice of the Third World be reflected in these decisions, without either becoming "tyranny of the majority" or being brushed aside as irrelevant and unnecessary? These questions should engage the attention of those who are interested in a lasting peace which can only be achieved if there is a structure of justice in the world.

Our objective is a more limited one: to review briefly the international economic structures which are necessary in order to provide the equality of opportunity between nations which is at the heart of the issue of international economic justice.

WORLD DEVELOPMENT AUTHORITY

To begin with, there is a need to establish a single World Development Authority (WDA) where decisions on international economic issues can be coordinated. This should be under the aegis of the United Nations and have complete jurisdiction over all international economic institutions, old and new. The WDA should be run by a board elected periodically by the U.N. General Assembly, representing the interests of various national blocs.[1]

[1] In a way, this is implicit in the Report of the Group of Experts on the Structure of the United Nations System: *A New United Nations Structure for Global Economic Cooperation,* U.N., New York, May 1975. This Group suggested the appointment of a Director-General for Development and Economic Cooperation, next to the U.N. Secretary General, and

The major tasks of the World Development Authority should be to:

(a) regulate short-term international credit;
(b) provide long-term development finance;
(c) create a framework for expansion of world trade;
(d) strive at a balance between world population increase and food production; and
(e) in general, act as a global economic planning commission in an advisory role.

Each of these functions would require either the creation of new institutions or the restructuring of the old, but it is better to proceed from these functions to the institutional structures than in the reverse order.

SHORT-TERM INTERNATIONAL CREDIT

At the national level, we are now used to the establishment of Central Banks which regulate the total supply of liquidity and, with varying success, the distribution of national credit to various sectors of the economy. At the international level, we still lack such a mechanism. As discussed earlier, international liquidity is created at present largely by the national decisions of the United States. An attempt was made in the early 1970s to create SDRs (Special Drawing Rights) as an international currency by the International Monetary Fund but this has been a once-for-all operation so far; its value was linked to a basket of reserve currencies of the rich nations; its volume ($11 billion) was decided by the needs and convenience of the rich nations, and its distribution, not surprisingly, was in favor of the developed world which received as much as three-fourths of the SDRs.

strengthening of the mandate and operations of the Economic and Social Council (ECOSOC). It would be more deisrable, however, to create an overall operational authority at the U.N. headquarters with broad economic powers.

In order to provide adequate short-term credit to meet the genuine needs of all parts of the world, rich and poor alike, it is absolutely necessary to agree on the concept of an International Central Bank. Such a Central Bank should have exclusive jurisdiction over the creation and regulation of international reserves.[2] Thus, national reserve currencies (dollars, sterling, etc.) should be gradually phased out of international payments because they subject vital international concerns on inflationary or deflationary policies to *ad hoc* national decisions and because they put a few countries (exclusively the richest nations at present) in a more privileged position, whose national currency is accepted as an international reserve, and place a vast majority of nations (Third World, OPEC, socialist bloc, and many industrialized countries) in a more unfavorable position since they cannot create their own credit. This leads to major international distortions. Equality of opportunity is clearly impossible in such a situation. The richest countries enjoy an unlimited access to international credit; the poorest countries keep nursing their "foreign exchange bottleneck." Even the international capital market is open only to those nations which are already creditworthy, despite a plethora of ever fresh proposals on how to increase the access of the poor developing countries to this capital market.

The strength of the tie-up of the present international credit system to a few rich nations became even more clear during 1974–75. While the OPEC members theoretically arranged a significant resource transfer from the industrialized countries through a quadrupling of oil prices, they could not accomplish such a transfer in actual practice. Since they did not have a reserve currency of their own, they had to put their financial surpluses in dollars, sterling, etc., and, as such, lost real control over their disposal. The industralized nations came to an understanding among themselves on a safety net of $25 billion to protect each other from the impact of short-term fluctuations in reserves. The control over the recycling of financial funds was

[2] Gold can no longer play this role because of its inelastic supply and extreme geographical concentration.

exercised by the industralized nations, not OPEC. The poor nations, which had fewer options to turn to, could not negotiate any safety nets of their own [3] and had to fall back on a few limited credit facilities established by the International Monetary Fund. The net result was that, due to the workings of the international credit system, the poor countries had to carry out many painful adjustments in their low consumption and development levels while the rich nations could postpone such adjustments since they could live off international credit.

If an equitable system is to be established, an International Central Bank must be set up with the power to create an international currency. This currency need not be backed up by either gold or a basket of reserve currencies or even by a stock of commodities. Just as in a national system, the real backing for the international currency is the production system of the world. Care should be taken that it is expanded in line with the growth needs of the world for production and exports. In estimating these needs, the Central Bank should allow for a much higher growth rate in the developing countries than the past trend. At least, the necessary working capital to achieve a high growth rate in the poor nations should be available: the rest is up to these countries themselves. This also means that the distribution of international credit between rich and poor nations should not be in relation to creditworthiness assessments or quotas based on their past wealth. The distribution must be in relation to future growth needs and potential. The access to the facilities of the Central Bank should be de-linked from past affluence (unlike the present quotas established in the International Monetary Fund) if the poor nations are to be afforded an equal opportunity to compete.

The affairs of the International Central Bank can be run in the larger interests of the world only if the same principles are accepted for its management as have already been implemented at the national level. The Central Banks within countries are usually managed by the state, since provision of credit is too es-

[3] Economic Commission for Latin America, "Possible Features of a Financial Safety Net for Latin America," July 31, 1975.

sential a service to be entrusted to the market system or to a handful of private interests. At the international level, this implies that the control over the Central Bank should be exercised by the entire international community through an acceptable formula which balances the interests of the poor and the rich nations. The important point is that capital subscriptions should not be the basis of either the control of this institution or the distribution of its credit. If the International Monterary Fund has to be restructured along these lines to become a genuine international central bank, the transformation in its basic concepts and operations will be truly profound. In order to evolve an operational proposal, it would be best to proceed from certain agreed principles on the basis of which international credit should be created, distributed and managed over time and then to explore whether such a system could be put in place through the reform of the International Monetary Fund or whether it would require an entirely fresh start.[4]

LONG-TERM FINANCE

Within national systems, deliberate efforts must be made to redirect investment flows if the productivity of the poorest sections of the society is to be increased. The situation is no different at the international level. The rich nations have by now built up a considerable stock of capital and technology. Even

---

[4] It is encouraging to note a remarkably courageous recent speech of the Managing Director of the International Monetary Fund, Mr. Witteveen, in which he supported the idea of a fundamental reform in the IMF so that "it would function both as the exclusive issuer of official international reserve assets and as a lender-of-last-resort to central banks." He also noted "the striking parallels between the development of domestic and international means of payment," commented on the need to reduce the role of gold and reserve currencies in international payments and to replace them by the creation of Special Drawing Rights, and frankly admitted that "it would be very difficult to obtain international consensus on such a major change in the international monetary system now." Address delivered to the International Financial Business Outlook Conference, Frankfurt, West Germany, October 28, 1975.

though the investment rates in rich and poor nations are roughly comparable at present (see the Statistical Appendix, Table 1), the absolute increase in the total income of the rich nations every year is about twenty times that in the poor nations because of initial disparities. If the disparities are to be reduced, the rate of growth in the developing countries must be stepped up considerably, for which they need a sizable supplement of longer-term development capital at least over the next two decades.

The traditional basis for the provision of supplemental long-term development finance to the developing countries has been the voluntary decision of the rich nations to set aside some funds for foreign assistance to be channeled bilaterally or through multilateral institutions. Besides the fact that such an arrangement is subject to shifting political winds in the rich nations, it introduces considerable uncertainty in the calculations of the developing countries about the level of development assistance. Nor can the developing countries acquire a significant control over the generation of such finance themselves since, as already discussed, there is no international central bank which could provide both short-term credit and long-term finance.

The need for evolving an entirely different framework for the provision of development finance has increased by recent political and economic developments in the rich nations. On the political level, there has been a great weakening of their will to provide additional long-term capital since their own economies are under considerable short-term pressure. On the economic front, their own need for long-term capital has also increased sharply, particularly in order to find viable substitutes for energy based on petroleum. In a stiff competition for scarce investment funds in a situation like this, it is natural that the developing countries would lose both in negotiating additional official development assistance and in gaining access to the international capital markets.

If the international system is to be relied on for the provision of supplemental development resources to the developing countries, there must be some way of a more assured and automatic access to these funds in the light of the growth needs of the developing countries and a greater control over the size and distribution of these funds. This principle seems to have been agreed upon at the Seventh U.N. Special Session—even though very reluctantly by the rich nations—since the final resolution affirms that "concessional financial resources to developing countries need to be increased substantially . . . and their flow made *predictable, continuous and increasingly assured* so as to facilitate the implementation by developing countries of long-term programs for economic and social development" [5] (italics supplied). The real question is how to give a practical shape to this principle.

One of the primary means to accomplish this objective would be to link the creation of international liquidity with the provision of development finance. There is no logical reason why the International Central Bank, proposed above, should not provide both short-term liquidity and long-term capital. The distinction between short- and long-term capital in this context, as has been observed within national orders, is both false and dangerous. They are freely substitutable and often treated as such by the developing countries. The real implications of such a proposal would be to set up an automatic system of international taxation since the poor nations will obtain the greater part of these funds from the International Central Bank which they will normally use to acquire capital goods and technology in the rich nations.

Another way of arranging automatic resource transfers is to devise a specific system of international taxation. The more practicable forms may be those where resources are new and additional (such as exploitation of continental shelfs and ocean beds), or where international taxation can be linked to activities which are coming under public criticism, such as international pollutants and armament spending. Since progressive taxation structures took several decades to develop even at the national

[5] Seventh U.N. Special Session, Resolution no. A/RES/3362(S-VII) on *Development and International Economic Cooperation,* p. 5, September 1975.

level, one can appreciate the problems involved in developing a system of international taxation which raises delicate issues of national sovereignty. Yet such a system is an essential part of the new economic order that the Third World is pressing for. And it can be established if the World Development Authority is empowered to prepare feasible proposals for international taxation, to be administered through an International Development Fund.

The heart of the issue of providing adequate long-term capital to the developing countries lies in establishing the principle of automatic transfer of resources from the rich to the poor nations, not in negotiating *ad hoc* increases in the current levels of foreign assistance. The acceptance of the former principle will be an essential part of a new order, comparable in its conceptual breakthrough to the prolonged national evolution to the time when the State—instead of Robin Hood—took over the responsibility for taxing the rich for the benefit of the poor. *Ad hoc* increases in foreign assistance, whether under the banner of the 0.7 percent official development assistance target or under alternative formulas, while helpful, will still constitute an extension of the old order.

It is likely to take several decades before the principle of automaticity is fully accepted. The groundwork for its acceptance can be gradually prepared in a step-by-step approach. First, the creation of international liquidity should definitely be linked to provision of development capital to the poorest nations. This will be considerably facilitated by the establishment of an International Central Bank, as proposed above, and should in fact be a part of the charter of such a bank. Over the course of the next decade, such a linkage can provide $5–10 billion a year automatically to the developing countries.

Second, new lobbies should be set up and encouraged to build up a climate of international opinion for the taxation of anti-humanitarian activities, such as armament spending and international pollutants, by the United Nations. Today there is a spending of about $250 billion on armaments which are one of the major consumers of world's resources at a time when we complain about their shortage and scarcity. Most of this expenditure is by the rich nations though the developing countries must own up to their guilt since they are also wasting about $40 billion on armaments. If a tax of, say, 10 percent is imposed, it will yield about $25 billion for an international development fund. Hopefully, the defense spending itself will decrease as a result of international taxation, thereby releasing resources even more directly for alternative uses. Similarly, there is considerable concern today about international pollution. If this concern is properly mobilized and results in international taxation, particularly on oil tankers, it can both discourage such pollution as well as become a source of sizable revenue. The principle for taxation in these cases will be the same as at the national level: if external diseconomies are created by private action, the State has the right to tax them. Whenever social diseconomies result on an international scale from the action of sovereign states, the United Nations should have the authority to impose a tax on such activities on behalf of the entire international community. The principle is a simple one. Its acceptance will require a revolution in mankind's thinking.

Third, the full potential of common property resources of mankind (such as oceans and space) should be carefully analyzed since this may well become a major source of development funds for the poor nations in the 1980s. The major promise lies in oil exploration in continental shelfs and in ocean bed mining.[6] The strategy of the developing countries should be to bring the exploitation of such resources under some form of international control. In this context, their current opposition to the establishment of an International Seabed Authority seems to be based on narrow considerations and is entirely mistaken. The developing world should, in fact, insist that such an Authority is created and given a strong mandate for the exploitation of ocean beds, including continental shelfs.

Fourth, since in the short-run there will be great opposition

[6] Arvid Pardo and Elisabeth Mann Borgese, *The New International Economic Order and the Law of the Sea* (Valletta: The Royal University of Malta, 1976).

by the rich nations to accept any form of direct income taxation by an international authority, one must think of some way of imposing such taxation indirectly. The proposals made above are various ways this objective can be achieved, without directly challenging national sovereignty. Another major avenue that has opened up recently is the possibility of taxing a scarce resource that the rich nations need desperately for their continued growth. The prime example of this is oil. The OPEC has successfully increased the price of oil and thereby imposed in effect an excise tax of about 2 percent on the consumption expenditure of the rich nations. One of the questions that the OPEC members must consider is whether they would wield such a taxation power exclusively in their own interests or also for the benefit of the poor nations (which were subjected to the same increase in oil prices as the rich nations had to bear). If the OPEC were to impose a "development levy" of only $1 per barrel, it could yield an additional revenue of $10 billion a year, assuming that the levy would be fully absorbed by the consuming nations. This revenue can be transferred to poor developing countries in proportion to their oil imports in a base year. The beauty of any such scheme is its essential simplicity. There are no disputes over burden-sharing among the OPEC members, and no need to evolve complicated allocation criteria. Essentially, the OPEC members would be acting as tax collectors on behalf of the Third World and creating a built-in political interest on the part of the Third World to support the OPEC in its present efforts to index the current level of their oil prices and to prevent them from declining in real terms.

Finally, it must be acknowledged that a fully automatic system of resource transfers can be evolved only after considerable experimentation with interim solutions. It should also be noted here that automaticity in raising development finance does not necessarily mean that there should be similar automaticity in providing this finance to the developing countries. The development finance must be channelled through international financial institutions, after they have been placed under more democratic control of the international community, according to some uni-

versally accepted criteria of basic human needs and national performance. These issues are discussed further in the next chapter.

INTERNATIONAL TRADE

In the field of trade, it appears that a good deal of energy is
being wasted by the Third World on the wrong issues. Stabilization of primary commodity prices or of export earnings has
often dominated the field. Yet stabilization of prices or earnings
does not confer an additional benefit in the long run. If this is
the only aim, it can be managed even by national action. Extra
earnings in boom periods can be conserved to cover lean years
through good economic management. And if national action is
not forthcoming in this field, why should we expect that it is
easier to arrange such action at the international level? In fact,
the developing countries are often working for higher earnings,
not more stable prices, even though this issue is often posed in
international forums in terms of commodity price stabilization.
But if the real aim is higher earnings—as it should be—then
the main action lies in additional processing of commodities,
diversification out of a few unstable commodities, greater control over the distribution channels for these commodities, etc.,
as discussed in chapter 8.

Again, far too much attention has focused on trade in primary raw materials rather than in processed goods, which may
well be the more promising area in the future. This emphasis is
evident in the confusion over the present debate on "indexing."
Some of the developing countries have started making the argument that the prices of their primary exports should be indexed
in terms of their manufactured imports. This is clearly the
wrong issue for non-oil exporting developing countries. There is
no logic in their freezing the present price relationships, both
because these are already unfavorable to them and because they
should have an interest in opting out of unprocessed raw material exports rather than in perpetuating the present patterns of
international division of labor. The comparative advantage in
the production of many processed goods in changing fast. In any

case, it would be folly to index a bad deal before it has been changed decisively.[7] Indexation is a technique to consolidate gains already made, not a device to make such gains, unless the developing countries feel that the normal, long-term market trends in primary raw materials are against them.

In discussing the problems of primary raw material producers and exporters, one must divide them into at least two distinct groups. At the one extreme are the poorest nations, below $200 per capita income, which are generally saddled with the weakest commodities (e.g., tea, jute, sisal) which face uncertain and poor long-term prospects. Commodity stabilization schemes are difficult to implement in these cases and are not likely to achieve much. The real solution for the poorest nations lies in devising a package of policies which shifts resources systematically out of traditional commodities into more productive channels and which encourages the export of commodities in a more processed form. On the other hand, the long-term prospects for the primary exports of richer developing countries look much brighter and there are greater possibilities of stabilizing their prices through international buffer stocks and even establishing these prices at higher real levels through supply management. In particular, the terms of trade for mineral producers are likely to improve. It should be recognized, however, that the higher commodity prices in this case would not only be at the expense of the rich nations but also tax the limited capacity of the very poorest nations.

In view of the widely different prospects for different commodities and countries, proposals have recently been prepared for an integrated approach. The Integrated Program for Commodities, prepared by the UNCTAD,[8] aims at stabilization of prices at an adequate level of ten major commodities (coffee,

---

[7] Indexing in the context of raw material prices and earnings of today makes just as much sense for the Third World as this slogan would have made for OPEC way back in 1960 when the price of oil was still less than $2.

[8] UNCTAD Integrated Program Proposal: TD/B/C. 1/184, June 24, 1975; TD/B/C. 1/184/Add. 1, June 27, 1975.

cocoa, tea, sugar, cotton, rubber, jute, hard fibers, cotton and tin) through a system of internationally held and managed stocks by creating a common fund of $3 billion for this purpose; a substantial improvement in the existing compensatory financing facility by enlarging its scope to cover not only periodic shortfalls in exports but partial reimbursement for increases in import costs; and a renewed effort to increase the scope and degree of domestic processing of primary products in developing countries and to accelerate diversification of their production and export structure. The UNCTAD proposals are the most ambitious attempt made so far to tackle the issue of commodity stabilization and diversification. Their best chance lies in deriving the financial resources for the common fund from the previously-proposed International Central Bank or from the OPEC members who are marginal consumers of the ten primary commodities in question. It is also worth recalling that the commodity stabilization schemes of the past have generally come apart on the bedrock of fundamental conflicts between producer and consumer interests. If such schemes are to be successful in future, their financing must be divorced from major raw material consumers and should ideally be linked to the creation of international liquidity, some of which can be invested in international commodity stocks.

However, the priority issues for the Third World in the field international trade are somewhat different. First, the primary emphasis should be on market access. The developing countries should seek a gradual but complete removal of *all* tariff and non-tariff barriers imposed by the industrialized nations by a specified date, say by 1985. This is likely to yield the most substantial gains from the export of primary as well as manufactured goods (the rough estimates ranging from $6 to $12 billion). And the case of the Third World is a strong one here. They are not seeking selective concessions but only asserting that market mechanism should be allowed to work freely. They can also argue, with implacable logic, that if neither their labor can move across international frontiers (because of immigration laws) nor the goods that their labor produces (because of current tariff and non-tariff restrictions), then there would be no recourse left but to raise the slogan of international land reforms. Within national orders, land reforms often become a political as well as an economic imperative. At the international level, one cannot see their feasibility at this stage, but long-term agitation for such a solution can arise if other avenues of market access are not increasingly thrown open to the Third World.

Second, the Third World must acquire greater control over the trading infrastructure of shipping, credit, distribution channels, etc. since, as was argued in chapter 8, the margins in international services are substantial. This control cannot be organized except through concerted action by the developing countries—for instance, by establishing their own joint international shipping lines, export credit agencies and other related services. Again, the financing for creating such a new trading infrastructure cannot realistically be expected to come from those established trading nations whose own interests are challenged thereby. It can either come from the OPEC or from the International Central Bank.

It is necessary, therefore, that a third arm of the World Development Authority should be established in the form of an International Trade Organization (which was also proposed in the 1940s as part of the restructuring that was taking place at that time). This organization should be given supreme responsibility for fixing specific targets for market access and for ensuring a greater role for the Third World in controlling and managing international trading infrastructure. It can also play a role in organizing an integrated program of international buffer stocks, as discussed earlier.

POPULATION AND FOOD

One of the essential features of any new economic order should be that, in the short run, no one should starve in a world which currently has the means to feed all its population and that, in the long run, the Third World countries should increasingly de-

velop the capacity to grow their own food. This issue was high-
lighted by the World Food Conference in 1974. The proposals
made at that time, and generally accepted by the international
community, were soundly conceived and need to be implemented.

In particular, there are two important proposals which deserve urgent attention in the context of a new international economic order. First, there must be a mechanism to provide immediate, short-term relief whenever crops fail in a poor country
for unforeseen reasons and famine threatens. The poor nations
cannot compete at such a time in a ruthless market mechanism.
They must be provided either the grains from an international
emergency reserve or the financial means to buy the grains at
the market price. There must be a built-in automaticity in such
a mechanism if the worst kind of human suffering is to be
avoided in periodic crises of this kind.[9]

Second, for the long run, there is no other solution but to
produce more food in the food-deficit developing countries, particularly in the poorest countries of South Asia and sub-Saharan
Africa,[10] and also to control their population growth. The last
two decades have witnessed a neglect of the food production sector in these countries which is almost criminal. It is true that
the economics of food grains production appeared to be unfavorable when PL480 surpluses were plentiful but, with the advantage of hindsight, one can see that the poor food-deficit countries mistook short-term generosity for long-term supply. This
mistake must be avoided especially if short-term rescue operations materialize in times of emergencies from the international
community. One of the important conclusions to come out of

[9] See also my observations in "The Triumph of Sanity" in *CERES*, 8, no. 3
(May–June 1975).
[10] Over 80 percent of the total net food deficit is in the poorest nations of
South Asia (India, Pakistan, Bangladesh, Sri Lanka) and sub-Saharan Africa
(Senegal, Mali, Chad, Niger, Mauritania and Upper Volta). The food deficit of these countries is likely to increase from 19 million tons in 1975 to
50 million tons by 1985 unless vigorous steps are taken to reverse the
current trends.

the World Food Conference was that international trade was too unpredictable and fragile a mechanism for meeting such an essential need as food at reasonably stable prices and that increased domestic production in the food-deficit countries was the only viable, long-term solution.

The proposed World Development Authority should, therefore, have a fourth arm—a World Food Authority—both to arrange short-term relief as well as to provide long-term finance, research, and technical assistance for increased food production in food-deficit countries. These proposals are not discussed in detail here because all the essential elements are included in the recommendations of the World Food Conference held in Rome in November 1974, viz., an annual minimum food aid target; adequate international and national stocks of food grains; and establishment of an International Fund for Agricultural Development.[11]

AGENDA FOR ACTION

A number of detailed proposals can be added to the above list—particularly in regard to the international coordination of policies in the field of energy, industrialization, transfer of technology, etc. However, the most essential features of any new economic order are the establishment of a World Development Authority, supported by an International Central Bank, an International Development Fund, an International Trade Organization and a World Food Authority. The structure of these institutions is not so important as the principles underlying them. To recapitulate, these are that: (i) the international community must assume a direct responsibility for the development of its poorest members; (ii) in order to acquire the financial means to do so, the international community should acquire jurisdiction over the creation of international reserves and powers of taxation

[11] See FAO, *The World Food Problem: Proposals for National and International Action* (Rome: November 1974). Also see Sartaj Aziz, ed., *Hunger, Politics, and Markets: The Real Issue in the Food Crisis* (New York: New York University Press, 1975).

over the rich nations; and (iii) the international community should use these powers to equalize the access of the poor nations to short-term credit, long-term development finance, international markets and trading infrastructure, and opportunities for increased productivity.

In this scheme of things, the establishment of an International Central Bank is the centerpiece. Unless the international community develops its own independent sources of finance and unless it is free from a financial veto from its richer members, its freedom of action is going to remain strictly limited. At the national level, the governments acquired their real economic power with the evolution of taxation systems and establishment of central banks. At the international level, a similar evolution is necessary. The most promising element in such an evolution is the establishment of an international central bank which could provide both short- and long-term finance to the developing countries and support new initiatives in the field of international trade and food production. If the Third World must focus its efforts on one major issue, as indeed it must, this is the issue it should take up.

We have proceeded in this chapter on the assumption—which may well prove to be too idealistic—that it would be possible to restructure the existing international institutions and to set up new ones through a peaceful, orderly dialogue. There are few examples in history where this has happened. If it comes to pass in our age and in this era, it would be a rare tribute to the wisdom and foresight of the present generation of mankind and to the great distance it has already traveled down the tortuous road of history.

·11· A NEW FRAMEWORK FOR INTERNATIONAL RESOURCE TRANSFERS

As DISCUSSED IN THE LAST CHAPTER, an important element in the debate on a new international economic order is the urgent need to develop a new framework for orderly resource transfers from the rich to the poor nations. Such a framework should be based on some internationally accepted needs of the poor rather than on the uncertain generosity of the rich. As was the case in the evolution of progressive national orders, provision of equality of opportunity to the poor nations should come to be regarded not as a token of "charity" but as a matter of right. While the last chapter discussed the ultimate objectives, this chapter explores some specific, interim solutions.

CHARACTERISTICS OF THE PRESENT "AID" ORDER

Before searching for a new basis for international resource transfers, it is useful to sketch out some of the implicit assumptions of the present order and what is wrong with them.

To begin with, the present resource transfers from the rich to the poor nations are totally voluntary, dependent only on the fluctuating political will of the rich nations. The volume and terms of most assistance are dictated by short-term decisions, with no longer-term perspective or assurances. As such, there is no agreed basis for resource transfers. "Aid" is given for a variety of reasons, including cold war considerations, international leadership, political impact, special relationships with former colonies, domestic and international economic interests, moral considerations—the relative weight of these factors changing greatly over time with each country. As an illustration, about 25 percent of total resource transfers at present are still governed by "special relationships" with a few former colonies (constituting only 3 percent of the total population of the developing world) [1] rather than by the relative poverty or growth needs of the developing countries.

The only international deal which presently exists on resource transfers is enshrined in the acceptance by the rich nations of a target of 1 percent of GNP, with 0.7 percent as Official Development Assistance (ODA) on fairly concessional terms. However, the acceptance of this target by the rich nations was grudgingly slow (with many nations still not officially subscribing to this target or, as with the United States, not having agreed to a date by which this target should be met). The actual performance has been most disappointing: official development assistance from 17 DAC countries actually declined from 0.52 percent of GNP in 1960 to 0.32 percent in 1975 and, according to some recent World Bank projections, is expected to decline further to 0.28 percent by 1980, given the present trends (see Table 7 in the Statistical Appendix).[2]

So far, international resource transfers have been regarded primarily as the responsibility of the Western industrialized nations. Centrally planned economies have given little aid bilaterally and have not participated in any major multilateral channels of assistance. The OPEC member countries are recent arrivals on the scene and have already started transferring significant amounts—an estimated $11 billion of total commitments in 1974 or over 5 percent of their combined GNP, though the disbursements are naturally slower and were about 2 percent of

---

[1] See Table 9 in the Statistical Appendix.

[2] According to the Resolution agreed at the seventh Special Session of the United Nations, the developed countries have been urged to implement the target of 0.7 percent by 1980. However, there were several reservations made by the developed countries, including the United States, Germany, and the United Kingdom which are seriously behind in their own implementation.

their GNP in 1974 (see Table 8 in the Statistical Appendix). They are, however, not yet systematically integrated into the overall framework of international resource transfers.

Sufficient attention has not been paid in the past to the terms of international assistance or to the concept of *net* transfer of resources. As a result, the developing countries have accumulated by now a total financial debt of over $120 billion, so that annual debt servicing is already taking away about half of the new assistance that the Third World receives (see Table 11 in the Statistical Appendix).

While foreign assistance has played an important role in the development of some countries at certain times, the overall contribution of this kind of resource transfer to the level and character of economic development remains shrouded in controversy. There have been repeated accusations by the developing countries that foreign assistance has at times been given in such a way as to undermine national resolve, create conflicts with national priorities, transfer irrelevant technologies, education systems and development concepts, tie the recipient down to the source of assistance at a prohibitive cost, promote the interests of a privileged minority in the recipient country rather than those of the vast majority. The critics of aid in the developed countries allege that aid is largely wasted, that it goes to support repressive governments (or even worse in their judgment, experiments in socialism), and that it discourages indigenous efforts to save and invest. These controversies are not an invariable guide to the truth in each case, but they generally illustrate how unhappy the recipients are with the present pattern of assistance, how thankless the donors regard their current task to be, and how urgent it is to get a new start.

SEARCH FOR A NEW FRAMEWORK

There must, therefore, be a search for a new framework for international resource transfers as an essential part of the effort to establish a new international economic order. Such a framework can only be negotiated over time, in a step-by-step approach, carefully balancing the interests and sensitivities of both donors and recipients.[3]

As discussed in chapter 10, the most important principle underlying a new framework must be a clear recognition by the international community that the resource transfers from the rich to the poor nations cannot continue to remain as totally voluntary acts of periodic generosity: an element of automaticity must be built into such resource transfers. Unless this is done, the evolution of the international economic order will continue to lag behind the evolution of progressive national orders by at least half a century and the pressure for the acceptance of the principle of automaticity will continue in one form or another. This does not mean, of course, that the world is yet ready, or need embrace, the concept of international taxation in its entirety, but at least a serious effort must begin to introduce some of the elements of automaticity in resource transfer through a variety of devices. As discussed in the last chapter, these devices can include: (i) a larger share of the liquidity created by the International Monetary Fund (whether through the Special Drawing Rights or through gold sales) can be made available for development either through the international financial institutions or directly to the developing countries; (ii) certain sources of international financing can be developed—such as a tax on nonrenewable resources, a tax on international pollutants, a tax on multinational corporation activities, rebates to country of origin of taxes collected on the earnings of trained immigrants from the developing countries, taxes on or royalties from commercial activities arising out of international commons, e.g., ocean beds, outer space, the Antarctic region; and various proposals for taxing international civil servants, consumer durables, and armament spending; (iii) if the rich industrialized nations are unwilling to tax themselves, others can collect and distribute these tax proceeds on the basis of what the rich nations con-

---

[3] A logical forum for such negotiations could well be the Joint Bank–Fund Development Committee established in 1974, but only after it has been restructured to reflect a greater voice for the Third World (including OPEC) and after it has been given a fresh mandate to consider the above-mentioned issues and to complete its report in a specified period of time.

sume—e.g., even a one dollar per barrel "development levy" by the OPEC can create a development pool of over $10 billion a year.

The devices can be many: the more difficult aspect is to convince the rich nations that a more automatic system of international resource transfers will be in their own interest in the longer run as it will greatly reduce the present conflicts and endless controversies over the quantum and form of "aid" between the rich and the poor nations.

The focus of international assistance must shift to the poorest countries and, within them, to the poorest segments of the population. These are generally the countries below $200 per capita income, mostly in South Asia and the sub-Saharan Africa, containing over one billion of the poorest people in the world. For higher income developing countries, what is important is their access to international capital market and expanding trade opportunities, not greater concessional assistance. If international assistance is so redirected, it is also essential that it be in the form of grants, without creating a reverse obligation of mounting debt service liability at a low level of poverty. Even the thought of the poorest sections of society repaying huge debts to the richest sections under the eyes of a benign government would be found abhorrent at the national level, but it is still tolerated at the international level because of the lamentable slow growth of our perceptions as an international community.

It would also be logical to link international assistance to national programs aimed at satisfying basic human needs, however treacherous the concept may prove to be in actual practice. This would give both a focus and direction to international assistance effort and make it a limited period affair till some of the worst manifestations of poverty—malnutrition, illiteracy, and squalid living conditions—are overcome, both through the international effort and the expanding ability of the national governments to launch a direct attack on mass poverty. These programs, however, should not be based on the concept of a simple income transfer to the poor—which would create permanent dependence—but on increasing the productivity of the poor and integrating them into the economic system. It is difficult to estimate how much investment it may take to bring the majority of mankind to the level of minimum human needs: much conceptual and empirical work still needs to be done.[4] But a very rough estimate shows that the target of providing basic minimum needs to all mankind over the next ten years may require a total investment of about $125 billion in 1974 prices (e.g., food and nutrition $42 billion, education $25 billion, rural and urban water supply $28 billion, urban housing $16 billion, urban transport $8 billion, population and health programs $6 billion).[5] Of course, these estimates will vary considerably depending on the style of development pursued by various countries. However, the merits of articulating such a target for removal of the worst manifestations of poverty are that it can be easily understood by the public (and, it is hoped, by the politicians) in the rich nations; it can be the basis of a shared effort between the national governments and the international community; it provides an allocative formula for concessional assistance; and it establishes a specific time period over which the task should be accomplished.

International assistance, on a more automatic and purely grant basis, should be accepted by the international community as a transitional arrangement only, to be terminated as soon as some of the worst manifestations of poverty are removed and institutional reforms are carried out to establish the main elements of the new international economic order, as discussed in the last chapter. This is necessary because the most essential element in the new international economic order is not so much the redistribution of past incomes and wealth as the distribution of future growth opportunities and because the main responsibility for developing their societies must be assumed by the

---

[4] Some work is currently getting organized in the Dag Hammarskjöld Foundation and the World Bank. The idea was originally initiated by Maurice Strong, Executive Director of the United Nations Environment Program (UNEP).

[5] See Table 5 in the Statistical Appendix.

Third World nations themselves. If each developing country is to shape its own pattern of development and its own life style, international assistance can be regarded only as a temporary supplement to domestic efforts, not a permanent crutch.

One of the key questions is who should provide this assistance and how the burdens should be shared. Obviously, the major part of the resource transfers should come from the richest nations, as measured by their per capita income. The problem for the next few years, however, is going to be that the rich industrialized nations—with an average per capita income of about $4,700 in 1975 for DAC members—may experience balance-of-payments difficulties while most of the liquid OPEC countries (other than Saudi Arabia, Kuwait, Libya, Qatar, and the United Arab Emirates, with an average per capita income of about $4,000) are hardly rich enough to provide large subsidy funds since their average per capita income is still less than $500. An obvious solution would be to combine the volume of lending from the OPEC with the availability of subsidy funds from the industrialized countries and from the richest OPEC nations. But such a formula is likely to provide resources at intermediate terms, with about 50 to 60 percent grant element, rather than the pure grants recommended above. However, this "second best" solution may be the only course available for the next few years unless some of the automatic mechanisms suggested earlier come into play.[6]

An effort should also be made to create a framework within which the richer socialist countries start playing a more substantial role in resource transfers than their present limited contribution. However, the basic decision and initiative on this is largely up to the socialist bloc itself.

---

[6] An interim Third Window facility in the World Bank has been established in July 1975, on somewhat similar principles. The World Bank will use the guarantee backing of mainly the industrialized nations to raise funds in the international capital market at 8 to 8.5 percent interest rate and subsidize them down to 4.5 percent (with seven years grace and thirty years repayment period) by raising subsidy funds from some of the OPEC members and the industrialized countries.

If the framework of international resource transfers is to be restructured along the lines indicated above, it is a logical corollary that multilateral channels should be used increasingly for directing this assistance in preference to bilateral channels. This will be consistent with greater automaticity in resource transfers, allocations based on poverty and need rather than on special relationships, and a more orderly system of burden-sharing for international resource transfers. Greater reliance on multilateral channels will also place a major responsibility on international financial institutions to accept such reforms as are essential to their efficient and equitable working. This is discussed later in this chapter.

In order to evolve a new framework of international assistance, it is also important to wipe the slate clean at least in two directions. First, arrangements must be made to provide a negotiating forum for an orderly settlement of past debts. This can be done by organizing a conference of principal creditors and debtors to discuss and agree on the principles for a major settlement to ease past burdens, particularly for the poorest countries. Second, since the concessions, leases, and contracts negotiated by the developing countries with the multinational corporations in the past often reflect their unequal bargaining strength, and since there is an environment of constant agitation and uncertainty surrounding foreign private investment at present, a mechanism should be provided to permit an orderly renegotiation of past contracts within a specified period of time under some international supervision. A United Nations report,[7] commissioned in 1974, provides a sensible framework within which a new code of conduct for both the multinationals and the developing countries should be negotiated and arrangements provided for international monitoring of agreements.

Let us be realistic. It is not going to be easy to negotiate all the above principles simultaneously or to implement them immediately. Moreover, a concrete blueprint for the reform of the

---

[7] U.N., Report of the Group of Eminent Persons to the Secretary-General, *The Impact of Multinational Corporations on Development and on International Relations* (New York, 1974).

present system can only emerge out of hard, tough bargaining which seeks to balance various conflicting interests. An "idealized" framework should include most of the principles mentioned above; a more practical framework will naturally have to settle for many compromises and "second best" solutions, at least in the short run.

IMPLICATIONS FOR THE WORLD BANK

Any new framework for international resource transfers that is negotiated will have major implications for the future of the international financial institutions, particularly for the World Bank, since it is the premier institution at present for the channeling of assistance to the developing countries. In fact, the primacy of the role of the World Bank in the coming decades will depend largely on how well and how quickly it can adjust to the fast changing situation and needs of the developing countries.

Before outlining the nature of the changes that the World Bank will have to face and accept, it would be useful to review very briefly the underlying philosophy of this institution since its inception in 1946. The World Bank started out primarily as a United States–sponsored effort for the reconstruction of Europe and Japan, not as an international effort to channel assistance to the developing countries.[8] As late as 1964, about one third of its disbursements were still to those developed countries which are no longer included in its lending program now (the so-called "past borrowers"). Over the last three decades, it has

---

[8] Note, for instance, the opening remarks of Lord Keynes at the first meeting of the Bretton Woods Commission on the World Bank: "It is likely, in my judgement, that the field of reconstruction from the consequences of war will mainly occupy the proposed Bank in its early days. But as soon as possible, and with increasing emphasis as time goes on, there is a *second* primary duty laid upon it, namely to develop the resources and productive capacity of the world, with special reference to the less developed countries." (Italics supplied; quoted in Edward S. Mason and Robert E. Asher, *The World Bank since Bretton Woods* (Washington, D.C.: The Brookings Institution, 1973.)

shown considerable dynamism and brilliant improvisations in the light of changing situations. At first, it became an intermediary (through the instrument of the IBRD lending) between the capital markets of the world and the more creditworthy among the developing countries which were still unable to raise a sufficient amount of capital on reasonable terms under their own guarantee. As debt burdens increased in the poorest countries, the World Bank established a "soft" window (International Development Assistance or IDA) in 1960 to provide long-term concessional resources to this group of countries (at 0.75 percent commitment charge for repayment periods of fifty years with ten years grace period). The Bank's sectoral priorities also changed with the changing requirements of its recipients. While it had provided mainly equipment and consultants for infrastructure projects in the earlier phase, it is promoting a direct attack on mass poverty in the last five years.[9] For instance, about two thirds of its total lending went to transport, power, and communications during 1964–68, but a similar proportion now goes into rural development, industry, education, water supply, nutrition, and population projects. It has increasingly phased out higher income developing countries above $1,000 per capita income and focused its attention on the very poorest countries below $200 per capita, subject only to the limitations of the total availability of concessional resources. Over 90 percent of the IDA resources are now directed to countries below $200 per capita income. Thus, the essential vitality of the World Bank has been reflected in its ability to adapt and improvise as the situation demanded.

The need to adapt will be much greater in the future. The general direction of change is already clear from the foregoing discussion and can be indicated rather briefly.

First, in order to become a truly international institution and to shed its image of a Western club, the World Bank must aim at universality of membership, both among its potential contributors and among its recipients. Some of the original rules of

[9] World Bank, *The Assault on World Poverty,* Washington, D.C., 1975.

the game, which make it difficult for new members to join the club, may therefore have to be changed. For instance, if the IBRD capital base is expanded at present, the existing members have the first right to preempt the additional capital subscriptions so that new members can be inducted or relative quotas changed only with the tacit permission of the existing members. Similarly, the voting rights in the IDA are based on cumulative contributions since its inception in 1960 so that if the OPEC, for instance, is willing to contribute even 50 percent to the next replenishment of IDA, it will obtain only about 10 percent of the total voting rights, which is not likely to encourage its participation unless the formula is revised. Again, a stumbling block in the way of the socialist countries in seeking membership in the World Bank has been the requirement that they must become members of the International Monetary Fund beforehand, which they have been rather reluctant to do and which is totally unnecessary for them to play their role in international resource transfers. The main point is that while it was inescapable that the World Bank should be conceived primarily as a Western club at the time of the Bretton Woods conference, it must now find ways of becoming truly international and actively negotiate the participation of richer OPEC and socialist countries in its affairs. In the emerging climate, universality of membership becomes one of the most important principles to pursue in the future evolution of the World Bank Group.

Second, new formulas must be found for the restructuring of voting rights in the World Bank (including IDA). While voting rights have been revised over time, they still essentially represent the balance of economic, financial, and political power which prevailed in the 1940s. For instance, the United Kingdom continues to have twice the voting power of Germany and nearly three times that of Japan; Belgium and the Netherlands together have more voting strength than the OPEC member countries combined; Iran has a lower voting power than India, and Pakistan nearly twice as much as Saudi Arabia, despite the fact that both India and Pakistan are by now aid recipients from Iran and Saudi Arabia. Overall, the developing countries (excluding OPEC) have only 31 percent of the total voting power. It is important, therefore, to carry out a general and thoroughgoing review of the voting power structure which replaces the historical past with current realities so that the OPEC members can be persuaded to play a larger role through existing financial institutions, the developing countries get an increased voice in international financial and development decisions, and the established lenders continue to have an important, though necessarily reduced, role in the running of the institution. It is not necessary to start out with preconceived formulas; what is really needed is to set out with a clear recognition of the need for change and to provide appropriate negotiating forums where acceptable formulas can be hammered out.

In this context, it is also important that the developing countries adjust their own thinking about their future role in the running of international financial institutions. There has been, at times, a demand for the U.N.-type pattern ("one state, one vote") to prevail in the Bretton Woods institutions as well. This is totally unrealistic. No lender is ever likely to put his money into an institution over whose lending policies he cannot exercise a reasonable control. If complete democratization of the financial institutions is regarded as an absolute objective, the institutions are hardly likely to attract significant financial contributions from potential donors. This has, in fact, been the fate of some U.N.-sponsored financial institutions. Moreover, an insistence on this kind of pattern of control is inconsistent with the developing countries' own policies on the domestic front. Whenever public development finance companies are set up within the developing countries, the normal pattern is for the governments to assume at least 51 percent of the control on the board of directors. And this is the case when the governments generally enjoy tremendous power to influence the running of these companies without even requiring a formal presence on their boards. The developing countries cannot show less responsibility just because it is somebody else's money and when they are the recipients, not the contributors, to international financial institutions.

An ideal pattern for the control of these international financial institutions would imply that the donor members should have the strong capability of influencing the disposal of their funds (which would specifically mean a voting right somewhat higher than 50 percent) and the recipient countries should have at least the probability, if not the certainty, of influencing the decisions of these institutions (which would argue for voting rights somewhat lower than 50 percent). The area of negotiation, therefore, lies somewhere between 40 to 50 percent voting rights for the recipient developing countries as against the current proportion of about 30 percent in the World Bank.[10] The real effort must be to evolve a new pattern somewhere in between the U.N.'s existing pattern of democracy without finance and the Bretton Woods' existing pattern of finance without democracy.

There is one important consideration, however, which could completely change the perspective on what has been said above. If the sources of funding of the World Bank Group change significantly and become more automatic, as discussed in chapter 10 and below, the pattern of international control over this institution has to be thoroughly re-examined. For instance, if the resources are derived from international taxation or royalties from the exploitation of ocean beds, there will be a powerful argument for a more broad-based control of the World Bank by the entire international community.

Third, there is a strong case for imparting more automaticity to the fund-raising efforts of the multilateral institutions like the World Bank. This is needed in order to free the World Bank increasingly from bilateral pressures and to enable it to play a truly multilateral role in the new international economic order. Thus, efforts must be made to link at least a part of the future IDA replenishments with the creation of an international currency (e.g., Special Drawing Rights), or with gold sales, or with some other sources of international taxation, as mentioned

[10] This is excluding some countries like Spain, Greece, Portugal, etc., which are included in the category of developing countries in the definition of the World Bank.

previously. For the IBRD, it would be logical that, instead of seeking the concerned government's permission before floating its bonds, it should have an automatic right to borrow in any capital market where the country has been enjoying an overall balance of payments surplus for a certain period. Such an automatic access to the international capital markets will enhance the role of the World Bank as an intermediary between the surplus markets and the developing countries and will, in fact, make Bank borrowings a part of the corrective mechanism for redressing persistent balance-of-payments surpluses.

Fourth, while the World Bank has shown considerable vitality and imagination in deepening and enlarging its activities in regard to its lending program (for instance, by turning its attention to productive programs for the lowest 40 percent of the population), it has not shown the same vitality in widening the range of its services (for example, buffer stock financing, export credit financing, use of its guarantee powers, etc.). The latter aspects are likely to become even more crucial in the 1970s as trade expansion comes to be recognized as an increasingly important supplement to resource transfers to provide the needed foreign exchange for the accelerated development of the developing countries.[11]

Fifth, though the IBRD and the IDA have served admirably as mechanisms for channeling assistance to the developing countries, it is becoming increasingly necessary to evolve a new mechanism for obtaining and directing assistance at terms intermediate between the IBRD and the IDA. The introduction of a "Third Window" in July 1975 (as mentioned above) was, therefore, a pragmatic and inevitable response to the changing circumstances. While the Third Window facility has been introduced essentially as an interim measure for fiscal year 1976, there can hardly be any doubt about the longer-term need for this type of assistance and about the considerable room for maneuver that it provides to the World Bank Group in blending

[11] Hollis B. Chenery, "Approaches to Development Finance," in Jan Pronk, ed., *Report on the Symposium on a New International Economic Order,* The Hague, May 22–24, 1975.

its assistance to a wide variety of developing countries which have vastly different capital needs and degrees of creditworthiness.

Finally, at some stage, consideration must also be given to a general review of the Articles of the World Bank which were conceived and drafted in the environment of the 1940s. This is becoming necessary as the basic economic situation of the developing countries is undergoing a fairly rapid change, calling for a much greater measure of flexibility in the World Bank operations. For instance, the original Articles expected, quite rightly at that time, that the bulk of the World Bank assistance would be in the form of projects and in foreign exchange, so that restrictions were built into the rules of the game against program lending and local cost financing. The World Bank has improvised pragmatically in its actual operations to get around these restrictions as the need arose; still the long shadow of the Articles is always there and the needed flexibility is often missing. Program lending and local cost financing still have to be justified, on a case-by-case basis, as deviations from a normal trend which is bound to influence the form and character of lending. One can find other instances of such restrictions in the original conception of the role of the World Bank: for example, procurement of goods and services restricted only to Bank members; extremely limited preference margin to developing countries for procurement within their own country; a strict financial rate of return criterion, etc. The Bank practice has moved considerably, though not sufficiently, away from some of these restrictive aspects of its Articles and its past tradition. But the Articles themselves may have to be reviewed, not only to bring them in conformity with the actual practice but to build into them enough flexibility to accommodate the needs of the 1970s and the fast changing role of the World Bank in the future.

We have discussed in this chapter the major considerations for rethinking the role of international resource transfers and for designing the institutional changes which suit the future needs of the Third World. This is a field in which the imagination can often run wild. The idealists would regard the establishment of a World Treasury as a logical evolution from the experience with national treasuries.[12] The pessimists may consider that even the present level of international resource transfers is not going to survive the growing concern of the rich nations with their own economic problems. In the immediate future, it would be the heart of realism to steer a middle course between such extremes and to build up, brick by brick, a new edifice for international cooperation. The proposals in this chapter offer only some of these bricks. The outcome of the present dialogue on the nature and form of resource transfers from the rich to the poor nations will obviously depend, in the last analysis, on the political vision and the enlightened self-interest of the entire international community. But let us face it. Political vision is one of the most scarce commodities in the world today. We can only hope it still exists.

[12] Jan Tinbergen, *Reviewing the International Order* (Rotterdam: Interim Report for the Club of Rome, June 1975).

STATISTICAL APPENDIX

TABLES

TABLE 1

Profile of the Rich and the Poor Nations

(*Data for 1974; values in 1974 U.S. Dollars*)

Demographic	Rich Nations [a]	OPEC [b]	Poor Nations [c]	World
1. Population (in billions)	1.1	.1	2.8	4.0
2. Percentage of total world population	27.5	2.5	70.0	100.0
3. Birth rate (per thousand)	17	n.a.	37	31
4. Death rate (per thousand)	9	n.a.	14	13
5. Infant mortality (per thousand)	25	n.a.	125	75
6. Life expectancy (years)	71	n.a.	52	55
Economic				
7. GNP ($ billion)	4,991	165	632	5,788
8. Percentage of total world GNP	86.2	2.9	10.9	100.0
9. GNP growth rate (1970–74)	3.6	7.7	5.5	4.5
10. Per capita income (1974 $)	4,537	1,650	226	1,447
11. Investment ($ billion)	1,098	31	114	1,243
12. Per capita investment ($)	100	31	4	31
13. Investment as a % of GNP	22.0	18.8	18.0	21.5
14. Exports [d] ($ billion)	808	101	134	1,043
15. Percentage of total world exports	77.5	9.7	12.8	100.0
Social				
16. Literate population (in millions)	7.58	18	746	1,522
17. Percentage of population	68.9	18.0	26.6	38.0
18. Malnourished population (in millions)	10	nil	900	910
19. Percentage of population	0.9	nil	32.1	22.8
20. Poorest population in millions below $100 per capita	nil	nil	942	942
21. Percentage of population	nil	nil	33.6	23.6

SOURCE: World Bank, *Prospects for Developing Countries, 1976–1980,* July 1975; World Bank, *World Economic Indicators,* July 1975; and United Nations, *World Population Prospects for 1970–2000,* as assessed in 1973.

[a] Includes Western Europe, socialist Europe, N. America, Oceania, and Japan.

[b] Algeria, Iran, Iraq, Kuwait, Libya, Qatar, Saudi Arabia, United Arab Emirates, Venezuela. Ecuador, Gabon, Indonesia, and Nigeria are excluded.

[c] Includes countries of the Third World and China but excludes OPEC members (except Indonesia and Nigeria).

[d] Excludes non-factor services.

Key Economic Indicators for the Third World

Asia	1974 Population (000 omitted)	Per Capita Income (1974 $)	GNP growth rate (1970–73)	Gross domestic investment as a % of 1973 GDP	Literacy rate (% of adults) (1972)
India	595,586	129	1.9	16.4	29
Indonesia	131,010	192	8.2	17.9	56
Bangladesh	76,200	88	−4.5	11.6	23
Pakistan	68,210	163	2.4	14.2	39
Philippines	41,300	327	6.7	19.8	72
Thailand	41,020	266	5.9	24.1	82
Turkey	38,854	614	8.7	19.5	92
Korea, Rep. of	33,459	433	11.1	26.0	n.a.
Iran	32,868	1,360	12.6	19.5	5
Burma	30,158	103	2.4	10.7	n.a.
Viet Nam, Rep. of	20,390	188	1.8	11.2	n.a.
Afghanistan	18,656	86	4.1	5.6 [a]	n.a.
China, Rep. of	15,700	637	11.7	25.2	82
Sri Lanka	13,393	130	1.7	17.2	n.a.
Nepal	12,320	96	1.3	n.a.	n.a.
Malaysia	12,000	564	6.9	18.1	60
Iraq	10,697	1,206	13.1	10.5	26
Khmer Rep.	7,725	111	−5.5 [b]	n.a.	n.a.
Syria	7,164	444	6.5	20.0 [c]	n.a.
Saudi Arabia	6,101	5,770	18.9	12.0	n.a.
Yemen AR	6,060 [a]	90 [a]	n.a.	n.a.	10
Hong Kong	4,249	1,183	7.9	26.5	n.a.
Laos	3,250	129	2.2	n.a.	n.a.
Lebanon	3,057	944	8.6	21.7	86
Papua New Guinea	2,650	362	8.0	27.7	n.a.
Jordan	2,620	332	1.2	26.5	59
Singapore	2,219	1,699	12.1	27.1	75
Yemen PDR	1,510 [a]	100 [a]	n.a.	n.a.	10
Kuwait	900	13,667	6.0	7.0	n.a.
Oman	644	748	−3.0	27.5	20
Fiji	560	627	6.9	25.2	n.a.
UAE	340	22,059	n.a.	n.a.	n.a.
Bahrain	245	1,218	n.a.	n.a.	n.a.
Qatar	190	10,526	24.0	n.a.	n.a.
Sub-Total	1,241,305	278		18.9	
Yugoslavia	21,130	1,179	9.2	25.3	n.a.
China, Peoples Rep. of [d]	786,440 [a]	170 [a]	n.a.	n.a.	n.a.
Sub-Total	2,048,875	246	n.a.	18.9	n.a.

SOURCES: World Bank Atlas estimates; Basic Economic Data Sheet (World Tables, Part I); Comparative Economic Data Tables (World Tables, Part II); Comparative Education Indicators, IBRD.

[a] Data for 1972   [c] Fixed investment only
[b] Growth rate 1970–72   [d] Data for 1973

TABLE 2 (continued)

Key Economic Indicators for the Third World

Africa	1974 Population (000 omitted)	Per Capita Income (1974 $)	GNP growth rate (1970–73)	Gross domestic investment as a % of 1973 GDP	Literacy rate (% of adults) (1972)
Nigeria	75,417	240	10.8	20.4	n.a.
Egypt AR	36,350	286	3.3	12.2	n.a.
Ethiopia	27,240	95	4.3	14.2	7
Zaire	20,135	123	4.9	21.9	13
Sudan	17,528	141	3.2	10.8	15
Morocco	16,880	330	4.3	14.8	20
Algeria	15,395	760	7.1	38.5	25
Tanzania	14,351	137	4.6	23.5	49
Kenya	12,910	199	6.3	25.4	35
Uganda	11,186	151	0.6	9.9	25
Ghana	9,560	345	4.1	6.1 [a]	n.a.
Mozambique	7,962 [a]	300	n.a.	13.4 [a]	n.a.
Malagasy Rep.	7,800	165	−1.2	13.0	n.a.
Cameroon	6,330	237	2.5	14.7	n.a.
Upper Volta	5,834	72	−0.3	13.9	5
Ivory Coast	5,762	424	6.1	21.8	n.a.
Tunisia	5,640	488	11.7	22.6	n.a.
Mali	5,477	80	2.0	18.5	10
Guinea	5,390	105	3.9	21.8	n.a.
Malawi	4,958	126	11.5	19.9	n.a.
Zambia	4,646 [d]	382	1.9	17.5	43
Niger	4,480	91	−5.5	7.2	n.a.
Senegal	4,160	313	2.6	18.7	10
Chad	3,952	82	−4.0	13.8	7
Rwanda	3,904 [a]	80	1.8	9.7	23
Burundi	3,655	103	2.5	4.0	n.a.
Somalia	3,118	96	5.9	27.4	5
Dahomey	3,027	120	2.0	24.6	11
Sierra Leone	2,853	207	−2.3	14.5	n.a.
Libya	2,300	4,956	3.1	29.6	n.a.
Togo	2,155	198	2.3	17.3	n.a.
CAR	1,748	206	1.4	19.7	n.a.
Liberia	1,500	361	3.9	13.9	15
Mauritania	1,290	215	2.5	14.0	10
Congo	1,199 [d]	338	2.7	31.3	50
Lesotho	996	151	n.a.	22.9	40
Mauritius	871	410	9.6	25.2	80
Botswana	653	219	12.8	56.9	n.a.
Gabon	528	1,138	9.5	28.2	n.a.
Gambia, The	506	152	0.9	19.3	n.a.
Swaziland	478	400	8.0	18.9	28
Equatorial Guinea	308 [a]	234	n.a.	n.a.	n.a.
Sub-Total	360,432	266	n.a.	19.7	n.a.

TABLE 2 (*continued*)

Key Economic Indicators for the Third World

Latin America	1974 Population (000 omitted)	Per Capita Income (1974 $)	GNP growth rate (1970–73)	Gross domestic investment as a % of 1973 GDP	Literacy rate (% of adults) (1972)
Brazil	103,981	850	11.1	20.0	67
Mexico	58,009	843	6.0	20.9	76
Argentina	24,646	1,637	4.4	19.9	n.a.
Colombia	24,538	516	7.0	19.7	74
Peru	14,952	665	6.2	15.0	72
Venezuela	11,701	2,299	5.1	28.4	81
Chile	10,404	1,049	1.4	16.5	n.a.
Ecuador	6,952	458	7.4	18.5	69
Bolivia	5,470	256	6.8	14.3	n.a.
Guatemala	5,284	595	7.6	14.5	n.a.
Dominican Rep.	4,561	608	10.5	19.6	51
Haiti	4,524	136	n.a.	6.2 [a]	n.a.
El Salvador	3,926	418	4.2	17.0	58
Uruguay	3,031	861	−0.1	9.8	n.a.
Honduras	2,864	362	5.0	18.0	52
Paraguay	2,479	410	5.8	19.0	79
Nicaragua	2,022	631	4.1	18.3	n.a.
Jamaica	1,944	1,065	4.3	23.7	n.a.
Costa Rica	1,919	792	5.1	25.9	89
Panama	1,619	1,038	7.4	29.9	n.a.
Trinidad & Tobago	1,069	1,530	4.7	28.6	90
Guyana	791	475	1.1	24.6	83
Surinam	406	924	n.a.	n.a.	n.a.
Barbados	241	967	0.9	20.1	n.a.
Sub-Total	297,333	888	n.a.	20.3	n.a.
Grand Total	2,706,640	319	n.a.	n.a.	n.a.

SOURCES: World Bank Atlas estimates; Basic Economic Data Sheet (World Tables, Part I); Comparative Economic Data Tables (World Tables, Part II); Comparative Education Indicators, IBRD.

[a] Data for 1972   [c] Fixed investment only
[b] Growth rate 1970–72   [d] Data for 1973

TABLE 3
Key Economic Indicators for the OPEC Members [a] (*Data for 1974; values in 1974 U.S. Dollars*)

Country	Population (million)	Total GNP ($ million)	Per Capita GNP ($)	Annual Petroleum Exports ($ million)	Per Capita Petroleum Reserves [b] (billion barrels)	Foreign Exchange Reserves [c] ($ billion)
a) *Richest* (above $2,500)						
United Arab Emirates	.34	7,500	22,059	6,400	99,706	0.4 [d]
Kuwait	.90	12,300	13,667	9,400	90,556	1
Qatar	.19	2,000	10,526	2,000	31,579	1 [d]
Saudi Arabia	6	35,200	5,770	30,400	28,377	14
Libya	2	11,400	4,956	7,200	11,565	4
Subtotal	9.43 (3)	68,400 (33)	7,253	55,400 (49)	32,665	20.4 (42)
b) *Middle Income* ($750–$2,500)						
Venezuela	12	26,900	2,299	10,900	1,282	7
Iran	33	44,700	1,360	20,600	2,012	8
Iraq	11	12,900	1,206	7,400	3,271	3
Algeria	15	11,700	760	4,300	500	2
Subtotal	71 (25)	96,200 (46)	1,355	43,200 (38)	1,752	20 (42)
c) *Poor* (below $250)						
Nigeria	75	18,100	240	9,400	277	6
Indonesia	131	25,100	192	5,000	114	1.5
Subtotal	206 (72)	43,200 (21)	210	14,400 (13)	174	7.5 (16)
Grand Total	286 (100)	207,800 (100)	727	113,000 (100)	1,676	47.9 (100)

SOURCE: Background material from World Bank Report on *Prospects for Developing Countries, 1976–1980*, July 1975; IMF, *International Financial Statistics*, September 1975.

NOTE: Figures in parentheses correspond to percentage distributions.
[a] Excludes Ecuador and Gabon.   [c] End of period 1974.
[b] Reserves at January 1975.   [d] IMF Regional Office estimate, end 1974.

TABLE 4

Third World's Share in the World's Natural Resources
(*Data for 1973; in thousand metric tons*)

Commodity	Third World	Total World	Third World's Share (percent)
Cocoa	1,355	1,355	100.0
Rubber	3,449	3,452	99.9
Coffee	4,186	4,193	99.8
Hard fibers	671	681	98.5
Jute	2,404	2,712	88.7
Tin	166	220	75.5
Tea	1,057	1,535	68.8
Rice	179,667	320,714	56.0
Bauxite	35,152	73,134	48.1
Cotton	5,840	13,080	44.6
Copper	2,833	7,533	37.6
Phosphate	32,345	97,199	33.3
Iron ore	211,500	835,900	25.3
Coarse grains (maize)	69,597	311,780	22.3
Wheat	71,786	377,017	19.0

SOURCES: The source for agricultural commodities is the FAO Production Yearbook, 1973, Vol. 27.

Bauxite: Metallgesellschaft A.G. Frankfurt/M, 1974, *Metal Statistics, 1963–1973.*

Phosphate: *ISMA* (International Superphosphate Manufacturers Association) publication 1974.

Tin: International Tin Council, *Statistical Tin Yearbook,* 1974.

Iron Ore: World Bank, *Price Forecasts for Major Primary Commodities,* July 1975.

Copper: World Bureau of Metal Statistics, *World Metal Statistics,* June 1975.

TABLE 5

Investment Requirements to Meet Minimum Human Needs in the Third World

(*Target Date 1985*)

Second Development Decade Targets	Physical Target	Approximate Annual Investment Required, 1975–85 (in US $ billion)
1. Nutrition	145 million tons of food grains	4.2
2. Education		2.5
3. Housing	for 35 million families	1.6
4. Drinking water		2.8
Rural	for over 1,000 million	
Urban	for 510 million	
5. Health and family planning programs	to decrease birth rate to 34 and death rate to 12 per thousand	0.6
6. Transport		0.8
	Total	12.5

SOURCE: Various World Bank staff estimates.

TABLE 6
Developing Countries Food Grain Production and Consumption

	1973			1975			1980			1985		
	Prod.	Cons.	GAP	Prod.	Cons.	GAP	Prod.	Cons.	GAP	Prod.	Cons.	GAP
Africa	44.8	48.4	− 3.6	47.1	52.2	− 5.1	53.3	62.8	− 9.5	63.9	75.7	−11.8
Latin America	70.1	68.9	1.2	74.2	74.0	0.2	85.6	88.3	− 2.7	100.3	105.3	− 5.0
Middle East	40.0	42.1	− 2.1	42.5	45.5	− 3.0	49.5	55.4	− 5.9	57.7	67.4	− 9.7
South & Southeast Asia	201.9	225.4	−23.5	211.7	241.0	−29.3	238.4	284.8	−46.4	281.7	348.1	−66.4
Total	356.8	376.8	−28.0	375.5	412.7	−37.2	426.8	491.3	−64.5	503.6	596.3	−93.2

SOURCES: Production and Consumption data for 1973 computed from FAO sources (see FAO, *Agricultural Commodity Projections 1970–1980*, vol. 2); 1975 and 1980 data from the World Food Conference production and consumption estimates (see FAO, *The World Food Problem: Item 8 of the Provisional Agenda*); 1985 production and consumption data are based on the World Industrial Food Plan developed by FAO.

TABLE 7

Flow of Official Development Assistance from the OECD Countries [a]

(As a percentage of Gross National Product)

	(Calendar years)				1980
	1960	1965	1970	1975	(projected)
Australia	.38	.53	.59	.55	.59
Austria		.11	.07	.16	.17
Belgium	.88	.60	.46	.55	.64
Canada	.19	.19	.42	.51	.64
Denmark	.09	.13	.38	.57	.70
Finland [b]		.02	.07	.20	.28
France	1.38	.76	.66	.60	.62
Germany	.31	.40	.32	.35	.25
Italy	.22	.10	.16	.14	.12
Japan	.24	.27	.23	.23	.18
Netherlands	.31	.36	.61	.72	.77
New Zealand [c]			.23	.36	.70
Norway	.11	.16	.32	.61	.75
Sweden	.05	.19	.38	.75	.87
Switzerland	.04	.09	.15	.15	.15
United Kingdom	.56	.47	.37	.33	.30
United States	.53	.49	.31	.23	.14
Grand Totals					
ODA ($ billion— nominal prices)	4.6	5.9	6.8	12.2	20.7
ODA ($ billion— constant 1975 prices	10.3	12.3	12.6	12.2	14.0
ODA Deflator [d]	.45	.48	.54	1.00	1.48
GNP ($T—nominal prices)	.9	1.3	2.0	3.8	7.3
ODA as percentage of GNP	.52	.44	.34	.32	.28

SOURCE: Robert S. McNamara, Annual Address to the Board of Governors, Washington, D.C., September 1, 1975.

[a] Countries included are members of OECD Development Assistance Committee. Figures for 1970 and earlier years are actual data from DAC. The projections for 1975 and 1980 are based on OECD and World Bank estimates of growth of GNP, on information on budget appropriations for aid, and on aid policy statements made by governments.

[b] Finland became a member of DAC in January, 1975, though it has provided assistance since 1965.

[c] New Zealand became a member of DAC only in 1973. ODA figures for New Zealand are not available for 1960 and 1965.

[d] Includes the effect of parity changes. Figures through 1970 are based on DAC's Statistics for 1973 and Earlier Years. Projected deflators for 1974, 1975, and 1980 are the same as those for GNP.

TABLE 8

Flow of Official Development Assistance from the OPEC Members [a]

Countries		Commitments		Disbursements	
		1973	1974	1973	1974
Algeria	$ million	43	137	20	20
	% of GNP	0.6	1.2	0.3	0.2
Iran	$ million	12	1,913	1	358
	% of GNP	0.1	4.3	0	0.8
Iraq	$ million	38	486	6	118
	% of GNP	0.4	3.8	0.1	1.0
Kuwait	$ million	100	728	38	91
	% of GNP	2.2	5.9	0.8	0.7
Libya	$ million	63	693 [b]	15	40
	% of GNP	1.1	6.1	0.3	0.4
Nigeria	$ million	1	8	1	3
	% of GNP	0	0	0	0
Qatar	$ million	111	63	—	107
	% of GNP	18.5	3.2	—	5.3
Saudi Arabia	$ million	113	2,031	20	112
	% of GNP	1.1	5.8	0.2	0.3
U.A.E.	$ million	244	688	33	53
	% of GNP	10.2	9.2	1.4	0.7
Venezuela	$ million	1	831	—	45
	% of GNP	0	3.1	—	0.2
Others [c]	$ million	5	59	—	—
	% of GNP	0.4	3.1	—	—
Total ODA	$ million	731	7,637	134	947 [d]
	% of GNP	0.8	4.1	0.1	0.5

SOURCE: World Bank estimates.

[a] Bilateral and multilateral ODA excludes war relief grants, budget support and reconstruction aid. Including these grants, budget support and reconstruction aid the total ODA commitment was 5 percent and disbursement 1 percent of total GNP in 1974.

[b] Includes provisional commitment to 1975 IMF Oil Facility.

[c] Trinidad and Tobago, Oman, Bahrain.

[d] Including war relief grants, budget support and reconstruction aid, disbursements of total ODA in 1974 amounted to 2,247.8, of this 2,034.8 corresponded to bilateral ODA. Bilateral other officials flows were 258.1. Therefore, total bilateral official flows from the OPEC members amounted to 2,293 in 1974 as detailed in Table 9.

TABLE 9

Distribution of Bilateral Official Flows

From New Donors (disbursements 1974) [a]	Total (Current $ million)	Annual Per Capita Flows ($)	As a Percentage of Total
To recipients below $200 per capita			
To countries with special relations [b]	9	1.2	—
To other countries	480	0.6	21
Subtotal	489	0.6	21
To recipients above $200 per capita			
To countries with special relations [b]	1,752	15.2	77
To other countries	52	0.5	2
Subtotal	1,804	7.8	79
Total [c]	2,293	2.2	100
From DAC Members (net disbursements 1970–73) [d]			
To recipients below $200 per capita			
To countries with special relations [e]	557	24.5	43
To other countries	2,480	2.3	43
Subtotal	3,037	2.8	53
To recipients above $200 per capita			
To countries with special relations [e]	1,115	39.4	19
To other countries	1,610	2.3	28
Subtotal	2,725	3.8	47
Total	5,762	3.2	100

SOURCE: World Bank estimates and the 1974 Report of the DAC Chairman.

[a] The following are included: Algeria, Iran, Iraq, Libya, Nigeria, Qatar, Saudi Arabia, United Arab Emirates and Venezuela. Kuwait is also included in the group although its assistance program has been established for a longer period.

[b] The countries included in this group are: Algeria, Bahrain, Egypt, Iraq, Jordan, Lebanon, Morocco, Sudan, Syria, Tunisia, Yemen AR, Yemen PDR.

[c] Bilateral ODA and bilateral other official flows (OOF) including war relief grants, budget support and reconstruction aid.

[d] Annual average for 1970–73.

[e] Refers to the 39 countries defined in the 1974 Report of the DAC Chairman as having a special bilateral relationship with a DAC Member.

TABLE 10

Geographical Distribution of International Liquidity
January 1, 1970–September 30, 1974
(in U.S. $ billion)

Sources	Size	Beneficiaries	
		Developed countries	Less developed countries
1. World Gold	8.1	6.6	1.4
Physical, measured in SDR's	0.3	−0.3	0.6
Official revaluation profits	7.7	6.9	0.9
2. International Decisions	8.0	4.8	3.2
SDR allocations	11.1	8.3	2.8
IMF credits	−2.4	−2.8	0.4
BIS credits	−0.7	−0.7	—
3. National "Reserve Currency" Accumulation	115.3	115.3	—
4. Total (1 + 2 + 3)	131.4	126.8	4.6
Net Reserve Gains or Losses (−)	8.1	−43.2	51.2
Reserve Assets	131.4	76.9	54.3
Reserve Liabilities (−) = 1 + 2	−123.3	−120.1	−3.2

SOURCE: Robert Triffin, "Size, Sources and Beneficiaries of International Reserve Creation: 1970–1974," *Economics and Diplomacy,* Ministry of Foreign Affairs of Japan, March 1975.

TABLE 11

External Debt Problem of the Third World
(in U.S. $ million)

	1967	1970	1973
1. Total external public debt [a]	50,747	73,739	118,893
of which: India	7,695	9,474	12,367
Brazil	3,434	4,862	9,297
Iran	1,830	4,130	7,047
Mexico	2,675	3,803	7,031
Indonesia	2,302	3,527	6,616
Pakistan	2,907	4,536	5,151
Algeria	1,402	1,986	4,789
Korea, Rep. of	1,199	2,522	4,413
Turkey	1,766	2,684	3,778
2. Total debt servicing	4,022	6,227	11,002
3. Debt servicing as a percentage of exports	15.3	18.5	14.3
of which: India	24.9	28.0	20.1
Brazil	16.0	15.3	13.9
Iran	4.9	11.5	10.6
Mexico	23.8	25.2	25.2
Indonesia	5.3	6.6	7.1
Pakistan	16.7	24.3	16.1
Algeria	6.0	7.4	11.3
Korea, Rep. of	8.2	23.4	13.9
Turkey	16.4	22.5	10.4
4. Debt servicing as a percentage of capital inflows [b]	50.6	68.0	68.5

SOURCE: World Bank, *Annual Report 1975* and unpublished staff papers.
[a] Outstanding, including undisbursed, of 86 developing countries.
[b] Disbursements on loans, grants and grantlike loans minus amortization on loans.

TABLE 12

Fluctuations in the Primary Exports of the Third World

Commodities [a]	Unit	Mean (1950–72)	Maximum Fluctuations (1950–1972)	
			Negative	Positive
Beef				
Value	$ million	260.0	31.4	56.5
Price	¢/kg.	152.7	27.3	27.0
Volume	1000 MT	462.3	34.6	89.4
Iron Ore				
Value	$ million	523.9	20.7	96.0
Price	$/MT	16.6	20.5	38.0
Volume	1000 MT	183.2	19.2	27.2
Timber				
Value	$ million	561.2	40.5	64.9
Price	$/m³	42.2	26.3	48.5
Volume	1000 MT	—	—	—
Copper				
Value	$ million	1,297.2	36.9	45.2
Price	¢/lb.	42.4	37.4	49.5
Volume	1000 MT	1,717.1	10.6	20.2
Tin				
Value	$ million	403.7	36.2	44.6
Price	¢/lb.	129.1	26.9	44.8
Volume	1000 MT	145.9	30.8	16.2
Bananas				
Value	$ million	353.1	15.2	18.3
Price	¢/kg.	12.6	18.2	11.6
Volume	1000 MT	3,461.0	−5.5	15.9
Sugar				
Value	$ million	1,352.9	19.0	38.0
Price	¢/lb.	5.2	25.4	60.9
Volume	1000 MT	—	—	—

SOURCE: World Bank estimates.

[a] Arranged in descending order according to coefficient of variation of export earnings.

TABLE 12 (continued)

Commodities [a]	Unit	Mean (1950–72)	Maximum Fluctuations (1950–1972)	
			Negative	Positive
Rubber				
Value	$ million	1,240.3	47.5	76.2
Price	¢/lb.	29.7	37.6	68.5
Volume	1000 MT	2,409.2	15.0	.5
Cocoa				
Value	$ million	553.9	26.4	53.7
Price	¢/lb.	33.5	35.4	55.4
Volume	1000 MT	918.7	20.8	25.5
Coffee				
Value	$ million	2,231.8	12.1	23.9
Price	¢/lb.	49.9	21.9	36.9
Volume	1000 MT	2,591.0	17.8	20.4
Rice				
Value	$ million	520.8	19.9	30.7
Price	$/MT	159.1	11.6	26.1
Volume	1000 MT	4,023.0	19.9	22.5
Jute				
Value	$ million	196.0	38.0	150.8
Price	$/MT	229.0	62.4	72.9
Volume	1000 MT	932.9	27.8	34.3
Tea				
Value	$ million	548.6	16.2	40.3
Price	¢/lb.	57.1	17.6	45.2
Volume	1000 MT	512.8	16.0	19.7
Cotton				
Value	$ million	1,275.2	18.0	20.0
Price	¢/lb.	34.1	12.7	15.7
Volume	1000 MT	1,875.2	20.2	27.4

SELECTED READINGS

(A number of works, dealing with the issues on which this book focuses, were cited in the text. Some others are listed below. The following is a select bibliography, providing to the interested reader some additional material to which he can turn.)

Adelman, Irma. *Economic Growth and Social Equity in Developing Countries.* Stanford, Calif.: Stanford University Press, 1973.

Barraclough, Geoffrey, "The Great World Crisis I," *New York Review,* January 23, 1975.

Beckerman, Wilfred. *In Defence of Economic Growth.* London: Jonathan Cape, 1974.

Bendavid, Avron. *Developed and Underdeveloped: A Radical View of Constructive Relationships.* The Hague, Netherlands: Institute of Social Studies, 1973.

Bergsten, C. Fred. *Toward a New International Economic Order.* Cambridge, Mass.: Lexington Books, 1974.

Brown, Lester. *By Bread Alone.* New York: Praeger, 1974.

Brown, Seyom. *New Forces in World Politics.* Washington, D.C.: Brookings Institution, 1974.

Bundy, William P. *The World Economic Crisis.* New York: Norton, 1975.

Chenery, H. B., "Restructuring the World Economy," *Foreign Affairs,* January 1975.

Chenery, H. B. et al., *Redistribution with Growth.* London: Oxford University Press, 1974.

Demeny, Paul, "The Populations of the Underdeveloped Countries," *Scientific American,* September 1974.

Elliott, Charles. *Patterns of Poverty in the Third World.* New York: Praeger, 1975.

Evans, Douglas. *New Forces in World Politics.* Washington, D.C.: Brookings Institution, 1975.

Falk, Richard A. *A Study of Future Worlds.* New York: Free Press, 1975.

Gardner, Richard. *New Structures for Economic Interdependence, The Proceedings of an International Conference.* United Nations and Rensselaerville, N.Y.: May 1975.

Gardner, Richard N. (Rapporteur). *"Group of Experts on the Structure of the United Nations System"* (ST/SG/AC 9/WP. 2, February 28, 1975).

International Institute for Environmental Affairs. *World Energy, the Environment and Political Action,* January 1973.

Lovejoy, Derek. *Appropriate Technology (UNITAR News* 6, No. 4, 1974).

Mendlovitz, Saul H. *On the Creation of a Just World Order.* New York: Free Press, 1975.

National Academy of Sciences. *Rapid Population Growth: Consequences and Policy Implications.* Report of a Committee of the Office of the Foreign Secretary (Roger Revelle, Chairman) vol. I, ch. 4. (Baltimore: Johns Hopkins University Press, July 1971.

Nerfin, Marc. *What Now: Report Prepared on the Occasion of the Seventh Special Session of the United Nations General Assembly.* Stockholm, 1975.

Paleman, T. T. and D. K. Freebairn. *Food, Regulation and Employment: The Impact of the Green Revolution.* New York: Praeger, 1973.

Pugwash Conference. *Report of the Working Group on Code of Conduct on Transfer of Technology,* Document TD/B/AC.11/L.12. Geneva, Switzerland, April 1–5, 1974.

Third World Forum, *Communique.* Karachi, 1975.

Third World Forum, Special Task Force. *"Proposals for a New International Economic Order."* Mexico City, August 21–24, 1975.

Tinbergen, Jan. *Reviewing the International Order.* Interim Report. Rotterdam, 1975.

Triffin, Robert. *Negotiating a World Monetary Order.* Introductory Remarks at the Second International Conference on "Society and Environment in Transition of the World Academy of Art and Science." New York, May 6–11, 1974.

Ward, Barbara. "The Fat Years and the Lean," *The Economist,* November 2, 1974.

World Food Conference. *The World Food Problem: Proposals for National and International Action.* Rome, 1974.

INDEX

241